The
South Cen
Bus Handbook

British Bus Publishing

Body codes used in the Bus Handbook series:

Type:
A	Articulated vehicle
B	Single-deck bus
C	Coach - High-back seating
D	Low floor double-deck bus (4-metre)
DP	Express - high-back seating in a bus body
H	Full-height double-deck
L	Low-height double-deck with side gangway upstairs
M	Minibus
N	Low-floor bus
O	Open-top bus (CO = convertible - PO = Partial open-top)

Seating capacity is then shown. For double-decks the upper deck first,

Door position:-
C	Centre entrance/exit
D	Dual doorway
F	Front entrance/exit
R	Rear entrance/exit (no distinction between doored and open)
T	Three or more access points

Equipment:-
L	Lift for wheelchair
T	Toilet

e.g. - H32/28F is a high-bridge bus with thirty-two seats upstairs, twenty-eight down and a front entrance/exit.
B43D is a bus with two doorways.

Re-registrations:-
Where a vehicle has gained new index marks the details are listed at the end of each fleet showing the current mark, followed in sequence by those previously carried starting with the original mark.

Other books in the series:
The Scottish Bus Handbook
The Ireland & Islands Bus Handbook
The North East Bus Handbook
The Yorkshire Bus Handbook
The Lancashire, Cumbria and Manchester Bus Handbook
The Merseyside and Cheshire Bus Handbook
The North and West Midlands Bus Handbook
The East Midlands Bus Handbook
The South Midlands Bus Handbook
The North and West Wales Bus Handbook
The South Wales Bus Handbook
The Chilterns and West Anglia Bus Handbook
The East Anglia Bus Handbook
The South West Bus Handbook
The South Central Bus Handbook
The South East Bus Handbook (New in Autumn 1998)

Annual books are produced for the major groups:
The 1998 Stagecoach Bus Handbook
The 1998 FirstBus Bus Handbook
The 1999 Arriva Bus Handbook (New in Autumn 1998)

Associated series:
The Hong Kong Bus Handbook
The Leyland Lynx Handbook
The Model Bus Handbook
The Toy & Model Bus Handbook - Volume 1 - Early Diecasts
The Fire Brigade Handbook (fleet list of each local authority fire brigade)
The Fire Brigade Handbook - Special Appliances Volume 1
The Fire Brigade Handbook - Special Appliances Volume 2

Contents

The South Central Bus Handbook

The South Central Bus Handbook is part of the Bus Handbook series that details the fleets of stage carriage and express coach operators. Where space allows other significant operators in the areas covered are also included. These handbooks are published by *British Bus Publishing* and cover Ireland, Scotland, Wales and England outside central London. The current list is shown on page 2 of this book. These provide comprehensive coverage of all the principal operators' fleets in the British Isles.

Considerable time has been expended to ensure the accuracy of the fleet detail. However, the author would be keen to learn of anything which is incorrect so we can ensure that future books reflect that information.

British Bus Publishing,
The Vyne,
16 St Margaret's Drive
Wellington
Telford,
Shropshire TF1 3PH

Series Editor: Bill Potter

Principal Editor for *The South Central Bus Handbook:* David Donati

Acknowledgements:
We are grateful to Andy Chown, Steve Curl, Robert Edworthy, Keith Grimes, Steve Sanderson, Tony Wilson, the PSV Circle and the majority of the operating companies for their assistance in the compilation of this book.
To keep the fleets up to date we recommend *Buses*, published monthly by Ian Allan while the news-sheets of the PSV Circle provide more in-depth information.

The front cover photograph is by Tony Wilson. The frontispiece picture shows the Plaxton-bodied Dennis Javelin on Bennetts, M8BSL.

Contents correct to August 1998
ISBN 1 897990 43 X
Published by *British Bus Publishing*
The Vyne, 16 St Margarets Drive, Wellington,
Telford, Shropshire, TF1 3PH

Fax & Evening orderline number for all books- ☎ *01952 255669* 💳 VISA

ALDERMASTON COACHES

Arlott Bros, Old Mill Farm, Aldermaston Wharf, Berkshire, RG7 5PP

1	JAX25W	Bedford YNV Venturer	Duple Dominant IV	C53F	1981	Bebb, Llantwit Fardre, 1982
3	H459FLD	Leyland Tiger TRCL10/3ARZA	Plaxton Paramount 3200 III	C53F	1990	Pan Atlas, 1993
4	M198PCF	LDV 400	LDV	M16	1995	Adrian Truck Hire, Reading, 1996
5	H458FLD	Leyland Tiger TRCL10/3ARZA	Plaxton Paramount 3200 III	C57F	1990	Pan Atlas, 1993
6	C116GVU	Leyland Tiger TRCTL11/3RZ	Plaxton Paramount 3200 II	C57F	1986	Freshfield, Stockport, 1996
7	A836PPP	Bedford YNT	Plaxton Paramount 3200	C53F	1984	Armchair, Brentford, 1985
9	CCG830V	Bedford YMT	Duple Dominant II	C53F	1980	Lever, East Knoyle, 1984
11	B413CMC	Leyland Tiger TRCTL11/3R	Plaxton Paramount 3200	C57F	1985	British Airways, Heathrow, 1986
12	B414CMC	Leyland Tiger TRCTL11/3R	Plaxton Paramount 3200	C57F	1985	British Airways, Heathrow, 1986
	B971FBL	Freight Rover Sherpa	Dormobile	M12	1985	
17	H675LOX	Leyland-DAF 200	Leyland-DAF	M12	1991	Leyland-DAF, Birmingham, 1992
	JBZ4909	Leyland Tiger TRCTL11/3R	Plaxton Paramount 3200	C53F	1983	Harrington, Bedworth, 1998

Previous Registrations:

C116GVU   C79XWK, A4FFC   JBZ4909   RNY309Y, VFN53, JUB675Y

Livery: Red and white

Aldermaston Coaches operate tendered school services in the Aldermaston area of the county latterly known as Berkshire, which was eliminated during the recent local authority changes. Seen here is B413CMC, a Plaxton-bodied Leyland Tiger previously used by British Airways at London Heathrow airport. It is seen in Aldermaston's all-white livery at the depot on Beenham Industrial Estate. *Aldermaston Coaches*

ALTONIAN

Warrens Transport Ltd, Mill Lane, Alton, Hampshire, GU34 2PY

Reg	Chassis	Body	Type	Year	Previous operator
CPE162Y	Bova EL26/581	Bova Europa	C53F	1983	Wallace Arnold, 1989
RIB4313	Neoplan N122/3	Neoplan Skyliner	CH57/20CT	1986	Durham Travel, 1997
C942DHT	Volvo B10M-61	Duple 320	C57F	1986	Turner, Bristol, 1994
D893MWR	Freight Rover Sherpa	Dormobile	B20F	1987	Yorkshire Rider, 1991
D851CNV	Bedford YNV Venturer	Caetano Algarve	C57F	1987	County, 1993
WLO471	Bedford YNV Venturer	Plaxton Paramount 3200 III	C57F	1987	Graham's, Bristol, 1995
E837EUT	Bedford YNT	Duple 320	C57F	1988	Castell, Caerphilly, 1995
E716CPC	Mercedes-Benz 811D	Robin Hood	M16	1988	Chivers, Elstead, 1993
YIB9078	Dennis Javelin 12SDA1907	Plaxton Paramount 3200 III	C53F	1988	East Surrey, 1996
YIB9073	Dennis Javelin 12SDA1907	Plaxton Paramount 3200 III	C53F	1988	Leisuretime, Crondall, 1996
997GAT	Van Hool T815H	Van Hool Alizée	C53FT	1988	Midland Fox, 1991
JHF682	Volvo B10M-61	Van Hool Alizée	C53F	1989	Park's, Hamilton, 1996
F548WGL	Dennis Javelin 12SDA1907	Duple 320	C54F	1989	Darley Ford Coaches, 1994
YIB9072	Dennis Javelin 12SDA1907	Plaxton Paramount 3200 III	C53F	1988	Coach Services, Thetford, 1996
YIB9079	Volvo B10M-61	Plaxton Paramount 3200 III	C57F	1989	Turner, Bristol, 1996
G960ATP	Dennis Javelin 8.5SDA1915	Plaxton Paramount 3200 III	C35F	1989	B Kavanagh, Urlingford, 1997
G821UMU	Leyland Swift LBM6T/2RS	Reeve Burgess Harrier	C37F	1989	Thompson, Uxbridge, 1995
RJI6617	Scania K113TRB	Plaxton Paramount 4000 III	CH55/18CT	1990	Siesta, Middlesbrough, 1995
H758DTM	Leyland Swift ST2R44C97T5	Reeve Burgess Harrier	C37F	1990	Ralph's, Langley, 1994
J528WTW	Mercedes-Benz 709D	Wadham Stringer Wessex	B24F	1992	Javelin, Battersea, 1997
R180BDT	Scania K124IB	Irizar Century 12.35	C49FT	1998	

Previous Registrations:

997GAT	E445MMM	RJI6617	G705LKW
CPE162Y	FUA373Y, 997GAT	WLO471	E831EUT, MIW5796, E906NAC
C942DHT	C942DHT, 244SYA	YIB9072	F373MUT
E716CPC	E480JLK, WET590, E81LLO, KXI599	YIB9073	F377MUT, HSV343, F377MUT
G960ATP	89-D-31617	YIB9078	E132PLJ
JHF682	F754ENE, LSK511, F285MGB	YIB9079	F326SHU, 2170MV, F326SHU
RIB4313	C173KET		

Livery: Cream, orange and brown

Depots: Alton (Papermill Lane), Four Marks (Ranch Farm, Willis Lane)

Carrying the cream, orange and brown colours of Altonian is **E837EUT**. Tightly pitched seating , standard for this Duple product, means this Bedford YNT carries 57 seated passengers within the 320 bod. Upto sixty-one seats could be fitted, however.
Steve Curl

AMPORT & DISTRICT

P J Tedd, Eastfield House, Thruxton, Andover, Hampshire, SP11 8ED

JIL3713	Volvo B10M-61	Plaxton Paramount 3200 III	C53F	1988	Limebourne, Battersea, 1993
JIL3969	Volvo B10M-60	Van Hool Alizée	C49FT	1989	Armchair, Brentford, 1996
MIL1170	Volvo B10M-60	Van Hool Alizée	C51FT	1990	
M923TYG	Mercedes-Benz 814D	Optare StarRider	C29F	1994	
M413DBY	Mercedes-Benz 814D	Optare StarRider	C29F	1994	
M685MRP	Volvo B10M-62	Plaxton Première 350	C53F	1994	Country Lion, Northampton, 1998
M4PJT	Volvo B10M-62	Van Hool Alizée	C51FT	1995	
M334KRY	Volvo B10M-62	Jonckheere Deauville	C53F	1995	Snowdon, Easington, 1997
P250AUT	Volvo B10M-62	Jonckheere Mistral 50	C53FT	1997	

Previous Registrations:

JIL3713	E314OMG	M685MRP	A17CLN
JIL3969	G869RNC	MIL1170	G822YJF

Livery: Cream, tan and brown

All the full-sized vehicles in the Amport and District fleet are based on the Volvo B10M chassis. In the case of MIL1170 a Van Hool Alizée body is fitted. It is seen at work during April 1998 in the Millbank area of central London. *Colin Lloyd*

ANGELA

Angela Coaches Ltd, Oak Tree Cottages, Lowford, Bursledon, Hampshire, SO3 8ES

B672TPO	Mercedes-Benz L608D	Robin Hood	C19F	1985	
TIB4901	Mercedes-Benz 811D	Optare StarRider	C21FT	1989	Wings, Uxbridge, 1993
MJI2379	Toyota Coaster HB31R	Caetano Optimo	C19F	1989	
WJI1727	Van Hool T815	Van Hool Alicron	C49FT	1991	Williamsons Motorways, 1997
DAZ4518	Toyota Coaster HZB50R	Caetano Optimo III	C21F	1994	
M145KJF	Toyota Coaster HZB50R	Caetano Optimo III	C21F	1995	Real Motors, S Newton, 1998
DAZ5045	Mercedes-Benz 814D	Cacciamali	C20FT	1995	Robin Hood demonstrator, 1995
VTW600	Iveco EuroRider 391.12.35	Beulas Stergo E35	C53F	1996	
RIB6581	Iveco EuroRider 391.12.35	Beulas Stergo E35	C49FT	1996	
RIB6582	Iveco EuroMidi CC95.18	Indcar	C30F	1996	
DAZ5046	Mercedes-Benz 814D	Robin Hood	C24F	1997	

Previous Registrations:

DAZ4518	From new	RIB6582	From new
DAZ5045	From new	TIB4901	F670SBY, WET342
DAZ5046	From new	VTW600	N129HPX
MJI2379	F342JTN	WJI1727	H761RNT
RIB6581	N181OUT		

Livery: Red and white

Depots :- Lowford (Oak Tree Cottages), Hedge End (Grove Farm, Upper Northam Drive)

The integral Van Hool T815 is marketed as the Alicron (lower floor-height) and Acron (normal-height) members of the T8 family. An example of the Alicron is seen here as Angela Coaches WJI1727. The T8 Alizée family body style was available in various heights, the largest being the one-and-a-half-deck Astral. *Colin Lloyd*

BENNETTS SILVERLINE

R S & M E Bennett, Orchard Garage, Oxford Road, Chieveley, Reading, RG20 8RU

FIL4904	Leyland Leopard PSU3G/4R	Plaxton Supreme IV Exp	C46F	1981	Armchair, Brentford, 1995
LBO6X	Bova EL26/582	Bova Europa	C53F	1981	Harris, Fleur-de-lis, 1998
ADC176A	Bova EL26/582	Bova Europa	C51F	1982	Albert Wilde, Heage, 1998
WBW736X	Leyland National 2 NL116AL11/1R		B52F	1982	Procord, Harwell, 1996
NIL8237	Bova EL26/582	Bova Europa	C53F	1982	Woods, Bognor Regis, 1998
SIB3054	Bova EL26/582	Bova Europa	C51F	1982	Andy James, Tetbury, 1998
PIW5455	Bova EL26/582	Bova Europa	C49FT	1983	Way, Wokingham, 1998
SJI1960	Bedford YNV Venturer	Plaxton Paramount 3200	C53F	1983	McGowan, Neilston, 1997
TJI6301	Leyland Tiger TRCTL11/3R	Plaxton Paramount 3500	C50F	1983	City of Oxford, 1995
TJI6302	Leyland Tiger TRCTL11/3R	Plaxton Paramount 3500	C50F	1983	Reading, 1994
TJI6307	Leyland Tiger TRCTL11/3R	Duple Dominant IV Express	C50F	1983	City of Oxford, 1995
TJI6308	Leyland Tiger TRCTL11/3R	Duple Dominant IV Express	C50F	1983	City of Oxford, 1995
C650XDF	Mercedes-Benz L608D	Alexander AM	B20F	1986	Cheltenham & Gloucester, 1996
C657XDF	Mercedes-Benz L608D	Alexander AM	B20F	1986	Cheltenham & Gloucester, 1996
C658XDF	Mercedes-Benz L608D	Alexander AM	B20F	1986	Cheltenham & Gloucester, 1996
C668JKG	Mercedes-Benz L608D	Plaxton Mini Supreme	C25F	1986	Debonair, Hoddesdon, 1994
E664AUD	Peugeot-Talbot Express	Talbot	M8	1988	Procord, Harwell, 1996
L4BSL	Bova FHD12.340	Bova Futura	C49F	1994	
M8BSL	Dennis Javelin 12SDA2131	Plaxton Première 320	C53F	1995	
N9BSL	Dennis Javelin 12SDA2155	Plaxton Première 320	C53F	1995	
N10BSL	MAN 11.190	Berkhof E'llence 1000 Midi	C32F	1997	
P11BSL	Dennis Javelin	Plaxton Première 320	C53F	1997	
P12BSL	Bova FHD12.340	Bova Futura	C49FT	1997	
P13BSL	Bova FHD12.340	Bova Futura	C49FT	1997	
R5BSL	Dennis Javelin	Plaxton Première 320	C53F	1998	

Previous Registrations:

ADC176A	VWX348X	SJI1960	VGM245Y, 3900PH, CPD214Y, TIB4686, CPD814Y
FIL4904	HJB469W	TJI6301	YPJ209Y
LBO6X	LBO6X, 2375NU		
NIL8237	BAR905X, 274FYP	TJI6302	YPJ210Y, RJI5703
PIW5455	FUA400Y, 5611PP, EGV587Y	TJI6307	EBW108Y
SIB3054	VWX349X, 307WHT	TJI6308	EBW109Y

Livery: Green and silver

For bus service work, Bennetts Silverline operate Mercedes-Benz L608D minibuses. After ten years service with Cheltenham & Gloucester, C650XDF joined the Bennetts fleet in 1996, together with another two vehicles of the same batch, all converted by Reeve Burgess. *Philip Lamb*

9

BRIJAN TOURS

B H Botley & N A Wheeler, The Coach Station, Claylands Road, Bishops Waltham, Southampton, SO32 1BH

4	LJI8154	DAF MB200DKFL600	Van Hool Alizée	C52F	1984	Midland Fox, 1991
18	YDL672T	Bristol VRT/SL3/6LXB	Eastern Coach Works	H43/31F	1979	Southern Vectis, 1995
19	YDL675T	Bristol VRT/SL3/6LXB	Eastern Coach Works	H43/31F	1979	Southern Vectis, 1995
20	WIB3420	DAF MB200DKFL600	Plaxton Paramount 3200 III	C53F	1986	AMR, Bedfont, 1995
21	SBZ1621	Freight Rover Sherpa	Carlyle	B20F	1987	Priory, Gosport, 1995
23	LIL9923	Leyland Tiger TRBTL11/3R	Plaxton Derwent II	DP54F	1986	MoD, 1996
24	P224PTP	Iveco EuroMidi CC95-E18	Indcar	C35F	1996	
27	UVY412	Iveco Daily 49.10	Robin Hood City Nippy	B25F	1988	Solent Blue Line, 1997
29	R9BJT	Dennis Javelin	Plaxton Première 320	C55F	1997	
30	H211TCP	DAF SB2305DHTD585	Duple 340	C57F	1991	Perrett, Shipton Oliffe, 1997
32	P866ADO	Mercedes-Benz Vario O814	Autobus Classique Nouvelle	C29F	1997	Autobus demonstrator, 1998
34	K337ABH	Mercedes-Benz 814D	Plaxton Beaver	C33F	1992	Elcock Reisen, Telford, 1998
35	S	Mercedes-Benz Vario O814	Plaxton Beaver 2	DP27F	1998	On order

Previous Registrations:

LJI8154	A310XNV		UVY412	F258CEY
LIL9923	82KF03, D156MEA		WIB3420	C283RSF
SBZ1621	D152NON			

Named vehicles:- 4 *Jamie*; 18 *Alfred*; 19 *Wilfred*; 20 *Louise*; 21 *Kath*; 23 *Vic*; 24 *Maie*; 25 Snowy; 27 Fred; 29 *Emma*; 30, Patricia; 31 *Tina*; 32 *Ginny*.

Livery:- Cream and red; blue and yellow (Solent Blue Line) 19, 21/7, 35; green (King Alfred) 18.

E866ADO
S9DJD

BriJan Tours vehicles carry fleet numbers as well as each vehicle being individually named. **P224KTP** is number 24 in the fleet and is named *Maie*. This Iveco EuroMidi was bodied by Indcar in 1996 and is seen in this picture taken at Thorpe Park. *David Heath*

BUDDENS

Buddens Coaches, 29 Premier Way, Abbey Park Industrial Estate, Romsey, Hampshire, SO51 9AQ

246KOT	Bedford VAL14	Duple Vega Major	C52F	1964	preservation, 1973
OSK774	Leyland Olympian ONTL11/2R	Eastern Coach Works	CH47/30F	1984	Northumbria, 1998
A3ALP	Neoplan N117/2	Neoplan Spaceliner	C49FT	1985	Beavis, Bussage, 1995
SJI8128	Scania K93CRB	Van Hool Alizée	C55F	1988	
SJI8115	Scania K113CRB	Van Hool Alizée	C16FT	1989	
SJI8116	Scania K113CRB	Van Hool Alizée	C16FT	1989	
SJI8122	Scania K113TRB	Van Hool Astrobel	CH6/10CT	1989	Shaw, Coventry, 1993
6258VZ	Scania K112TRS	Van Hool Astrobel	CH6/10CT	1989	Shaw, Coventry, 1992
SJI8120	Scania K113CRB	Van Hool Alizée	C16FT	1990	
SJI8123	Scania K113CRB	Van Hool Alizée	C16FT	1990	
SJI8125	Volvo B10M-60	Jonckheere Deauville	C16FT	1990	
SJI8127	Dennis Javelin 12SDA1919	Caetano Algarve II	C50FT	1990	Robinson, Clitheroe, 1995
SJI8118	Scania K113TLB	Berkhof Excellence 3000HD	CH6/10FT	1991	Ringleburg, Holland, 1995
SJI8124	Scania K113CRB	Jonckheere Deauville P50	C16FT	1991	
SJI8129	Scania K113CRB	Jonckheere Deauville P50	C16FT	1992	
J35UHP	Scania K113TRB	Van Hool Astrobel	CH57/17CT	1992	Shaw, Coventry, 1995
K544EHE	Scania K113TRB	Van Hool Alizée	C16FT	1993	
K545EHE	Scania K113TRB	Van Hool Alizée	C16FT	1993	
K215CBD	MAN 16.290	Jonckheere Deauville	C16FT	1993	
K216CBD	MAN 16.290	Jonckheere Deauville	C16FT	1993	
K540EHE	Scania K113TRB	Van Hool Alizée	C16FT	1993	
K238PRV	Leyland-DAF 400	Leyland-DAF	M16	1993	Churchfields, Salisbury, 1995
L737EPC	Ford Transit VE6	Ford	M10	1994	private owner, 1994
M3BUD	Scania K113CRB	Berkhof Excellence 1000LD	C16FT	1995	
M302VET	Scania K93CRB	Berkhof Excellence 1000L	C55F	1995	
M305VET	Scania K93CRB	Berkhof Excellence 1000L	C55F	1995	
M682LRU	Scania K113CRB	Berkhof Excellence 1000LD	C51FT	1995	
M683LRU	Scania K113CRB	Berkhof Excellence 1000LD	C51FT	1995	
M684LRU	Dennis Javelin 10SDA2139	Berkhof E'llence 1000 Midi	C38FT	1995	
M149KJF	Toyota Coaster HZB50R	Caetano Optimo III	C21F	1995	
M15BUD	Scania K113TRA	Berkhof Excellence 3000HD	CH6/10FT	1995	

The latest body design from Belgian coachbuilder Berkhof is the Axial. It features a much more rounded frontal appearance when compared with its predecessor, the Excellence. P194KJM has an Axial body mounted on a Dennis Javelin chassis. This Buddens vehicle undertakes touring work on behalf of Insight whose name is the more prominent on the coach
Colin Lloyd

M497XWF	Scania K113CRB	Irizar Century 12.35	C49FT	1995
M499XWF	Scania K113CRB	Irizar Century 12.35	C49FT	1995
N908DWJ	Scania K113CRB	Irizar Century 12.35	C49FT	1996
N909DWJ	Scania K113CRB	Irizar Century 12.37	C49FT	1996
N910DWJ	Dennis Javelin 10SDA2163	Berkhof E'llence 1000 Midi	C41F	1996
N911DWJ	Dennis Javelin 12SDA2134	Berkhof Excellence 1000L	C49FT	1996
N912DWJ	Dennis Javelin 12SDA2134	Berkhof Excellence 1000L	C49F	1996
N913DWJ	Mercedes-Benz 814D	Robin Hood	C25F	1996
N916DWJ	Scania K113CRB	Van Hool Alizée	C49FT	1996
N917DWJ	Scania K113TRB	Irizar Century 12.37	C16FT	1996
N918DWJ	Scania K113TRB	Irizar Century 12.37	C16FT	1996
N919DWJ	Scania K113CRB	Irizar Century 12.35	C49FT	1996
N920DWJ	Scania K113CRB	Irizar Century 12.35	C49FT	1996
N921DWJ	Scania K113CRB	Van Hool Alizée	C51FT	1996
P977HWF	Neoplan N212H	Neoplan Jetliner	C35FT	1996
P122GHE	Scania K113CRB	Irizar Century 12.35	C49FT	1997
P124GHE	Scania K113CRB	Irizar Century 12.35	C49FT	1997
P125GHE	Scania K113CRB	Berkhof Axial	C49FT	1997
P126GHE	Scania K113CRB	Berkhof Axial	C49FT	1997
P988HWF	Dennis Javelin	Neoplan Transliner	C49F	1997
P989HWF	Dennis Javelin	Neoplan Transliner	C49F	1997
P193KJM	Dennis Javelin	Berkhof Axial	C49F	1997
P194KJM	Dennis Javelin	Berkhof Axial	C49F	1997
P242KJM	Dennis Javelin	Berkhof Axial	C49F	1997
297OJT	Scania K124IB	Berkhof Axial	C49FT	1998

Previous Registrations:

297OJT	From new	SJI8122	G100XAC, 3KOV, G317EHP
6258VZ	1KOV, F532VVC	SJI8123	H833RWJ
A3ALP	684ALP	SJI8124	H399ERP
SJI8115	F151DET	SJI8125	H49VNH
SJI8116	F152DET	SJI8127	H624FNB
SJI8118	VJ-79-NB	SJI8128	F162DET
OSK774	A103FPL	SJI8129	J529JNH
SJI8120	G699LKW		

Allocations and liveries:-   White, brown and yellow or yellow/brown graduated

Grand European (white)	N908DWJ					
Insight (white)	N911DWJ	N912DWJ	P988HWF	P989HWF	P193KJM	P194KJM
Phoenix (Band bus fleet, silver yellow and brown)	SJI8115	SJI8116	SJI8118	SJI8120		
	SJI8124	SJI8125	SJI8129	K215CBD	K216CBD	K544EHE
	K545EHE	M15BUD	N917DWJ	N918DWJ		

Buddens operate a number of coaches for transporting pop groups around Europe. They have many specialist features including sleeping areas and executive seating. A number of the *Band Bus* fleet are double deckers. SJI8122 is a Scania K113TRB tri-axle vehicle which carries a Van Hool Astrobel body seating only six on the upper deck and ten on the lower deck. It carries the Phoenix livery given to this specialist operation.
David Donati

Opposite:- **Two of Buddens Scania coaches in fleet livery are Berkhof-bodied M682LRU and the Irizar example N919DWJ.**
Colin Lloyd/Ralph Stevens

BURGHFIELD MINI COACHES

G JM AC & S McCouid, Burghfield Farm, Mill Road, Burghfield Bridge, RG30 3SS

DYA49A	Mercedes-Benz 811D	Optare StarRider	C29F	1987	Optare demonstrator, 1988
DYA199A	Mercedes-Benz 811D	Robin Hood	C29F	1988	Oakley Coaches, 1992
DYA197A	Dennis Javelin 8.5SDL1903	Plaxton Paramount 3200 III	C35F	1988	Oram, Hersham, 1992
E106JES	Ford Transit VE6	Steedrive	M16	1988	Pettrie, Lennoxtown, 1993
E503YSU	Ford Transit VE6	Dormobile	M16	1988	Wilson, Gourock, 1993
E129AAL	Ford Transit VE6	Mellor	M16L	1988	Nottinghamshire CC, 1995
F382KVM	Ford Transit VE6	Pearl	M8	1988	Lex Vehicle Leasing, Sale, 1993
DYA79A	Mercedes-Benz 507D	Reeve Burgess	C20F	1988	Buckland, Hurst, 1989
DYA97A	Mercedes-Benz 507D	Reeve Burgess	C16F	1988	Buckland, Hurst, 1989
DYA92A	Mercedes-Benz 811D	Optare StarRider	C29F	1989	
UJI2184	Dennis Javelin 8.5SDL1903	Duple 320	C35F	1989	Country Lion, Northampton, 1995
F299GDB	Ford Transit VE6	Pearl	M8L	1989	private owner, 1993
G234DFX	Ford Transit VE6	Horseman	M8L	1989	private owner, 1995
G471OKP	Ford Transit VE6	Crystals	M8L	1989	Kent CC, 1995
G217TKK	Ford Transit VE6	Crystals	M8L	1989	Kent CC, 1995
G518RKM	Ford Transit VE6	Crystals	M8L	1989	Kent CC, 1995
DYA272A	Ford Transit VE6	Dormobile	M16	1989	Wings, Uxbridge, 1992
G703XLY	Ford Transit VE6	Dormobile	M16	1989	Hill, Hersham, 1996
G705XLY	Ford Transit VE6	Dormobile	M16	1989	LB Harrow, 1996
G674YLP	Ford Transit VE6	Dormobile	M16	1989	LB Harrow, 1996
G838PJA	Ford Transit VE6	Mellor	M16	1989	Munro, Uddingston, 1993
UJI6316	Leyland Swift LBM6T/2RS	Elme Orion	C31F	1989	Crusader, Clacton 1996
UJI6317	Leyland Swift LBM6T/2RS	Reeve Burgess Harrier	C37F	1989	Smith, Liss, 1996
SJI7473	Leyland Swift LBM6T/2RS	Reeve Burgess Harrier	C29F	1989	Country Lion, Northampton, 1994
DYA93A	Mercedes-Benz 811D	Optare StarRider	C29F	1989	

Optare of Leeds produced the StarRider body for the Mercedes-Benz 811D chassis. This model was produced in bus and coach formats and found buyers in many companies large and small. Showing the single-leaf door that was only fitted to coach versions is DYA92A, which is a member of the Burghfield Mini Coaches fleet. *Colin Lloyd*

For coaching applications, the Mercedes-Benz 811D chassis was up-rated in power output into the 814D model. One of three similar vehicles in the Burghfield Mini Coaches fleet is P37KWA. It carries 32 seats in the Plaxton Beaver body. *David Heath*

G961CJB	Bedford Midi	Dormobile	M8	1990	
DYA238A	Dennis Javelin 8.5SDL1903	Duple 320	C35F	1990	Maynes, Buckie, 1992
G561HAX	Ford Transit VE6	Pearl	M8	1990	Bown Leasing, Caerphilly, 1993
G574HAX	Ford Transit VE6	Pearl	M8	1990	Bown Leasing, Caerphilly, 1993
G59WCF	Ford Transit VE6	Zodiac	M8	1990	van 1994
G226TKK	Ford Transit VE6	Crystals	M8L	1990	Kent CC, 1995
G803BLF	Ford Transit VE6	Dormobile	M8L	1990	LB Harrow, 1996
G804BLF	Ford Transit VE6	Dormobile	M8L	1990	LB Harrow, 1996
G805BLF	Ford Transit VE6	Dormobile	M8L	1990	LB Harrow, 1996
G435ETW	Ford Transit VE6	Dormobile	M16	1990	Nunn, Totton, 1993
G681DLJ	Ford Transit VE6	Dormobile	M16	1990	van, 1995
G682DLJ	Ford Transit VE6	Dormobile	M16	1990	van, 1995
DYA26A	Ford Transit VE6	Ford	M11	1991	
DYA27A	Ford Transit VE6	Ford	M11	1991	
DYA28A	Ford Transit VE6	Ford	M11	1991	
DYA52A	Ford Transit VE6	Ford	M11	1991	
DYA54A	Ford Transit VE6	Ford	M11	1991	
P36KWA	Mercedes-Benz 814D	Plaxton Beaver	C32F	1996	
P37KWA	Mercedes-Benz 814D	Plaxton Beaver	C32F	1996	
R176TKU	Mercedes-Benz 814D	Plaxton Beaver	C33F	1997	
R710NMO	Mercedes-Benz Sprinter 412D	Crest	C16F	1998	
R711NMO	Mercedes-Benz Sprinter 412D	Crest	C16F	1998	

Previous Registrations:

DYA26A	H324HLM	DYA97A	F132TRU
DYA27A	H326HLM	DYA197A	E135PLJ
DYA28A	H330HLM	DYA199A	E151JBK
DYA49A	E812SUM	DYA238A	G350VAS
DYA52A	H327HLM	DYA272A	G211JWG, WET476
DYA54A	H329HLM	SJI7473	F21DVV, A16CLC, F655ENH
DYA79A	F340SMD	UJI2184	F25DVV, A14CLC, F766ENH
DYA92A	F938AWW	UJI6316	G931HRN
DYA93A	G906XJB	UJI6317	F578RML

CARTERTON COACHES

Carterton Coaches (Witney) Ltd, 32 Corn Street, Witney, OX8 7BN

NAL53P	Leyland Fleetline FE30AGR	Alexander AD	H44/34F	1976	Swanbrook, Cheltenham, 1993
OBN502R	Leyland Fleetline FE30AGR	Northern Counties	H43/31F	1977	Beestons, Long Melford, 1996
RJI6612	Bedford YMT	Plaxton Supreme IV	C53F	1979	Senior, Witney, 1998
NDD113W	Bedford YMT	Plaxton Supreme IV Exp	C53F	1980	Swanbrook, Cheltenham, 1993
A463JJF	Fiat 60F10	Caetano Beja	C18F	1984	McDougall, Hoddesdon, 1994
A494JEC	Kässbohrer Setra S215H	Kässbohrer	C53F	1983	Stainton, Kendal, 1997
MIL3726	Volkswagen LT55	Optare City Pacer	B25F	1987	Beeston, Long Melford, 1996
M738KCU	Ford Transit V6	Ford	M8	1995	private owner, 1998

Previous Registrations:

A494JEC	A707DEC, LIB3768	MIL3726	D377JUM	RJI6612	ELP553T

Livery:- White, yellow, orange and red, to be replaced by white, brown and aquamarine and new fleetname 'Rebound'

Depot:- Downs Road, Witney

Seen here carrying the Rebound fleetname, incorrect registration A404JEC, A494JEC is a new addition to the Carterton Coaches fleet. It is a Kässbohrer Setra S215H, the more popular of the models from this German manufacturer. Of interest is the television aerial on the roof of the coach. The Rebound fleetname and new livery will be extended through the fleet in due course. *David Heath*

CHARLTON SERVICES

NGJ, NHM & PD Holder, The Garage, High Street, Charlton-on-Otmoor,
Oxfordshire, OX5 2UQ

AAU136A	Leyland Leopard PSU5/4R	Plaxton Panorama Elite III	C57F	1973	Lewis, Llanrhystyd, 1992
NWT639P	Leyland Leopard PSU3C/4R	Plaxton Supreme III	C53F	1976	Ranger, Farnborough, 1987
VGJ317R	Leyland Leopard PSU5A/4R	Plaxton Supreme III	C55F	1977	Epsom Coaches, 1984
VPP958S	Leyland Leopard PSU5C/4R	Plaxton Supreme III	C57F	1978	Biss Bros, Bishops Stortford, 1985
EBM440T	Leyland Leopard PSU5C/4R	Plaxton Supreme IV	C57F	1979	Squirrell, Hitcham, 1995
EDF269T	Leyland Leopard PSU5C/4R	Plaxton Supreme IV	C57F	1979	Shamrock & Rambler, 1984
WWM930W	Leyland Atlantean AN68B/1H	Willowbrook	H44/34F	1981	Rainbow, Westbury, 1996
CSU243	Leyland Tiger TRCTL11/3R	Plaxton Paramount 3200	C57F	1983	
OJI3907	Leyland Tiger TRCTL11/3R	Plaxton Paramount 3200	C57F	1983	B J, Abbey Wood, 1988
GAZ8573	Leyland Tiger TRCTL11/3R	Plaxton Paramount 3500	C53F	1983	Lee, Rowlands Gill, 1995
A113MUD	Leyland Tiger TRCTL11/3RH	Plaxton Paramount 3200E	C51F	1984	Oxford Bus Company, 1996
WXI6274	Mercedes-Benz L307D	Reeve Burgess	M12	1984	William Ramsay, Elsrickle, 1988
GJI7173	Leyland Tiger TRCTL11/3RH	Plaxton Paramount 3500 II	C46FT	1985	Cheltenham & Gloucester, 1993
OXI9100	Leyland Royal Tiger RT	Plaxton Paramount 3500	C55F	1986	Horseman, Reading, 1992
TJI6278	Leyland Tiger TRCTL11/3RH	Plaxton Paramount 3500 II	C51F	1986	Brighton & Hove, 1995
UJI2436	Leyland Tiger TRCTL11/3RH	Plaxton Paramount 3500 II	C51F	1986	Brighton & Hove, 1995
CSU432	Mercedes-Benz 609D	Whittaker Europa	C23F	1988	Llynfi, Maesteg, 1997
F516GGJ	Volvo B10M-60	Van Hool Alizée	C53F	1989	Epsom Coaches, 1998
3103PH	Volvo B10M-60	Van Hool Alizée	C53F	1989	Epsom Coaches, 1998

Previous Registrations:

3103PH	F517GGJ	OJI3907	YFG366Y
AAU136A	FAU46L	OXI9100	C801FMC
CSU243	FJO603Y	TJI6278	C378PCD
CSU432	E823WWF	UJI2436	C379PCD
GAZ8573	10RU, GNF980Y	WXI6274	A841UGB
GJI7173	B215NDG, 511OHU, B177SFH, 3103PH		

Livery: Two-tone blue

The two-tone blue colours of Charlton Services are carried here by 3103PH. It is one of a pair of Van Hool Alizée coaches purchased from Epsom Coaches in 1998. Both are mounted on Volvo B10M chassis that brought to an end the established practice of operating mostly Leyland products for the large coaches.

CHENEY COACHES

Cheney Coaches Ltd, Cheney House, Thorpe Close, Overthorpe Ind Est, Banbury,
Oxfordshire, OX16 8UZ

URH13R	Bedford YMT	Plaxton Supreme III Express	C53F	1977	Dorset CC, 1994
RIB5124	Leyland Leopard PSU3E/4R	Plaxton Viewmaster III	C49F	1978	Clark, Stairfoot, 1997
CDT587T	Leyland Leopard PSU3E/4R	Plaxton Viewmaster III	C53F	1978	Clark, Stairfoot, 1997
9785SM	Bedford YMT	Plaxton Supreme IV	C53F	1979	Tappins, Didcot, 1994
PDN873	Bedford YMT (Cummins)	Plaxton Supreme IV	C53F	1979	Tappins, Didcot, 1994
VPF742	Bedford YMT (Cummins)	Plaxton Supreme IV	C53F	1979	Tappins, Didcot, 1994
OGL849	Bedford YMT	Plaxton Supreme IV	C53F	1979	Tappins, Didcot, 1993
JDX574V	Bedford YMT	Duple Dominant II Express	C53F	1979	Sanders, Holt, 1995
KJU771V	Bedford YMT	Duple Dominant II	C53F	1980	Martin, Kettering, 1996
DVJ398W	Bedford YLQ	Plaxton Supreme IV Exp	C53F	1980	Newbury, Ledbury, 1996
RFC443W	Bedford YLQ	Plaxton Supreme IV Exp	C45F	1980	Dorset Police, 1994
WCA941W	Leyland Leopard PSU5C/4R	Plaxton Supreme IV	C57F	1980	Bostocks, Congleton, 1998
WCA942W	Leyland Leopard PSU5D/4R	Plaxton Supreme IV	C57F	1980	Bostocks, Congleton, 1998
B586EGT	Renault-Dodge S56	Dormobile	B22FL	1985	LB Merton, 1993
TAZ4988	TAZ D3200	TAZ Dubrava	C49FT	1985	Safeguard, Guildford,1993
NIW6518	Volvo B10M-61	Van Hool Alizée	C53F	1986	Rossendale (Ellen Smith), 1997
SJI2764	Neoplan N122/3	Neoplan Skyliner	CH57/20DT	1986	Williams, Cambourne, 1998
TAZ5002	TAZ D3500	TAZ Dubrava	C49F	1988	McTavish, Dalmuir, 1997
TAZ4999	TAZ D3200	TAZ Dubrava	C49FT	1989	Jan's, Soham, 1996
TAZ4990	TAZ D3200	TAZ Dubrava	C53F	1989	Dave Allen, Whiston, 1997
IIL1355	Leyland Tiger TRCL10/3ARZM	Duple 320	C55F	1989	Maynes, Manchester, 1997
URT682	Leyland Tiger TRCTL11/3ARZ	Duple 320	C53F	1989	Bennetts-Silverline, 1997
YSU975	Leyland Tiger TRCTL11/3ARZ	Duple 320	C53F	1989	?, 1997
TAZ5001	TAZ D3500	TAZ Dubrava	C49FT	1989	SMC, Garston, 1996
G243CLD	TAZ D3200	TAZ Dubrava	C53F	1990	McTavish, Dalmuir, 1997
G22UWL	Ford Transit VE6	Jubilee	M12	1990	
H787JFC	Ford Transit VE6	Ford	M8	1990	
H562FLE	Mercedes-Benz 609D	North West Coach Sales	C19FL	1990	Capital, Heathrow, 1996
K373HHK	Ford Transit	Ford	M14	1993	
N399LEW	LVD Convoy	Jubilee	M16	1996	Demonstrator, 1998

Previous Registrations:

9785SM	YAN817T	SJI2764	D323NWG
CDT587T	KUY777PYA, 616PYA, 4465KM	TAZ4988	F794TBC, DSK558, F199UPC,
G243CLD	G576WUT, SNR430		YSU975, F189UPC
IIL1355	F55HNC	TAZ4990	F872ONR
NIW6518	C322DND	TAZ4999	F880ONR
NSU914	KPR329W	TAZ5001	G711VRY
OGL849	YAN823T	TAZ5002	88KK1400, 88KK1115, E982UMS
PDN873	YAN818T	URT682	F785GNA
RFC443W	KPR329W, NSU914	VPF742	YAN819T
RIB5124	UDW44S, 7586UM, KCX920S	YSU975	G801RNC

Livery:- White, blue and red

NIW6518, a Van Hool Alizée is now part of the Banbury based Cheney fleet. It was previously in the Rochdale-based coach fleet of Ellen Smith which forms the contracts and tours division of Rossendale

TAZ4999 has a very appropriate registration number. This plate was sourced, like many throughout the mainland from Northern Ireland, and is now affixed to a TAZ Dubrava coach. This model was Mercedes-Benz licensed and built in Yugoslavia. The break up of that country and the associated civil war has ended the availability of this inexpensive coach.

CHILTERN QUEENS

Chiltern Queens Ltd, Long Toll, Greenmore Hill, Woodcote, Oxfordshire, RG8 0RP

OJO835M	Leyland Leopard PSU3B/4R	Plaxton Derwent	B55F	1974	
VBW581	Leyland Leopard PSU5A/4R	Plaxton Supreme III	C57F	1976	
RFC10T	Leyland Leopard PSU3E/4R	Duple Dominant II Express	C49F	1978	Oxford Bus Company, 1989
RFC12T	Leyland Leopard PSU3E/4R	Duple Dominant II Express	C49F	1978	Oxford Bus Company, 1990
WUD815T	Leyland Leopard PSU3E/4R	Duple Dominant II Express	C49F	1978	Oxford Bus Company, 1990
591STT	Leyland Leopard PSU3E/4R	Plaxton Supreme IV Exp	C53F	1979	
YFC18V	Leyland Leopard PSU3E/4R	Duple Dominant II Express	C49F	1979	Oxford Bus Company, 1991
BBW20V	Leyland Leopard PSU3E/4R	Duple Dominant II Express	C49F	1979	Oxford Bus Company, 1993
BBW22V	Leyland Leopard PSU3E/4R	Duple Dominant II Express	C49F	1979	Oxford Bus Company, 1992
2969HJ	Leyland Leopard PSU3E/4R	Plaxton Supreme IV	C53F	1979	Regis, Challow, 1996
MUD25W	Leyland Leopard PSU3E/4R	Duple Dominant II Express	C49F	1981	Oxford Bus Company, 1993
PPJ65W	Leyland Leopard PSU5C/4R	Wadham Stringer Vanguard	B54F	1982	M o D, 1993
PJH582X	Leyland Leopard PSU3E/4R	Plaxton Supreme III	C53F	1982	
EBW106Y	Leyland Tiger TRCTL11/3R	Duple Dominant IV Express	C51F	1983	Oxford Bus Company, 1995
EBW107Y	Leyland Tiger TRCTL11/3R	Duple Dominant IV Express	C51F	1983	Oxford Bus Company, 1996
B911SPR	Volvo B10M-61	Plaxton Paramount 3200 II	C53F	1985	Excelsior, Bournemouth, 1987
TSV804	Volvo B10M-61	Jonckheere Jubilee	C49FT	1986	Gunton, Ongar, 1994
C644SJM	Volvo B10M-61	Plaxton Paramount 3200 II	C53F	1986	
C114PUJ	Volvo B10M-61	Caetano Algarve	C49FT	1986	Selwyn Hughes, Llanfair C, 1993
D504NWG	Mercedes-Benz L608D	Alexander AM	B20F	1986	RoadCar, 1995
D506NWG	Mercedes-Benz L608D	Alexander AM	B20F	1986	RoadCar, 1995
D262HFX	Volvo B10M-61	Plaxton Paramount 3200 III	C53F	1987	Excelsior, Bournemouth, 1988
D34ENH	Volvo B10M-61	Duple 340	C55F	1987	Country Lion, Northampton, 1994
E533PRU	Volvo B10M-61	Plaxton Paramount 3200 III	C48FT	1987	
F344TSC	Mercedes-Benz 811D	Alexander AM	DP29F	1988	Challenger, Bridgnorth, 1992
F986TTF	Mercedes-Benz 811D	Optare StarRider	B33F	1989	Davron Travel, Caversham, 1991
H788RWJ	Scania K93CRB	Plaxton Paramount 3200 III	C55F	1990	

Previous Registrations:

2969HJ	EBM443T	PPJ65W	50AC08	TSV804	C28GNK
591STT	UUD623T	C114PUJ	C690KDS, SEL4X	VBW581	SFC32P

Livery: Red and white; two-tone green and white (coaches)

Chiltern Queens is a long established operator of local bus services. The operation was formed in 1955 as successor to Kemp's Motor Services and a network of services centred on Woodcote is operated. Pictured here are Caetano Algarve C114PUJ and Mercedes-Benz minibus D506NWG.
Ralph Stevens

Seen at Reading station is MUD25W. This Leyland Leopard was part of the substantial fleet of dual-purpose vehicles bought by the National Bus Company. This Duple Dominant-bodied example was previously in the Oxford fleet a source for many Chiltern Queens vehicles over the years.
Ralph Stevens

CITYLINE / WYCOMBE BUS

The City of Oxford Motor Services Ltd, 395 Cowley Road, Oxford, OX4 2DJ

Part of Go-Ahead Group Ltd.

1	R1OXF	Volvo B10M-62	Plaxton Première 350	C53F	1997		
2	R2OXF	Volvo B10M-62	Plaxton Première 350	C53F	1997		
3	R3OXF	Volvo B10M-62	Plaxton Première 350	C53F	1997		
4	R4OXF	Volvo B10M-62	Plaxton Première 350	C53F	1997		

5-12 Volvo B10M-62 Plaxton Excalibur C53F 1998

5	R5OXF	7	R7OXF	9	R9OXF	11	R11OXF	12	R12OXF
6	R6OXF	8	R8OXF	10	R10OXF				

41	M627FNS	Volvo B10M-60	Jonckheere Deauville P599	C52F	1995	Clarkes of London, 1997
42	M628FNS	Volvo B10M-60	Jonckheere Deauville P599	C52F	1995	Clarkes of London, 1997
43	M629FNS	Volvo B10M-60	Jonckheere Deauville P599	C52F	1995	Clarkes of London, 1997
44	M630FNS	Volvo B10M-60	Jonckheere Deauville P599	C52F	1995	Clarkes of London, 1997

50-55 Volvo B10M-62 Plaxton Premiére 350 C53F 1993

50	L150HUD	52	L152HUD	53	L153HUD	54	L154HUD	55	L155HUD
51	L151HUD								

56	N156BFC	Volvo B10M-62	Plaxton Premiere 350	C53F	1995
57	N157BFC	Volvo B10M-62	Plaxton Premiere 350	C53F	1995
58	N158BFC	Volvo B10M-62	Plaxton Premiere 350	C53F	1995

59-63 Volvo B10M-60 Plaxton Paramount 3500 III C51F 1991 Shearings, 1995

59	UJI1759	60	UJI1760	61	UJI1761	62	UJI1762	63	UJI1763

201-224 Leyland Olympian ONLXB/1R* Eastern Coach Works H47/28D* 1982-83 *220-4 are ONLXB/1R(6LXCT)
*218 is H47/25D

201	VJO201X	206	VJO206X	211	WWL211X	216	BBW216Y	221	CUD221Y
202	VJO202X	207	WWL207X	212	WWL212X	217	BBW217Y	222	CUD222Y
203	VJO203X	208	WWL208X	213	BBW213Y	218	BBW218Y	223	CUD223Y
204	VJO204X	209	WWL209X	214	BBW214Y	219	CUD219Y	224	CUD224Y
205	VJO205X	210	WWL210X	215	BBW215Y	220	CUD220Y		

225-229 Leyland Olympian ONLXB/1RH Alexander RL H47/26D 1988

225	E225CFC	226	E226CFC	227	E227CFC	228	E228CFC	229	E229CFC

230-235 Leyland Olympian ON2R50G16Z4 Alexander RL H47/29F* 1990 *230 is H47/30F

230	G230VWL	232	G232VWL	233	G233VWL	234	G234VWL	235	G235VWL
231	G231VWL								

236	FWL778Y	Leyland Olympian ONLXB/1R	Eastern Coach Works	H45/32F	1983	UKAEA, Harwell, 1991
237	FWL779Y	Leyland Olympian ONLXB/1R	Eastern Coach Works	H45/32F	1983	UKAEA, Harwell, 1991
238	FWL780Y	Leyland Olympian ONLXB/1R	Eastern Coach Works	H45/32F	1983	UKAEA, Harwell, 1991
239	FWL781Y	Leyland Olympian ONLXB/1R	Eastern Coach Works	H45/32F	1983	UKAEA, Harwell, 1991
240	D822UTF	Leyland Olympian ONLXB/1RH	Eastern Coach Works	CH39/25F	1986	The Bee Line, 1990
241	D823UTF	Leyland Olympian ONLXB/1RH	Eastern Coach Works	CH39/25F	1986	The Bee Line, 1990
242	D824UTF	Leyland Olympian ONLXB/1RH	Eastern Coach Works	CH39/25F	1986	The Bee Line, 1990

Opposite, top:- **CityLine acquired thirteen Northern Counties-bodied Volvo B10Bs from London General in 1997. These carried Select index marks with the London operator that were exchanged for local Oxford marks. Pictured in the University City is 648, K122BUD.** *Colin Lloyd*
Opposite, bottom:- **M629FMS is one of the CityLink Oxford-London Express coaches that compete with Stagecoach's *London Tube* services as well as rail services provided by Go-Ahead's Chiltern rail services.** *Ralph Stephens*

Wright's five years of manufacturing low floor buses helped the Oxford Bus Company refine the specification of the new fleet of ten Crusader-bodied Dennis Darts which are to be used on Oxford city route 401. They are 10-metres in length with 30 seats and space for a further 30 standing passengers. Pictured showing the ramp feature is 401, R401FFC.

301-305

Leyland Lynx LX112L10ZR1S   Leyland Lynx   B49F   1988   The Bee Line, 1990

301	F556NJM	302	F557NJM	303	F558NJM	304	F559NJM	305	F560NJM

385	JWV127W	Leyland National 2 NL116L11/1R	B52F	1980	Brighton & Hove, 1996
386	JWV128W	Leyland National 2 NL116L11/1R	B52F	1980	Brighton & Hove, 1996
387	GUW445W	Leyland National 2 NL106AL11/2R	B41F	1981	London General, 1996
388	GUW453W	Leyland National 2 NL106AL11/2R	B41F	1981	London General, 1996
389	GUW482W	Leyland National 2 NL106AL11/2R	B41F	1981	London General, 1996
390	GUW451W	Leyland National 2 NL106AL11/2R	DP40F	1981	London General, 1996
391	GUW458W	Leyland National 2 NL106AL11/2R	DP40F	1981	London General, 1996
392	GUW495W	Leyland National 2 NL106AL11/2R	DP40F	1981	London General, 1996

401-410

Dennis Dart SLF   Wright Crusader   N30D   1998

401	R401FFC	403	R403FFC	405	R405FFC	407	R407FFC	409	R409FFC
402	R402FFC	404	R404FFC	406	R46FFC	408	R408FFC	410	R410FFC

421-427

Dennis Dart SLF   Plaxton Pointer   N36F*   1996   *or N31F plus wheelchair.

421	N521MJO	423	N523MJO	425	P525YJO	426	P526YJO	427	P527YJO
422	N522MJO	424	N524MJO						

501-520

Dennis Dart 9SDL3054   Marshall C37   B36D   1995

501	M501VJO	505	M505VJO	509	M509VJO	513	M513VJO	517	M517VJO
502	M502VJO	506	M506VJO	510	M510VJO	514	M514VJO	518	M518VJO
503	M503VJO	507	M507VJO	511	M511VJO	515	M515VJO	519	M519VJO
504	M504VJO	508	M508VJO	512	M512VJO	516	M516VJO	520	M520VJO

601-624   Volvo B10B   Plaxton Verde   B51F   1995-96

601	N601FJO	606	N606FJO	611	N611FJO	616	N616FJO	621	N621FJO
602	N602FJO	607	N607FJO	612	N612FJO	617	N617FJO	622	N622FJO
603	N603FJO	608	N608FJO	613	N613FJO	618	N618FJO	623	N623FJO
604	N604FJO	609	N609FJO	614	N614FJO	619	N619FJO	624	N624FJO
605	N605FJO	610	N610FJO	615	N615FJO	620	N620FJO		

625	N413NRG	Volvo B10B	Plaxton Verde	B51F	1995
626	N414NRG	Volvo B10B	Plaxton Verde	B51F	1995
627	N415NRG	Volvo B10B	Plaxton Verde	B51F	1995
628	N416NRG	Volvo B10B	Plaxton Verde	B51F	1995

629-643   Volvo B10B   Plaxton Verde   B45D   1997

629	P629FFC	632	P632FFC	635	P635FFC	638	P638FFC	641	P641FFC
630	P630FFC	633	P633FFC	636	P636FFC	639	P639FFC	642	P642FFC
631	P631FFC	634	P634FFC	637	P637FFC	640	P640FFC	643	P643FFC

644-656   Volvo B10B   Northern Counties Paladin   B43D   1993   London General, 1997

644	K118BUD	647	K121BUD	650	K124BUD	653	K127BUD	655	K129BUD
645	K119BUD	648	K122BUD	651	K125BUD	654	K128BUD	656	K130BUD
646	K120BUD	649	K123BUD	652	K126BUD				

703	H189RWF	Mercedes-Benz 811D	Reeve Burgess Beaver	B21F	1990	London Central, 1995
704	H191RWF	Mercedes-Benz 811D	Reeve Burgess Beaver	B21F	1990	London Central, 1995

708-727   Mercedes-Benz 811D   Alexander AM   B28F   1990-91   London General, 1996-97

708	G108PGT	711	G711PGT	715	G115PGT	718	G118PGT	724	G124PGT
709	G109PGT	712	G712PGT	716	G116PGT	719	G119PGT	727	H427XGK
710	G110PGT	714	G114PGT	717	G117PGT	720	G120PGT		

755w	E755VJO	MCW MetroRider MF150/26	MCW	B25F	1987	
768w	F505CBO	MCW MetroRider MF150/105	MCW	B25F	1987	Merthyr Tydfil, 1989

769-783   Optare MetroRider MR09   Optare   B25F*   1990   *769-74 are B23F

769w	G769WFC	772w	G772WFC	775w	G775WFC	778	G778WFC	781	G781WFC
770w	G770WFC	773w	G773WFC	776w	G776WFC	779	G779WFC	782	G782WFC
771w	G771WFC	774w	G774WFC	777	G777WFC	780	G780WFC	783	G783WFC

950-975   Leyland Titan TNLXB2RRSp   Leyland   H44/26D*   1981-83   London Buses, 1993   *970 are H44/24D

950	GYE280W	960	OHV711Y	968	NUW661Y	970	KYN308X	975	A869SUL
956	KYV519X	966	KYV381X						

999	PWL999W	Leyland Olympian B45/TL11/2R	Alexander RL	H50/34D	1980	Leyland demonstrator, 1987

Ancilliary vehicles:

T1	BBW21V	Leyland Leopard PSU3E/4R	Duple Dominant II Express	C49F	1979
T2	BBW23V	Leyland Leopard PSU3E/4R	Duple Dominant II Express	C49F	1979
T4	VUD33X	Leyland Leopard PSU3E/4R	Willowbrook Warrior (19—)	B48F	1982

Previous Registrations:

F505CBO	F105CWG	K127BUD	K10KLL
K118BUD	K100KLL	K128BUD	K11KLL
K119BUD	K2KLL	K129BUD	K12KLL
K120BUD	K3KLL	K130BUD	K13KLL
K121BUD	K4KLL	UJI1759	H959DRJ
K122BUD	K5KLL	UJI1760	H954DRJ
K123BUD	K6KLL	UJI1761	H957DRJ
K124BUD	K70KLL	UJI1762	H960DRJ
K125BUD	K8KLL	UJI1763	H958DRJ
K126BUD	K9KLL		

Liveries: Red, white and blue (Buses); dark blue, yellow and white (City Link); green, white and blue (Park & Ride)

On order:- 20 Dennis Trident double-deck buses and 15 Volvo B10.

Allocation:

Cowley Road, Oxford (City Line) - *CityLink (all Volvo coaches)*

Volvo coach	1	2	3	4	5	6	7	8
	9	10	11	12	41	42	43	44
	50	51	52	53	54	55	56	57
	58	59	60	61	62	63		
MetroRider	777	778	779	780	781	782	783	
Dart	401	402	403	404	405	406	407	408
	409	410	501	502	503	504	505	506
	507	508	509	510	511	512	513	514
	515	516	517	518	519	520		
Volvo B10B	601	602	603	604	605	606	607	608
	609	610	611	612	613	614	615	616
	617	618	619	620	621	622	623	624
	625	626	627	628	629	630	631	632
	633	634	635	636	637	638	639	640
	641	642	643	644	645	646	647	648
	649	650	651	652	653	654	655	656
Titan	950	956	960	966	968	970	975	
Olympian	201	202	203	204	205	206	207	208
	209	210	211	212	213	214	215	216
	217	218	219	220	221	222	223	224
	225	226	227	228	229			

Newlands Road, High Wycombe (Wycombe Bus)

Mercedes-Benz	703	704	708	709	710	711	712	714
	715	716	717	718	719	720	724	727
Dart	421	422	423	424	425	426	427	
National	385	386	387	388	389	390	391	392
Lynx	301	302	303	304	305			
Olympian	230	231	232	233	234	235	236	237
	238	239	240	241	242	999		

Unallocated:

MetroRider	755	768	769	770	771	771	773
	775	776					

Oxford has pioneered Park & Ride services and a well established network of routes has been developed. The Oxford Bus Company use a fleet of double-deckers for these operations in a distinctive green white and blue livery. Eastern Coach Works-bodied Leyland Olympian 210, WWL210X is seen in this scheme. Dennis Trident low-floor double deckers have been ordered for Park & Ride in the city.

COLISEUM

Coliseum Coaches Ltd, Botley Road Garage, West End, Southampton, SO30 3JA

MIB653	Volvo B10M-61	Jonckheere Jubilee	C57F	1988
MIB649	MAN 16.290	Jonckheere Jubilee	C53F	1989
435SFC	Kässbohrer Setra S215HD	Kässbohrer Tornado	C32FT	1990
VOI890	Kässbohrer Setra S215HR	Kässbohrer Rational	C53F	1990
HIL7978	MAN 10.180	Jonckheere Deauville	C32FT	1992
MIB652	MAN 16.290	Jonckheere Deauville	C49FT	1993
MIB650	Volvo B10M-62	Van Hool Alizée	C46FT	1995
MIB651	Volvo B10M-62	Van Hool Alizée	C46FT	1995
WCR474	Iveco EuroRider 391.12.35	Beulas Stergo E35	C49FT	1995
WCR833	Iveco EuroRider 391.12.35	Beulas Stergo E35	C49FT	1996
KIB8111	Iveco EuroRider 391.12.35	Beulas Stergo E35	C49FT	1997
VFJ687	Dennis Javelin	Neoplan Transliner	C49F	1998
636VHX	Dennis Javelin	Neoplan Transliner	C53F	1998
S	MAN 18.350	Neoplan Transliner	C49FT	1998
S	MAN 18.350	Neoplan Transliner	C32FT	1998

Previous Registrations:

MIB653	E210GNV	VOI890	G237GDC	all others	from new

Named vehicle:- 435SFC *Statesman (to be re-named Emperor when the new MAN coaches arrive).*

Livery:- Silver, mauve and magenta

Iveco have been trying to establish their Italian built chassis in the United Kingdom in recent years. The EuroRider is a coach chassis which has achieved some market penetration. Coliseum have bought three of this type, all of which are fitted with Beulas Stergo coachwork. The oldest of the trio is WCR474. *David Donati collection*

COUNTYWIDE TRAVEL

Countywide Travel Ltd, 16 Stoneham Lane, Swaythling, Southampton, SO16 2NP

NIB7625	Leyland Leopard PSU3C/4R	Willowbrook	B48F	1976	Mayne, Manchester, 1996
PJT262R	Leyland National 11351A/1R		B49F	1976	Marchwood Motorways, 1997
PJT271R	Leyland National 11351A/1R		B49F	1976	Marchwood Motorways, 1996
VFB617T	Bedford YMT	Caetano Alpha	C53F	1979	Marchwood Motorways, 1996
D259JPR	Ford Transit	Deansgate	M12	1987	Marchwood Motorways, 1995
F730OOT	Iveco Daily 49.10	Robin Hood City Nippy	B23F	1988	Marchwood Motorways, 1996
F851YJX	DAF SB2305DHTD585	Plaxton Paramount 3200 III	C53F	1989	Marchwood Motorways, 1995
UDZ7334	DAF SB2300DHS585	Caetano Algarve	C53F	1989	Logan, Dunloy, 1996
H186EJF	Toyota Coaster HDB30R	Caetano Optimo II	C21F	1991	Marchwood Motorways, 1995
J137LLK	Toyota Coaster HDB30R	Caetano Optimo II	C18F	1991	Capital, West Drayton, 1996
N305FOR	Iveco TurboDaily 59-12	Mellor	B29F	1996	Marchwood Motorways, 1996
P616LTP	Iveco TurboDaily 59-12	Mellor	B29F	1997	
R163GNW	DAF DE33WSSB3000	Ikarus Blue Danube	C55F	1998	
R164GNW	DAF DE33WSSB3000	Ikarus Blue Danube	C55F	1998	

Previous Registrations:

NIB7625   NTX362R   UDZ7334   G745BCV

Livery:- Grey, black and yellow

Depot:- Provincial Way, Basingstoke.

The Countywide Travel fleet contains a number of buses and coaches previously operated by Marchwood Motorways. One of the coaches obtained in this way is F851YJX. A Plaxton Paramount-bodied DAF, the West Yorkshire registration mark indicates that the vehicle was supplied by Hughes-DAF, the coach dealer which now is part of the Arriva group. *Colin Lloyd*

COURTNEY

Courtney Coaches Ltd, Terranova House, Kiln Lane, Bracknell, RG12 5EU

TXI8764	Volvo B10M-61	Van Hool Alizée	C53F	1985	Dereham Coachways, 1996
MIL4530	Volvo B10M-61	Van Hool Alizée	C53F	1985	Chivers, Elstead, 1996
D613WEY	Freight Rover Sherpa	Dormobile	B16F	1986	Cerbydau Carreglefn, 1996
SIB8342	Volvo B10M-61	Van Hool Alizée	C49FT	1987	Birmingham Coach Co, 1996
D898YCF	Mercedes-Benz L307D	Devon Conversions	M12	1987	Buckland, Hurst, 1989
F888XOE	Freight Rover Sherpa	Carlyle Citybus 2	B20F	1988	Merry Hill Minibuses, 1998
F254MGB	Volvo B10M-60	Van Hool Alizée	C49FT	1989	Meon Valley Cs, Moreton, 1997
F221DDY	Leyland Swift LBM6T/2RS	Wadham Stringer Vanguard	C33F	1989	Gatwick Parking, 1997
G277BEL	Toyota Coaster HB31R	Caetano Optimo	C21F	1989	Ayreville, Plymouth, 1995
G800RNC	Leyland Tiger TRCTL11/3ARZ	Duple 320	C53F	1989	Shearings, 1993
G802RNC	Leyland Tiger TRCTL11/3ARZ	Duple 320	C53F	1989	Shearings, 1993
G343WHY	Mercedes-Benz 609D	Made-to-Measure	C26F	1990	Redwood Travel, West Byfleet, 1998
H329POG	Scania K113TRB	Van Hool Astrobel	CH53/14CT	1990	Birmingham Coach Co, 1998
H640UWE	Mercedes-Benz 609D	Whittaker Europa	B19F	1991	Silverwing, Brislington, 1995
J907GTC	Mercedes-Benz 609D	Autobus Classique	C21F	1992	Silverwing, Brislington, 1995
L89EWO	Mercedes-Benz 814D	Crystals	C33F	1994	Bebb, Llantwit Fardre, 1996
P991RNV	Mercedes-Benz 711D	Olympus	C24F	1994	van, 1998
P992RNW	Mercedes-Benz 711D	Olympus	C24F	1994	van, 1998
P18CCL	Mercedes-Benz 611D	Olympus	C24F	1996	

Previous Registrations:

D613WEY	D738PTU, GEY124	MIL4530	B481UNB, JXI507
F221DDY	F131UMD, A15GPS	SIB8342	D848KVE
H329POG	H133ACU, KSU473, H682FCU	TXI8764	B916BGA, 341AYF, B94EGG
	H10WLE		

Livery:- white with multigraphics.

This Courtney coach carries an elaborate multigraphic livery. One of two double-deck coaches in the fleet, this vehicle is a tri-axle Scania K113TRB. The Van Hool body type for this chassis is the Astrobel, which has only 14 seats in the lower saloon. H329POG, which was photographed at Chessington, was new to Busways for its Newcastle to London Clipper service. *David Heath*

DAISH'S HOTEL

Daish's Hotel Ltd, 79A High Street, Shanklin, Isle of Wight, PO37 6NP

ONE	F905YNV	Volvo B10M-60	Jonckheere Deauville	C51FT	1989	West Kingsdown Coaches, 1994
TWO	F904YNV	Volvo B10M-60	Jonckheere Deauville	C51FT	1989	West Kingsdown Coaches, 1994
THREE	G168RBD	Volvo B10M-60	Jonckheere Deauville	C51FT	1990	Silver Fox, Renfrew, 1996
FOUR	G43HDW	Volvo B10M-60	Jonckheere Deauville	C51FT	1990	Escort Cs, Middlesbrough, 1996
FIVE	G457MGG	Volvo B10M-60	Jonckheere Deauville	C51FT	1990	Barnard Castle, Newsham, 1998

Livery:- White, blue and turquoise

EASSON'S

Easson's Coaches (Southampton) Ltd, 44 Wodehouse Road, Southampton, Hampshire, SO19 2EQ

WNR63	Volvo B10M-61	Van Hool Alizée	C53F	1987	Shearings, 1992
E68MCR	Mercedes-Benz 811D	Robin Hood	C24F	1988	
VIJ68	Kässbohrer Setra S210HD	Kässbohrer	C39F	1988	
F69RBK	Ford Transit VE6	Ford	M11	1988	
64AAE	Kässbohrer Setra S215HRI	Kässbohrer Rational	C35FT	1990	
67DNR	Van Hool T815H	Van Hool Alicron	C49FT	1993	
66BXC	Kässbohrer Setra S250	Kässbohrer Special	C49FT	1995	
P76MOR	Mercedes-Benz Sprinter 312D	Mercedes-Benz	M16	1997	
P77ECL	Mercedes-Benz 814D	Robin Hood	C24F	1997	
P77EAS	Volvo B10M-62	Plaxton Excalibur	C52F	1997	
TOK65	Neoplan N212H	Neoplan Jetliner	C37FT	1998	

Previous Registrations:

64AAE	G841AOW	TOK65	From new
66BXC	M75BOR	VIJ68	E68MTB
67DNR	K73OOW	WNR63	D546MVR

Livery:- Tan, brown and red

It is unusual, but by no means unique, for a hotel to operate its own coach fleet but Daish's Hotel of Shanklin has taken this step for the conveyance of patrons. The fleet of Volvo B10M coaches are all of a similar age and specification. F905YNV is numbered *one* and, in common with the other four coaches, carries a Jonckheere Deauville body. *Don Vincent*

The Kässbohrer Setra coach business was acquired by Daimler-Benz in 1995. The combined bus and coach arm of this German conglomerate is now known as EvoBus but the Setra name continues to be used on vehicle produced at Ulm. Eassons have four Setra coaches in service. S250 model M75BOR is now registered 66BXC and is seen with its former registration mark in this view. *David Donati collection*

FIRST BEELINE
FIRST LONDON BUSLINES

The Berks Bucks Bus Co Ltd, MacMillan House,
Paddington Station, London W2 1TY

D201	K279XJB	Dennis Dart 9.8SDL3017	Plaxton Pointer	B40F	1993	
D202	K281XJB	Dennis Dart 9.8SDL3017	Plaxton Pointer	B40F	1993	
D203	K282XJB	Dennis Dart 9.8SDL3017	Plaxton Pointer	B40F	1993	
D204	K283XJB	Dennis Dart 9.8SDL3017	Plaxton Pointer	B40F	1993	
D205	L205GMO	Dennis Dart 9.8SDL3035	Plaxton Pointer	B37F	1993	
D206	L206GMO	Dennis Dart 9.8SDL3035	Plaxton Pointer	B37F	1993	
D207	L207GMO	Dennis Dart 9.8SDL3035	Plaxton Pointer	B37F	1993	
D208	L208GMO	Dennis Dart 9.8SDL3035	Plaxton Pointer	B37F	1993	

D601-632

Dennis Dart — Plaxton Pointer — B37F — 1996

601	N601XJM	608	N608XJM	615	N615XJM	621	N621XJM	627	P627CGM
602	N602XJM	609	N609XJM	616	N616XJM	622	N622XJM	628	P628CGM
603	N603XJM	610	N610XJM	617	N617XJM	623	N623XJM	629	P629CGM
604	N604XJM	611	N611XJM	618	N618XJM	624	N624XJM	630	P630CGM
605	N605XJM	612	N612XJM	619	N619XJM	625	N625XJM	631	P631CGM
606	N606XJM	613	N613XJM	620	N620XJM	626	N626XJM	632	P632CGM
607	N607XJM	614	N614XJM						

DML633-653

Dennis Dart SLF — Marshall Capital — N37F — 1997-98

633	R633VLX	638	R638VLX	642	R642TLM	646	R646TLM	650	R650TLM
634	R634VLX	639	R639VLX	643	R643TLM	647	R647TLM	651	R651TLM
635	R835VLX	640	R640VLX	644	R644TLM	648	R648TLM	652	R652TLM
636	R636VLX	641	R641VLX	645	R645TLM	649	R649TLM	653	R653TLM
637	R637VLX								

L7	P407MLA	Dennis Dart SLF	Plaxton Pointer	N34F	1996	CentreWest, 1997

L211-217

Dennis Dart SLF — Plaxton Pointer — N37F — 1996

211	N211WRD	213	N213WRD	215	N215WRD	216	N216WRD	217	N217WRD
212	N212WRD	214	N214WRD					

L237	P237NLW	Dennis Dart SLF	Plaxton Pointer	N37F	1997	CentreWest, 1997
L238	P238NLW	Dennis Dart SLF	Plaxton Pointer	N37F	1997	CentreWest, 1997
L239	P239NLW	Dennis Dart SLF	Plaxton Pointer	N37F	1997	CentreWest, 1997
LA506	G55XLO	Leyland Olympian ONCL10/1RZ	Alexander RL	H47/28F	1989	
LA507	G56XLO	Leyland Olympian ONCL10/1RZ	Alexander RL	H47/28F	1989	

LN501-505

Leyland Olympian ONCL10/1RZ — Northern Counties — H45/29F — 1989

501	F172LBL	502	F173LBL	503	F174LBL	504	F175LBL	505	F176LBL

LX800	F101GRM	Leyland Lynx LX112L10ZR1R	Leyland Lynx	DP48F	1988	CentreWest, 1997
LX801	K801CAN	Leyland Lynx LX2R11V18Z4S	Leyland Lynx 2	B51F	1992	Stagecoach South, 1992
LX802	K802CAN	Leyland Lynx LX2R11V18Z4S	Leyland Lynx 2	B51F	1992	Stagecoach South, 1992
LX803	D751DLO	Leyland Lynx LX112TL11ZR1S	Leyland Lynx	B49F	1987	
LX804	D752DLO	Leyland Lynx LX112TL11ZR1S	Leyland Lynx	B49F	1987	
LX805	D753DLO	Leyland Lynx LX112TL11ZR1S	Leyland Lynx	B49F	1987	
LX806	D754DLO	Leyland Lynx LX112TL11ZR1S	Leyland Lynx	B49F	1987	
LX807	809DYE	Leyland Lynx LX112TL11ZR1R	Leyland Lynx	DP48F	1988	CentreWest, 1997
LX808	D756DLO	Leyland Lynx LX112TL11ZR1S	Leyland Lynx	B49F	1987	
LX809	292CLT	Leyland Lynx LX112TL11ZR1R	Leyland Lynx	DP48F	1988	CentreWest, 1996

RB551	K651DBL	Renault S75	Plaxton Beaver	B18FL	1992	
RB552	K652DBL	Renault S75	Plaxton Beaver	B18FL	1992	
RB553	K653DBL	Renault S75	Plaxton Beaver	B18FL	1992	

First BeeLine continue to operate the Reading to Heathrow Rail/Air link. It was started many years ago by the Alder Valley company from which was split the Bee Line operation. No.798, N798WAN is a Scania K113CRB that carries a special green and grey dedicated livery on its Berkhof Excellence coachwork. *Ralph Stevens*

The Renault S75 is a larger and more robust vehicle than the more common S56. Both models can trace their design back to the Commer Walk-Thru van. A batch of 90 Wright-bodied S75 midibuses were placed in service with what is now the CentreWest company in London in 1990. FirstGroup have now cascaded forty-nine of the batch to Bee Line. All still carry their London fleet numbers as shown by RW34, HDZ5434. *Mark Lyons*

RW1-53 Renault S75 Wright B28F 1990 CentreWest, 1997

1	HDZ5401	11	HDZ5411	22	HDZ5422	33	HDZ5433	44	HDZ5444
2	HDZ5402	13	HDZ5413	23	HDZ5423	34	HDZ5434	45w	HDZ5445
3	HDZ5403	14	HDZ5414	24	HDZ5424	35	HDZ5435	47	HDZ5447
4	HDZ5404	15	HDZ5415	25	HDZ5425	36	HDZ5436	48	HDZ5448
5	HDZ5405	16w	HDZ5416	26	HDZ5426	37	HDZ5437	49	HDZ5449
6	HDZ5406	17	HDZ5417	27	HDZ5427	38	HDZ5438	50	HDZ5450
7	HDZ5407	18	HDZ5418	29	HDZ5429	39	HDZ5439	51	HDZ5451
8	HDZ5408	19	HDZ5419	30	HDZ5430	42	HDZ5442	52	HDZ5452
9	HDZ5409	20	HDZ5420	31	HDZ5431	43	HDZ5443	53	HDZ5453
10	HDZ5410	21	HDZ5421	32	HDZ5432				

SB740-746 Scania K113CRB Berkhof Excellence 2000 C53F 1991

740	TJI4830	742	TJI4832	744	TJI4834	745	TJI4835
741	TJI4831	743	TJI4833					746	TJI4836

SB791-798 Scania K113CRB Berkhof Excellence 1000LD C53F 1995

791	M791TCF	793	M793TCF	795	N795WAN	797	N797WAN	798	N798WAN
792	M792TCF	794	M794TCF	796	N796WAN				

SN810-819 Scania L113CRL Northern Counties Paladin N51F 1988

810	M810PGM	812	M812PGM	814	M814PGM	816	M816PGM	818	M818PGM
811	M811PGM	813	M813PGM	815	M815PGM	817	M817PGM	819	M819PGM

TP768	TJI4838	Leyland Tiger TRCTL11/3ARZA	Plaxton Paramount 3200 III	C53F	1988	Luton & District, 1993
VJ782	TJI4822	Volvo B10M-60	Jonckheere Deauville P50	C55F	1989	Alder Valley, 1992
VJ783	TJI4823	Volvo B10M-60	Jonckheere Deauville P50	C55F	1989	Alder Valley, 1992
VJ786	TJI4826	Volvo B10M-60	Jonckheere Deauville P50	C55F	1989	Alder Valley, 1992
VJ788	TJI4828	Volvo B10M-60	Jonckheere Deauville P50	C55F	1989	Alder Valley, 1992
VJ789	TJI4829	Volvo B10M-60	Jonckheere Deauville P50	C55F	1989	Alder Valley, 1992
VJ790	TJI4820	Volvo B10M-60	Jonckheere Deauville P50	C55F	1989	Alder Valley, 1992

Ancilliary vehicles:

LS470	GUW470W	Leyland National 2 NL106AL11/2r(Volvo)	DP43F	1981	First CentreWest, 1986
LS497	GUW497W	Leyland National 2 NL106AL11/2r(Volvo)	DP43F	1981	First CentreWest, 1986

Previous Registrations:

292CLT	F102GRM	TJI4829	F759OJH
809DYE	D105NDW	TJI4830	F740TDP
HDZ5401 etc	From new	TJI4831	F741TDP
TJI4820	F760OJH	TJI4832	F742TDP
TJI4822	F772OJH	TJI4833	F743TDP
TJI4823	F773OJH	TJI4834	F744TDP
TJI4826	F756OJH	TJI4835	F745TDP
TJI4828	F758OJH	TJI4836	F746TDP

Livery: FirstGroup:- Stone, purple and magenta (new low floor vehicles); yellow, blue and orange (First Beeline); green and grey (RailAir); yellow, two-tone brown and orange (First London Buslines);

Opposite,top:- **Pictured at Bracknell bus station is Northern Counties-bodied Leyland Olympian L505, F176LBL. It has been painted in a special scheme for BAA's Heathrow Airport, where the vehicle is frequently found.** *Malc McDonald*
Opposite, bottom:- **In 1988 The Bee Line took delivery of ten Scania L113s with Northern Counties bodywork. These, including SN813, M813PGM seen here, carry the bright yellow, blue and orange livery introduced by Bee Line before they became part of FirstGroup.** *Malc McDonald*

Allocations

Bracknell (Market Street) - The Bee Line

Renault	RW42	RW43	RW47	RW48	RW49	RW50	RW51	RW52
	RW53							
Dart	L211	L212						
Lynx	LX800	LX801	LX802	LX803	LX804	LX808	LX809	
Scania Coach	SB740	SB741	SB742	SB743	SB744	SB745	SB746	SB791
	SB792	SB793	SB794	SB795	SB796	SB797	SB798	
Scania Bus	SN810	SN811	SN812	SN813	SN814	SN815	SN816	SN817
	SN818	SN819						
Olympian	LN501	LN502	LN503	LN504	LN505	LA506	LA507	

Slough (Stanley Cottages) - The Bee Line

Renault	RW1	RW2	RW3	RW4	RW5	RW6	RW7	RW8
	RW9	RW10	RW11	RW13	RW14	RW15	RW17	RW18
	RW19	RW20	RW21	RW22	RW23	RW24	RW25	RW26
	RW27	RW29	RW30	RW31	RW32	RW33	RW34	RW35
	RW36	RW37	RW38	RW39	RW44			
Dart	D201	D202	D203	D204	D205	D206	D207	D208
	L213	L214	L215	L216	L217			
Lynx	LX805	LX806	LX807					
Tiger	TP768							
Volvo	VJ782	VJ783	VJ786	VJ788	VJ789	VJ790		

Southall (Bridge Road) - London Buslines

Renault	RB551	RB552	RB553					
Dart	D601	D602	D603	D604	D605	D606	D607	D608
	D609	D610	D611	D612	D613	D614	D615	D616
	D617	D618	D619	D620	D621	D622	D623	D624
	D625	D626	D627	D628	D629	D630	D631	D632
	DML633	DML634	DML635	DML636	DML637	DML638	DML63	
	DML640	DML641	DML642	DML643	DML644	DML645	DML646	
	DML647	DML648	DML649	DML650	DML651	DML652	DML635	
	L7	L237	L238	L239				

Unallocated

National (trainers)	LS470	LS497
Renault	RW16	RW45

The Bee Line purchased four 37-seat Plaxton Pointer-bodied Dennis Darts in 1993. One of the quartet is D208, L208GMO shown here in the green, yellow and grey livery applied to buses dedicated to services 74 & 75 which link Heathrow and Slough with Maidenhead and High Wycombe.
Malc McDonald

FIRST CITYBUS

Southampton Citybus Ltd, 226 Portswood Road, Southampton, SO17 2BE

102	F102RTR	Leyland Lynx LX112L10ZR1S	Leyland Lynx	B47F	1989
104	G104WRV	Leyland Lynx LX2R11C15Z4R	Leyland Lynx	B47F	1990
105	G105WRV	Leyland Lynx LX2R11C15Z4R	Leyland Lynx	B47F	1990
106	G106WRV	Leyland Lynx LX2R11C15Z4R	Leyland Lynx	B47F	1990
108	G108WRV	Leyland Lynx LX2R11C15Z4R	Leyland Lynx	B47F	1990

109-113   Leyland Lynx LX2R11C15Z4R   Leyland Lynx   B47F*   1990   *112/3 are DP47F

109	G109XOW	110	G110XOW	111	G111XOW	112	G112XOW	113	G113XOW

114	K114PRV	Volvo B10B	Northern Counties Paladin	B51F	1993
115	M967GDU	Volvo B10B	Plaxton Verde	B51F	1994 Plaxton demonstrator, 1995

212-231   Leyland Atlantean AN68A/1R   East Lancashire   H45/31F   1977-78

212	MCR212R	225	PBP225S	229	PBP229S	230	PBP230S	231	PBP231S
224	PBP224S	228	PBP228S						

232-266   Leyland Atlantean AN68A/1R   East Lancashire   H45/31F   1979-81   265/6 are H40/31F

232	UPO232T	239	UPO239T	246	UPO246T	253	YRV253V	260	YRV260V
233	UPO233T	240	UPO240T	247	YRV247V	254	YRV254V	261	YRV261V
234	UPO234T	241	UPO241T	248	YRV248V	255	YRV255V	262	DBK262W
235	UPO235T	242	UPO242T	249	YRV249V	256	YRV256V	263	DBK263W
236	UPO236T	243	UPO243T	250	YRV250V	257	YRV257V	264	DBK264W
237	UPO237T	244	UPO244T	251	YRV251V	258	YRV258V	265	DBK265W
238	UPO238T	245	UPO245T	252	YRV252V	259	YRV259V	266	DBK266W

267-276   Leyland Atlantean AN68C/1R   East Lancashire   H40/31F   1981-82

267	FTR267X	269	FTR269X	271	FTR271X	273	KOW273Y	275	KOW275Y
268	FTR268X	270	FTR270X	272	KOW272Y	274	KOW274Y	276	KOW276Y

277	A277ROW	Dennis Dominator DDA171	East Lancashire	H46/30F	1984
289	E289HRV	Leyland Olympian ONLXB/1RH	East Lancashire	DPH43/27F	1987
290	E290HRV	Leyland Olympian ONLXB/1RH	East Lancashire	DPH43/27F	1987

The former Southampton City fleet is now part of FirstGroup. Seen before 'First' identity was applied, 115, M967GDU is a Plaxton Verde-bodied Volvo B10B that was previously used throughout the country as a demonstrator for Plaxton. It is seen operating on express service 747 which runs to Portsmouth where FirstGroup have the Provincial fleet. *Philip Stephenson*

The large pod on the roof of this Dennis Dart indicates that it is powered by compressed natural gas (CNG). FirstGroup are experimenting with this type of environmentally-friendly fuel at a number of locations. In the Southampton fleet there are ten vehicles purpose built to be powered by CNG including 336, N165GOT, shown here. *Malc McDonald*

291-296

	Volvo Olympian YN2RV18Z4			Northern Counties Palatine	H47/30F	1996			
291	P291KPX	293	P293KPX	294	P294KPX	295	P295KPX	296	P296KPX
292	P292KPX								

301-305

	Dennis Dart 9SDL3002			Duple Dartline	B36F	1990			
301	G301XCR	302	G302XCR	303	G303XCR	304	G304XCR	305	G305XCR

306	H306DRV	Dennis Dart 9SDL3002	Carlyle Dartline	B35F	1990	
307	G895XPX	Dennis Dart 8.5SDL3003	Wadham Stringer Portsdown	B31F	1990	Wadham Stringer demo, 1990
308	H308DRV	Dennis Dart 9SDL3002	Reeve Burgess Pointer	B35F	1991	

309-313

	Dennis Dart 9SDL3011			Plaxton Pointer	B35F	1993			
309	L309RTP	310	L310RTP	311	L311RTP	312	L312RTP	313	L313RTP

314-329

	Dennis Dart 9SDL3051*			Plaxton Pointer	B35F	1994-95 *314/5 are 9SDL3031			
314	M314YOT	318	M318YOT	321	M321YOT	324	N324ECR	327	N327ECR
315	M315YOT	319	M319YOT	322	M322YOT	325	N325ECR	328	N328ECR
316	M316YOT	320	M320YOT	323	M323YOT	326	N326ECR	329	N329ECR
317	M317YOT								

330-339

	Dennis Dart			Plaxton Pointer	B35F	1996			
330G	N159GOT	332G	N161GOT	334G	N163GOT	336G	N165GOT	338G	N167GOT
331G	N160GOT	333G	N162GOT	335G	N164GOT	337G	N166GOT	339G	N168GOT

Opposite, top:- **Atlantean 261, YRV261V**, represents the CityBus double-deck fleet. It well reflects its municipal origins with the East Lancashire-bodied Leyland Atlantean, a combination much respected for quality of build if not style. As with the other 'First' fleets, the livery on older vehicle will continue with local colours. The lower picture shows the style applied to new low floor buses, chosen after much research into the passengers preferred colours. The vehicle seen is **414, R414WPX**. *Mark Lyons*.

400	N615DWY	Dennis Dart 9.8SDL3054	Plaxton Pointer	B40F	1995	Hughes-DAF, 1996		
401	N465ETR	Dennis Dart 9.8SDL3054	Plaxton Pointer	B40F	1995			
402	N466ETR	Dennis Dart 9.8SDL3054	Plaxton Pointer	B40F	1995			
403	N467ETR	Dennis Dart 9.8SDL3054	Plaxton Pointer	B40F	1995			
404	P404KOW	Dennis Dart SLF	Plaxton Pointer	N37F	1996			
405	P405KOW	Dennis Dart SLF	Plaxton Pointer	N37F	1996			
406	P406KOW	Dennis Dart SLF	Plaxton Pointer	N37F	1996			
407	P407KOW	Dennis Dart SLF	Plaxton Pointer	N37F	1996			

408-427

		Dennis Dart SLF	Plaxton Pointer 2	N37F	1998

408	R408WPX	412	R412WPX	416	R416WPX	420	R420WPX	424	R424WPX
409	R409WPX	413	R413WPX	417	R417WPX	421	R421WPX	425	R425WPX
410	R410WPX	414	R414WPX	418	R418WPX	422	R422WPX	426	R426WPX
411	R411WPX	415	R415WPX	419	R419WPX	423	R423WPX	427	R427WPX

710	AAE653V	Leyland National 2 NL116L11/1R		B52F	1980	Brewers, 1997
711	AAE663V	Leyland National 2 NL116L11/1R		DP47F	1980	Brewers, 1997

Ancilliary vehicles:

002	C433BHY	Ford Transit 190	Dormobile	B16F	1986	White Horse Ferries, 1995
003	C443BHY	Ford Transit 190	Dormobile	B2F	1986	White Horse Ferries, 1995
—	CTM406T	Leyland Leopard PSU3E/4R	Duple Dominant II	C53F	1979	Hants & Sussex, 1996

Livery:- FirstGroup:- stone, purple and magenta (new low floor vehicles); red.

A number of Leyland Lynx single deck buses were sold by Southampton after a very short period in service. However, FirstGroup have retained the remaining vehicles of this now established type including 110, G110XOW.*Richard Godfrey*

FIRST PROVINCIAL

The Provincial Bus Company Ltd, Hoeford, Gosport Road, Fareham PO16 0ST

| 100 | VCL461 | Mercedes-Benz 609D | Reeve Burgess Beaver | DP20F | 1988 | Diesel-electric Hybrid vehicle |
| 147w | H463GTM | Iveco Daily 49.10 | Mellor | B21F | 1990 | Blue Admiral, 1996 |

160-165

Iveco TurboDaily 59.12   WS Coachbuilders Wessex II B27F   1993

| 160 | K160PPO | 162 | K162PPO | 163 | K163PPO | 164 | K164PPO | 165 | K165PPO |
| 161 | K161PPO | | | | | | | | |

166-207

Iveco TurboDaily 59.12   Marshall C31   B27F   1993-95

166	L166TRV	175	L175TRV	183	M183XTR	191	M191XTR	199	M199XTR
167	L167TRV	176	L176TRV	184	M184XTR	192	M192XTR	201	M201XTR
168	L168TRV	177	L177TRV	185	M185XTR	193	M193XTR	202	M202XTR
169	L169TRV	178	L178TRV	186	M186XTR	194	M194XTR	203	M203XTR
170	L170TRV	179	M179XTR	187	M187XTR	195	M195XTR	204	M204BPO
171	L171TRV	180	M180XTR	188	M188XTR	196	M196XTR	205	M205BPO
172	L172TRV	181	M181XTR	189	M189XTR	197	M197XTR	206	M206BPO
173	L173TRV	182	M182XTR	190	M190XTR	198	M198XTR	207	M207BPO
174	L174TRV								

208-213

Iveco TurboDaily 59-12   Marshall C31   B26D   1994   Blue Admiral, 1996

| 208 | M642HDV | 210 | M644HDV | 211 | M645HDV | 212 | M646HDV | 213 | M647HDV |
| 209 | M643HDV | | | | | | | | |

221-259

Iveco TurboDaily 59-12   Mellor Duet   B26D   1992-93 Blue Admiral, 1996

221	K701UTT	229	K710UTT	237	K802WFJ	245	K912VDV	253	K921VDV
222	K703UTT	230	K712UTT	238	K819WFJ	246	K914VDV	254	K922VDV
223	K704UTT	231	K715UTT	239	K619XOD	247	K915VDV	255	K923VDV
224	K705UTT	232	K716UTT	240	K621XOD	248	K916VDV	256	K928VDV
225	K706UTT	233	K723UTT	241	K622XOD	249	K917VDV	257	K929VDV
226	K707UTT	234	K728UTT	242	K623XOD	250	K918VDV	258	K930VDV
227	K708UTT	235	K729UTT	243	K633XOD	251	K919VDV	259	K931VDV
228	K709UTT	236	K801WFJ	244	K911VDV	252	K920VDV		

260-271

Iveco TurboDaily 59-12   Mellor-Duet   B26D   1993   Blue Admiral, 1996

260	L311BOD	263	L314BOD	266	L317BOD	268	L320BOD	270	L323BOD
261	L312BOD	264	L315BOD	267	L319BOD	269	L322BOD	271	L324BOD
262	L313BOD	265	L316BOD						

307	PCG920M	Leyland National 1151/2R/0403	B44D	1972	
312	JBP129P	Leyland National 11351/2R	B44D	1975	
314	JBP132P	Leyland National 11351/2R	B44D	1975	
315	JBP133P	Leyland National 11351/2R	B44D	1975	
316	MJT880P	Leyland National 11351/1R	B49F	1976	Hants & Dorset, 1983
317	RUF37R	Leyland National 11351A/2R	B44D	1977	Rennies, Dunfermline, 1988
318	SPR39R	Leyland National 11351A/1R	B49F	1977	Hants & Dorset, 1983
319	SPR40R	Leyland National 11351A/1R	B49F	1977	Hants & Dorset, 1983
320	SPR41R	Leyland National 11351A/1R	B49F	1977	Hants & Dorset, 1983
321	RJT147R	Leyland National 11351A/1R	B49F	1977	Hants & Dorset, 1983
322	RJT148R	Leyland National 11351A/1R	B49F	1977	Hants & Dorset, 1983
323	LTP634R	Leyland National 11351A/2R	B44D	1977	
324	MOW636R	Leyland National 11351A/2R	B44D	1977	
325	MOW637R	Leyland National 11351A/2R	B44D	1977	
327	PTR238S	Leyland National 11351A/2R	B44D	1977	
329	WFX257S	Leyland National 11351A/1R	DP48F	1978	Hants & Dorset, 1983
330	SBK740S	Leyland National 11351A/2R	B44D	1978	
331	UFX847S	Leyland National 11351A/1R	B49F	1977	Hants & Dorset, 1983
332	UFX848S	Leyland National 11351A/1R	B49F	1977	Hants & Dorset, 1983
333	VFX980S	Leyland National 11351A/1R	B49F	1978	Hants & Dorset, 1983
334	TPX41T	Leyland National 11351A/2R	B44D	1979	
336	UPO443T	Leyland National 11351A/1R	B44D	1979	
337	UPO444T	Leyland National 11351A/2R	B44D	1979	

Displaying the FirstGroup's corporate bus livery is First Provincial 622, R622YCR. This Dennis Dart SLF low floor is intended for services 17 & 18 as can be seen by the route lettering on the cantrail. The Hard in Portsmouth is the location of this view.

338	EEL893V	Leyland National 11351A/1R(Volvo)			B52F	1979	Hants & Dorset, 1983
401	A301KJT	Leyland National 2 NL116L11/1R			DP47F	1984	
402	A302KJT	Leyland National 2 NL116L11/1R			DP47F	1984	

403-411

Leyland National 2 NL116L11/1R — B49F* — 1980-81 — KCB Network, 1996
*403/4 are B52F

403	MDS855V	405	MDS857V	408	MDS867V	410	SNS827W	411	YFS306W
404	MDS856V	406	MDS863V	409	WAS766V				

413-418

Leyland National 2 NL116L11/1R — B49F — 1981 — KCB Network, 1996

413	AST151W	415	AST154W	416	AST156W	417	ST158W	418	AST159W
414	AST153W								

419	SWX534W	Leyland National 2 NL116AL11/1R		B52F	1981	KCB Network, 1996
420	UWY66X	Leyland National 2 NL116AL11/1R		B52F	1981	KCB Network, 1996
421	AAE645V	Leyland National 2 NL116L11/1R		B52F	1980	City Line, 1997
422	AAE652V	Leyland National 2 NL116L11/1R		B52F	1980	City Line, 1997
424	BOU3V	Leyland National 2 NL116L11/1R		B52F	1980	First Badgerline, 1998
427	BOU4V	Leyland National 2 NL116L11/1R		B52F	1980	First Badgerline, 1998
501	SFJ101R	Bristol VRT/SL3/6LXB	Eastern Coach Works	H43/31F	1977	Western National, 1993
502	NTC573R	Bristol VRT/SL3/6LXB	Eastern Coach Works	H43/27D	1977	City Line, 1994
503	RHT503S	Bristol VRT/SL3/6LXB	Eastern Coach Works	H43/27D	1978	City Line, 1994
504	RHT504S	Bristol VRT/SL3/6LXB	Eastern Coach Works	CO43/27D	1978	City Line, 1994

Opposite, top:- **FirstGroup have been undertaking trials with various types of fuel. Operating with First Provincial is 100, VCL461, which is hybrid vehicle that can operate with diesel and battery power. It is seen at the 1997 Showbus event at Duxford, which is considered the premier event for bus enthusiasts.** *Keith Grimes*
Opposite, bottom:- **First Provincial operate an ACE Cougar. Numbered 600, it is seen with locally-built bodywork by Wadham Stringer.** *Gerry Mead*

The UVG factory at Waterlooville was recently purchased from the Receivers by Salvador Caetano of Portugal. The new owners intend to continue production of the UrbanStar body for Dennis Dart chassis. First Provincial 601, N601EDP is one of a batch of seven such vehicles built in 1995. *Ivor Norman*

506w	UVX2S	Bristol VRT/SL3/6LXB	Eastern Coach Works	H39/31F	1977	Badgerline, 1994
507	UTO836S	Bristol VRT/SL3/501(6LXB)	Eastern Coach Works	H43/31F	1977	Western National, 1993
509	AFJ748T	Bristol VRT/SL3/6LXB	Eastern Coach Works	H43/31F	1979	Western National, 1993
510	AFJ752T	Bristol VRT/SL3/6LXB	Eastern Coach Works	H43/31F	1979	Western National, 1993
511	AFJ763T	Bristol VRT/SL3/6LXB	Eastern Coach Works	H43/31F	1979	Western National, 1993
512	AHU514V	Bristol VRT/SL3/6LXB	Eastern Coach Works	H43/27D	1980	Southampton Citybus, 1997
513	LWU471V	Bristol VRT/SL3/6LXB	Eastern Coach Works	H39/31F	1980	Rider York, 1995
594	MOD571P	Bristol VRT/SL3/6LXB	Eastern Coach Works	O43/31F	1976	Western National, 1993

600	H523CTR	ACE Cougar	Wadham Stringer Portsdown	B41F	1990

601-607   Dennis Dart 9.8SDL3054   UVG Urban Star   B40F   1995

601	N601EBP	**603**	N603EBP	**605**	N605EBP	**606**	N606EBP	**607**	N607EBP
602	N602EBP	**604**	N604EBP						

608-623   Dennis Dart SLF   Plaxton Pointer 2   N37F   1997-98

608	R608YCR	**612**	R612YCR	**615**	R615YCR	**618**	R618YCR	**621**	R621YCR
609	R609YCR	**613**	R613YCR	**616**	R616YCR	**619**	R619YCR	**622**	R622YCR
610	R610YCR	**614**	R614YCR	**617**	R617YCR	**620**	R620YCR	**623**	R623YCR
611	R611YCR								

624-635   Dennis Dart SLF   Plaxton Pointer 2   N40F   On order

624	S624...	**627**	S627...	**630**	S630...	**632**	S632...	**634**	S634...
625	S625...	**629**	S629...	**631**	S631...	**633**	S633...	**635**	S635...
626	S626...								

710-729   Mercedes-Benz 709D   Plaxton Beaver   B27F   1996

710	N710GRV	**714**	N714GRV	**718**	N718GRV	**722**	P722KCR	**726**	P726KCR
711	N711GRV	**715**	N715GRV	**719**	N719GRV	**723**	P723KCR	**727**	P727KCR
712	N712GRV	**716**	N716GRV	**720**	N720GRV	**724**	P724KCR	**728**	P728KCR
713	N713GRV	**717**	N717GRV	**721**	N721GRV	**725**	P725KCR	**729**	P729KCR

801-821	Mercedes-Benz 811D		Carlyle		B29F	1991		
801 H171GTA	**805**	H175GTA	**809**	H179GTA	**812**	H787GTA	**815**	H991FTT
803 H173GTA	**806**	H176GTA	**811**	H783GTA	**813**	H788GTA	**821**	H997FTT

Ancilliary vehicles:

949	B449WTC	Ford Transit 190		Dormobile	B16F	1985	Badgerline, 1995
966	D562HPO	Renault-Dodge G13		Wadham Stringer Vanguard	B39F	1986	MoD, 1997
967	B631XOW	Dodge G13		Reeve Burges	B39F	1984	AmAf, 1998

Previous Registrations:

B631XOW	?	D562HPO	80KF30	VCL461	E350AMR

Livery:- FirstGroup:- stone, purple and magenta (new low floor vehicles); cream and red.

On order:- 4 Volvo B10BLE/Wright Renown

Allocations

Hilsea (London Road)

Iveco	208	209	210	211	212	213	221	222
	223	224	225	226	227	228	229	230
	231	232	233	234	235	236	237	238
	239	240	241	242	243	244	245	246
	247	248	249	250	251	252	253	254
	255	256	257	258	259	260	261	262
	263	264	265	266	267	268	269	270
	271							
Mercedes-Benz	100	710	711	712	713	714	715	716
	717	718	728	729	801	803	805	806
	809	811						
	812	813	815					

Hoeford (Gosport Road)

Iveco	160	161	162	163	164	165	166	167
	168	169	170	171	172	173	174	175
	176	177	178	179	180	181	182	183
	184	185	186	187	188	189	190	191
	192	193	194	195	196	197	198	199
	201	202	203	204	205	206	207	
Mercedes-Benz	719	720	721	722	723	724	725	726
	727							
Dart	601	602	603	604	605	606	607	608
	609	610	611	612	613	614	615	616
	617	618	619	620	621	622	623	
National	307	312	314	315	316	317	318	319
	320	321	322	323	324	325	327	328
	329	330	331	332	333	334	336	337
	338	401	402	403	404	405	406	408
	409	410	411	413	414	415	416	417
	418	418	420	421	422	424	427	
ACE	600							
Bristol VR	501	502	503	504	506	507	509	510
	511	513	594					

Unallocated

Iveco	147
Bristol VR	506

FLEET COACHES

Fleet Coaches Ltd, 3 Crookham Road, Fleet, Hampshire, GU13 8DP

	YLC896S	Bedford YMT	Duple Dominant II	C53F	1978	Wilder, Feltham, 1982
	WSV489	Volvo B58-56	Duple Dominant II Express	C53F	1982	Newton, Dingwall, 1986
F2	F232DWF	Volvo B10M-61	Plaxton Paramount 3200 III	C53F	1988	
G4	G51WPF	Volvo B10M-60	Plaxton Paramount 3200 III	C53F	1990	
H1	H896JPG	Volvo B10M-60	Plaxton Paramount 3200 III	C53F	1991	
J1	J411AWF	Volvo B10M-60	Van Hool Alizée	C53F	1992	
J2	J412AWF	Volvo B10M-60	Van Hool Alizée	C53F	1992	
K1	K811EET	Volvo B10M-60	Van Hool Alizée	C53F	1992	
L1	L671OHL	Volvo B10M-62	Plaxton Première 320	C53F	1994	
L2	L672OHL	Volvo B10M-62	Plaxton Première 320	C53F	1994	
L3	L673OHL	Volvo B10M-62	Plaxton Première 320	C53F	1994	
N1	N901ABL	Volvo B10M-62	Berkhof Axial	C53F	1996	
N2	N902ABL	Volvo B10M-62	Berkhof Axial	C53F	1996	
N3	N903ABL	Volvo B10M-62	Berkhof Axial	C53F	1996	

Previous Registrations:

WSV489   ESB662X, 7622WF, OSJ83X

Livery:- Two-tone blue

Depots:- Fleet (Crookham Road) and Fleet (St James Road)

The Volvo B10M is the preferred chassis of Fleet Coaches. L672OHL carries Plaxton Premiére coachwork. This example is a 320 model built to a height of 3.2 metres. This view, taken in central London, shows the fleet number allocated as L2, an interesting numbering scheme using the registration year letter of the coach followed by the coach number that year. *Colin Lloyd*

FRIMLEY

I N Stone, Unit 1 Stubbs Industrial Estate, Hollybush Lane, Aldershot, Hampshire.
G G Stone, 11 Worsley Road, Frimley, Surrey.

NIL7247	Leyland National 1151/2R/0403		B25F	1972	Capital, West Drayton, 1997
WFM823L	Leyland National 1151/2R/0403		B21F	1972	Capital, West Drayton, 1997
GFJ658N	Leyland National 11351/2R		B24D	1975	Capital, West Drayton, 1997
KJD521P	Leyland National 10351A/2R		B24D	1976	Capital, West Drayton, 1997
OJD877R	Leyland National 10351A/2R		B24D	1977	Capital, West Drayton, 1997
PRE36W	Dennis Dominator DDA120	East Lancashire	H43/32F	1981	Maidstone & District, 1995
A108TRP	Leyland Tiger TRCTL11/3R	Plaxton Paramount 3200 E	C50FT	1983	S'coach United Counties, 1998
NIJ2636	DAF SB2300DHS585	Jonckheere Jubilee	C51F	1984	North Quay, N Walsham, 1997
E23ETN	DAF SB2300DHS585	Duple 340	C53F	1988	Capital, West Drayton, 1995
GIL8488	Dennis Javelin 11SDL1905	Duple 320	C53F	1988	The Shires, 1996
NIL7252	Dennis Javelin 12SDA1907	Duple 320	C57F	1988	Coombs, Weston-s-Mare, 1997
NIL7253	Dennis Javelin 12SDA1907	Duple 320	C57F	1988	Coombs, Weston-s-Mare, 1997
NIL7249	LAG G355Z	LAG Panoramic	C49FT	1989	Western National, 1997
NIL7251	Bova FHD12.—	Bova Futura	C—F	1990	??, 1997

Livery: .Green replacing silver and blue.

Previous Registrations:

GIL8488	E38SBO	NIL7251	?
NIJ2636	B502CBD	NIL7252	F682CYC
NIL7247	WFM815L, *CAP15*, WFM815L	NIL7253	F683CYC
NIL7248	?		
NIL7249	F767XNH		

Although registered in north-east England, E23ETN spent time with two operators in London before
moving to Surrey. This SB2300 coach is the rear engined variant of the DAF chassis and carries a 340
body constructed at the now-demolished Duple factory in Blackpool. This Frimley vehicle is seen in
Cardiff bus station. *Richard Eversden*

GANGE'S COACHES

J H T Gange, 77 Place Road, Cowes, Isle of Wight, PO31 7AE

HDL255E	Bedford VAM3	Duple Bella Venturer	C45F	1967	Moss, Sandown, 1993
FPR705E	Bedford VAS5	Duple Vista 29	C29F	1967	Arnold, Ventnor, 1996
ODL438M	Ford Transit 130	Strachan	B16F	1974	Preece, Totland Bay, 1989
LHO420T	Ford R1014	Duple Dominant II	C45F	1978	Marchwood Motorways, 1985
JDL724W	Bedford YMT	Duple Dominant II	C53F	1980	Paul, Sandown, 1994
NDL600W	Mercedes-Benz L508D	Robin Hood	C21F	1981	
A207JTT	Leyland Tiger TRCTL11/3R	Plaxton Paramount 3200	C53F	1983	Neill, East Cowes, 1990
B498JDL	Bedford YNT	Plaxton Paramount 3200	C53F	1984	Moss, Sandown, 1994
C984UDL	Peugeot-Talbot Express	Made-to-Measure	M14	1986	C H Gange, Cowes, 1992
D126YDL	Mercedes-Benz L608D	Plaxton Mini Supreme	C25F	1986	
4817F	Leyland Tiger TRCTL11/3RZ	Duple 340	C57F	1986	Moss, Sandown, 1994
H687EDL	Ford Transit VE6	Ford	M8	1991	

Previous Registrations:
4817F   D467YDL

Livery: Cream, red and madder

Named vehicle:- 4817F *Island Princess.*

Opposite:- **Retained in immaculate condition is Duple Bella Venturer HDL255E. Built on a Bedford VAM chassis, the styling won Duple many awards in the mid 1960s especially when fitted to the twin-steering axle Bedford VAL.**

GRAND TOURS

Kim's Tours Ltd, Grand Hotel, Culver Parade, Sandown, Isle of Wight, PO36 8QA

A136GTA	Volvo B10M-61	Van Hool Astral	CH47/11DT	1984	Pointon, Nuneaton, 1997
GIL8939	Dennis Dorchester SDA807	Duple Caribbean	C46F	1984	Jack Scott, Sandown, 1997
GIL8674	Scania K92CRB	Van Hool Alizée	C55F	1988	The Kings Ferry, 1997
H51SYG	Scania K93CRB	Plaxton Paramount 3200 III	C53F	1990	Steel's, Skipton, 1996
J517LRY	DAF SB2305DHS585	Caetano Algarve II	C53F	1992	Moor-Dale, Newcastle, 1998
N589GBW	Dennis Javelin 12SDA2146	Caetano Algarve II	C51FT	1996	Maidstone & District, 1998

Previous Registrations:
GIL8674   F163DET   GIL8939   A595GPD

Livery:- White

Depot:- Sandown (Broadway Garage, New Street)

Opposite:- **Grand Tours fleet of coaches includes GIL8939, a Duple Caribbean-bodied Dennis Dorchester**

GRAYLINE

Hartwool Ltd, Station Approach, Bicester, Oxfordshire, OX6 7BZ

NRU308M	Bristol VRT/SL2/6LX	Eastern Coach Works	H44/31F	1974	Buckinghamshire RC, 1995
YPB834T	Bedford YMT	Plaxton Supreme IV	C53F	1979	Oxon Travel, Bicester, 1996
KIB7027	Leyland Leopard PSU5C/4R	Duple Dominant II	C53F	1979	Prentice & McQuillan, 1991
EOI4376	Leyland Leopard PSU3F/4R	Plaxton Supreme IV Exp	C53F	1981	United, 1993
MJI1677	DAF SB2300DHS585	Berkhof Esprite 340	C53F	1985	Limebourne, Battersea, 1988
MJI1679	DAF SB2300DHS585	Berkhof Esprite 340	C53F	1985	Limebourne, Battersea, 1988
E215PWY	Volkswagen LT55	Optare City Pacer	B25F	1987	Coach House Travel, 1995
E512PWR	Volkswagen LT55	Optare City Pacer	B25F	1987	Thanet Bus, Ramsgate, 1998
E904LVE	Volkswagen LT55	Optare City Pacer	B25F	1987	CoastLine, Bude, 1997
MJI1676	Bova FHD12.290	Bova Futura	C49F	1988	Embling, Guyhirn, 1992
E68SUH	Volkswagen LT55	Optare City Pacer	B25F	1988	Rees & Williams, 1995
449BHU	Bova FHD12.290	Bova Futura	C55F	1989	Majestic, Shareshill, 1992
SPV860	Bova FHD12.290	Bova Futura	C55F	1990	
MJI1678	Bedford YMT	Duple Dominant II	C53F	1980	APT, Rayleigh, 1996
98CLJ	Dennis Javelin 12SDA2101	Caetano Algarve II	C53F	1993	Euroline, Radford, 1995
L195YDU	Dennis Javelin 12SDA2136	Caetano Algarve II	C53F	1994	Supreme, Coventry, 1997
N681AHL	Scania K93CRB	Berkhof Excellence 1000L	C55F	1995	
P159FJO	Scania K113CRB	Van Hool Alizée	C53FT	1997	
R524EUD	MAN 11.220 HOCLR	Berkhof Ex'llence 1000 Midi	C35F	1998	
R621VNN	MAN 24.400	Noge Catalan 3.70	C53FT	1998	

Previous Registrations:

449BHU	F690ONR	KIB7027	EAP937V	MJI1678	KBC6V
98CLJ	K105UFP	MJI1676	F109YFL	MJI1679	B684BTW
EOI4376	NDC242W	MJI1677	B682BTW	SPV860	G441WFC

Livery:- White, blue and red

Grayline operate local bus services in Oxford under the Local Link banner. E904LVE seen here displaying the Fox logo associated with this operation. This Optare CityPacer is one of a substantial number placed in service by Cambus during the early days of privatisation. Since leaving Cambus, this particular vehicle has been operated by Coastline of Bude before moving to Oxfordshire. *Colin Lloyd*

HELLYERS

Hellyers of Fareham Ltd, 8 West Street, Fareham, Hampshire, PO16 0BH

CTM412T	Leyland Leopard PSU3B/4R	Plaxton Supreme IV	C53F	1979	
LVS441V	Leyland Leopard PSU3E/4R	Plaxton Supreme IV	C53F	1980	
LVS442V	Leyland Leopard PSU3E/4R	Plaxton Supreme IV	C53F	1980	
IAZ4816	Leyland Tiger TRCTL11/3R	Plaxton Supreme V	C51F	1981	
TJI4929	DAF MB200DKFL600	Plaxton Paramount 3300 II	C53F	1986	
TJI4926	Leyland Tiger TRCTL11/3R	Van Hool Alizée	C50FT	1986	
TJI4927	Leyland Tiger TRCL10/3ARZM	Plaxton Paramount 3200 III	C53F	1988	Shearings, 1995
TJI7513	LAG G355Z	LAG Panoramic	C49FT	1989	
G274BEL	Toyota Coaster HB31R	Caetano Optimo	C21F	1989	
G283BEL	Dennis Javelin 12SDA1907	Duple 320	C57F	1990	
G284BEL	Dennis Javelin 12SDA1916	Plaxton Paramount 3200 III	C57F	1990	
M576JBC	Dennis Javelin 12SDA2136	Caetano Algarve II	C53F	1990	
M904OVR	Dennis Javelin	Neoplan Transliner	C53F	1995	Timeline, Leigh, 1998
M889WAK	Volvo B10M-62	Plaxton Première 350	C53F	1995	Renshaw, Withington, 1997
N956DWJ	Volvo B10M-62	Plaxton Première 350	C49FT	1996	Tellings-Golden Miller, 1998
P31KWA	Volvo B10M-62	Plaxton Première 350	C49FT	1996	Sovereign, Dover, 1998
P102GHE	Scania K113CRB	Van Hool Alizée	C49F	1997	
P781BJF	Dennis Javelin	Caetano Algarve II	C53F	1997	
P953DNR	Toyota Coaster BB50R	Caetano Optimo IV	C21F	1997	
R146COR	Dennis Dart SLF	Plaxton Pointer 2	N39F	1998	
R867SDT	Scania K113TRB	Irizar Century 12.37	C49FT	1998	
R868SDT	Scania K113TRB	Irizar Century 12.37	C49FT	1998	
S377SET	Scania K113TRB	Irizar Century 12.37	C49FT	1998	

Previous Registrations:

IAZ4816	UUR345W	TJI4929	C788MVH
TJI4926	C262EME	TJI7513	F507YNV
TJI4927	F725ENE		

Livery:- Silver and orange; white (Hovertravel) R146COR; white (Grand UK) P781BJF; (Byngs International) G283BEL, TJI4926.

Depot:- Fareham (F1 Fort Wallington Ind Est)

Hellyers of Fareham have the contract to provide a bus service to link between, Portsmouth & Southsea rail station and the Isle of Wight hovercraft service terminal at Clarence Pier. Dennis Dart SLF R146COR was purchased for this operation. It carries Pointer 2 bodywork which was re-modelled by Ogle Design for Plaxton when the super low floor version was conceived.
David Heath

HEYFORDIAN

Heyfordian Travel Ltd, Orchard Lane, Upper Heyford, Oxfordshire, OX5 3LB

	Reg	Chassis	Body	Seats	Year	History
	FIL7662	Leyland Leopard PSU3A/4R	Plaxton Panorama Elite	C52F	1970	
	FIL8317	Bedford YMT	Plaxton Supreme III Express	C53F	1976	Hills of Tredegar, 1982
	FIL8441	Bedford YMT	Plaxton Supreme III Express	C53F	1976	Hills of Tredegar, 1982
	FBZ7356	Bedford YMT	Plaxton Supreme III Express	C53F	1976	Hills of Tredegar, 1982
	NIL4580	Bedford YMT	Plaxton Supreme III	C53F	1977	Frostway, Upper Heyford, 1987
	7298RU	Bedford YMT	Plaxton Supreme III	C53F	1978	Premier, Watford, 1987
	7223MY	Bedford YMT	Plaxton Supreme III	C53F	1978	Smith, Rickmansworth, 1987
	7396LJ	Bedford YMT	Plaxton Supreme III	C53F	1979	Frostway, Upper Heyford, 1987
	HSV720	Bedford YMT	Plaxton Supreme IV	C53F	1979	Premier, Watford, 1987
	481HYE	Bedford YMT	Plaxton Supreme IV	C53F	1979	Premier, Watford, 1987
	9197WF	Bristol VRT/SL3/6LXB	Alexander AL	H44/31F	1979	Cardiff Bus, 1994
	7034KW	Bristol VRT/SL3/6LXB	Alexander AL	H44/31F	1979	Cardiff Bus, 1994
	3762KX	Bristol VRT/SL3/6LXB	Alexander AL	H44/31F	1980	Cardiff Bus, 1994
	9945NE	Bristol VRT/SL3/6LXB	Alexander AL	H44/31F	1980	Cardiff Bus, 1994
w	VSF438	Bedford YMT	Plaxton Supreme IV	C53F	1981	Smith, Rickmansworth, 1987
	748ECR	Bedford YMT	Plaxton Supreme IV	C53F	1981	Smith, Rickmansworth, 1987
	943YKN	Bedford YMT	Plaxton Supreme IV	C53F	1981	Smith, Rickmansworth, 1987
	FBZ7357	Bova EL26/581	Bova Europa	C53F	1981	Alder Valley South, 1991
	3078RA	Bova EL26/581	Bova Europa	C53F	1982	Crusader, Clacton, 1984
	4068MH	Bova EL26/581	Bova Europa	C53F	1982	The Londoners, Nunhead, 1987
	6940MD	Bova EL26/581	Bova Europa	C53F	1982	The Londoners, Nunhead, 1987
	3139KV	Bova EL26/581	Bova Europa	C53F	1983	Wallace Arnold, 1987
	6230NU	Bova EL26/581	Bova Europa	C53F	1983	Wallace Arnold, 1987
	2482NX	Bova EL26/581	Bova Europa	C53F	1983	Wallace Arnold, 1987

There are two of these tri-axle double deck coaches in the Heyfordian fleet. Both are Neoplan Skyliners that have been purchased from other operators. 6595KV was once in the Selby based fleet of Voyager International. It is seen at work in central London. *Colin Lloyd*

A quartet of former Cardiff Bristol VR double deckers are in the Heyfordian fleet. They are utilised on intersite transport for Oxford Brookes University. The Alexander AL bodywork of 9197WF is suitably lettered for the contract which, in common with many Heyfordian vehicles, has received a *cherished* index mark. *Andrew Jarosz*

2705TD	Bova EL26/581	Bova Europa	C40F	1983	Eastern National, 1987
PVV316	Bova EL26/581	Bova Europa	C52F	1983	Tourmaster, Dunstable, 1987
5057VC	Bova EL26/581	Bova Europa	C53F	1983	
5701DP	Bova EL26/581	Bova Europa	C53F	1983	
2779UE	Bova EL26/581	Bova Europa	C52F	1983	Grayline, Bicester, 1984
8779KV	Leyland Tiger TRCTL11/3R	Plaxton Paramount 3200E	C53F	1983	Wingates, Formby, 1998
1430PP	Leyland Tiger TRCTL11/3R	Plaxton Paramount 3200E	C53F	1983	Wingates, Formby, 1998
7209RU	Leyland Tiger TRCTL11/3R	Plaxton Paramount 3200E	C53F	1983	Wingates, Formby, 1998
3150MC	Leyland Tiger TRCTL11/3R	Plaxton Paramount 3200E	C53F	1983	Wingates, Formby, 1998
1636VB	Leyland Tiger TRCTL11/2R	Plaxton Paramount 3200E	C49F	1983	D&G, Rachub, 1998
TJI6303	Leyland Tiger TRCTL11/3RH	Plaxton Paramount 3500E	C50F	1984	Bennett's Silverline, 1998
TJI6304	Leyland Tiger TRCTL11/3RH	Plaxton Paramount 3500E	C50F	1984	Bennett's Silverline, 1998
TJI6305	Leyland Tiger TRCTL11/3RH	Plaxton Paramount 3500E	C50F	1984	Bennett's Silverline, 1998
7958NU	Dennis Dorchester SDA805	Plaxton Paramount 3200	C44FT	1984	South Yorks Coachline, 1998
4827WD	Scania K112CRS	Jonckheere Jubilee P599	C51FT	1984	BTS Borehamwood, 1991
HIL2295	Scania K112CRS	Jonckheere Jubilee P599	C49FT	1984	Goodwin, Stockport, 1992
ESU940	Scania K112CRS	Jonckheere Jubilee P599	C51FT	1984	Goodwin, Stockport, 1994
868AVO	Scania K112CRS	Jonckheere Jubilee P599	C49FT	1984	Hardings, Huyton, 1992
1264LG	Scania K112CRS	Jonckheere Jubilee P50	C53F	1985	
5089LG	Scania K112CRS	Jonckheere Jubilee P50	C53F	1985	
XCT550	Scania K112CRS	Jonckheere Jubilee P599	C51FT	1985	Cross Gates Coaches, 1992
6960TU	Scania K112CRS	Jonckheere Jubilee P599	C57F	1985	Cresswell, Moira, 1991
2185NU	Bova EL29/581	Bova Europa	C53F	1985	Main Line, Tonyrefail, 1987
8216FN	DAF SB2300DHS585	Plaxton Paramount 3200 II	C53F	1985	
7845LJ	DAF MB200DKFL600	Plaxton Paramount 3200 IIE	C51F	1985	Trent (Barton), 1998
SJI4428	Scania K112CRS	Jonckheere Jubilee P599	C51FT	1985	Constable, Long Melford, 1995
2110UK	Leyland Tiger TRCTL11/3RH	Duple 340	C51F	1986	Crosville Cymru, 1995
SJI5861	Leyland Tiger TRCTL11/3RH	Duple 340	C49FT	1987	Trelawney Tours, Hayle, 1995
LDZ2502	Scania K112CRS	Jonckheere Jubilee P599	C49FT	1987	Gillespie, Kelty, 1992
LDZ2503	Scania K112CRS	Jonckheere Jubilee P599	C51FT	1987	Buddens, Romsey, 1992

9769UK	Volvo B10M-61	Duple 340	C53F	1988	Westbus, Ashford, 1993
8548VF	Volvo B10M-61	Duple 340	C53F	1988	Westbus, Ashford, 1993
9682FH	Volvo B10M-61	Duple 340	C53F	1988	Westbus, Ashford, 1993
FIL7664	Volvo B10M-61	Duple 340	C53F	1988	Westbus, Ashford, 1995
8252MX	DAF SD3000DKV601	Plaxton Paramount 3500 III	C53F	1989	City Line, 1998
4128AP	DAF SD3000DKV601	Plaxton Paramount 3500 III	C53F	1989	City Line, 1998
6595KV	Neoplan N122/3	Neoplan Skyliner	CH57/20DT	1989	Voyager, Selby, 1992
2622NU	Toyota Coaster HB31R	Caetano Optimo	C21F	1990	
1435VZ	Hestair Duple SDA1512	Duple 425	C57F	1990	Limebourne, Battersea, 1994
4078NU	Neoplan N122/3	Neoplan Skyliner	CH57/22CT	1991	Oak Hall, Caterham, 1995
H848AHS	Volvo B10M-60	Paramount 3500 III	C53F	1991	Turner, Bristol, 1998
YAY537	Volvo B10M-60	Van Hool Alizée	C49FT	1992	Durham City Coaches, 1996
2462FD	Toyota Coaster HZB50R	Caetano Optimo III	C18F	1994	
9467MU	MAN 10-190	Caetano Algarve II	C33FT	1994	
L740YGE	Volvo B10M-62	Jonckheere Deauville 45	C49FT	1994	Park's, Hamilton, 1995
L743YGE	Volvo B10M-62	Jonckheere Deauville 45	C49FT	1994	Park's, Hamilton, 1995
L745YGE	Volvo B10M-62	Jonckheere Deauville 45	C49FT	1994	Park's, Hamilton, 1996
N808NHS	Volvo B10M-62	Jonckheere Deauville 45	C53FT	1996	Park's, Hamilton, 1998
N809NHS	Volvo B10M-62	Jonckheere Deauville 45	C53FT	1996	Park's, Hamilton, 1998

Previous Registrations:

1264LG	B157YBW	8216FN	From New
1430PP	NBD104Y	8252MX	F135LJO
1435VZ	G648YVS	8548VF	E174OMU
1636VB	RNY305Y	868AVO	A52JLW
2110UK	C72KLG	8779KV	NBD103Y
2185NU	B246YKX	9197WF	WTG364T
2462FD	L535XUT	943YKN	UNK102W
2482NX	FUA398Y	9467MU	L26CAY
2622NU	G152ELJ	9682FH	E175OMU
2705TD	BGX649Y	9769UK	E173OMU
2779UE	FWL782Y	9945NE	CTX390V
3078RA	DEV807X	ESU490	A60JLW
3139KV	FUA395Y	FBZ7356	MHB854P, 4827WD, UFC144P
3150MC	CDG207Y, 498FYB, RBD636Y	FBZ7357	KEP640X
3762KX	CTX387V	FIL7297	SUD464P
4068MH	JAB311X	FIL7662	VUD384H
4078NU	H297GKN	FIL7664	E171OMU
4128AP	F139LJO	FIL8317	MHB852P
481HYE	KPP9V	FIL8441	MHB853P
4827WD	A59JLW, ESU930, A545TMJ	HIL2295	A131XNH
5057VC	From New	HSV720	KPP8V
5089LG	B156YBW	LDZ2502	D313VVV
5701DP	From New	LDZ2503	D312VVV
6230NU	FUA396Y	NIL4580	OPC39R, 7298RU, DFC884R
6595KV	F625OWJ, NIW2235	PVV316	JRO615Y
6940MD	YMV351Y	SJI4428	B505CBD, RDU4, B989MAB
6960TU	B71MLT, C47CKR	SJI5861	D272FAS, SJI1998
7034KW	WTG379T	TJI6303	A115PBW
7209RU	NBD105Y, 83CBD, RBD397Y	TJI6304	A116PBW
7223MY	CMJ99T	TJI6305	A117PBW
7298RU	CMJ3T	VSF438	KPP100V
7396LJ	YOG965T	XCT550	B504CBD, HYY3, B984MAB
748ECR	UNK101W	YAY537	F483OFT
7845LJ	B623JRC		
7958NU	B674GWY		

Livery: Ivory, orange, red, yellow and black.

Depots:- Rabans Lane Ind Est, Aylesbury; Harefield Marine, Harefield;Bellfield Road, High Wycombe;Lamarsh Road, Oxford,Orchard Lane, Upper Heyford Downs Road, Witney.

HODGE'S

Hodge's Coaches (Sandhurst) Ltd, 100 Yorktown Road, Sandhurst, GU17 8BH

HRY698V	Bedford YMT	Plaxton Supreme IV	C53F	1980	Ron's, Ashington, 1993
5134PH	Volkswagen LT35	Devon Conversions	M8	1991	Alamo Car Hire, 1994
6967PH	DAF SB2700DHS585	Caetano Algarve II	C53F	1992	
8896PH	DAF SB2700DHS585	Caetano Algarve II	C53F	1992	
1598PH	MAN 18.370	Berkhof Excellence	C53F	1994	
5881PH	MAN 18.370	Berkhof Excellence	C53F	1994	
9958PH	MAN 11.190	Berkhof E'llence 1000 Midi	C35F	1994	
7107PH	Toyota Coaster HZB50R	Caetano Optimo III	C21F	1995	
9489PH	MAN 10.180	Berkhof E'llence 1000 Midi	C35F	1995	
3900PH	DAF DE33WSSB3000	Berkhof Excellence 1000	C53F	1996	
4402PH	DAF DE33WSSB3000	Berkhof Excellence 1000	C53F	1996	
4631PH	Toyota Coaster HZB50R	Caetano Optimo III	C21F	1996	
2568PH	Volvo B10M-62	Berkhof Axial	C51FT	1998	
8874PH	Volvo B10M-62	Berkhof Axial	C51FT	1998	
5226PH	Volvo B10M-62	Berkhof Axial	C51FT	1998	

Livery:- Dark blue and champagne

Previous Registrations:

2568PH	R984PMO	5881PH	L715FPE
3900PH	N460VPH	6967PH	K796KPJ
4402PH	N461VPH	8874PH	R985PMO
5134PH	H182GTT	8896PH	K795KPJ
5226PH	R986PMO		

For carrying small groups, a number of operators are specifying scaled-down versions of full-sized coaches as an alternative to van-derived midicoaches. Hodge's of Sandhurst is one such operator. 9489PH carries Berkhof Excellence coachwork with 35 seats installed. The body is mounted on a MAN chassis. *Colin Lloyd*

HOME JAMES

Home James Coach Travel Ltd, Rushington Business Park, Rushington, Totton, Southampton, SO4 4AH

SJI4431	Bristol VRT/SL3/6LX	Eastern Coach Works	H43/31F	1976	Beestons, Hadleigh, 1998
OAP16W	Dennis Dominator DDA134	East Lancashire	H43/31F	1981	Brighton, 1996
BPO109W	Ford R1114	Plaxton Supreme IV	C49F	1981	Southampton Inst of FE, 1996
NSU513	Volvo B10M-61	Van Hool Alizée	C49FT	1983	Hardings, Huyton, 1990
B552AKE	Mercedes-Benz L608D	Reeve Burgess	C21F	1985	Lucketts, Fareham, 1997
C588VAA	Volkswagen LT28	Robin Hood	M8L	1986	Parkinsons Disease Soc, 1997
D248KKL	Ford Transit VE6	Dormobile	M7L	1987	The Cedar School, 1996
G52CAB	Mercedes-Benz 811D	Devon Conversions	C19F	1987	Motor Touring, Bratton, 1994
G112APC	Toyota Coaster HB31R	Caetano Optimo	C21F	1989	
HJI8686	Neoplan N122/3	Neoplan Skyliner	CH53/18CT	1990	Trathens, Plymouth, 1996
G551SKP	Renault Master T35D	Robin Hood	M10	1990	Rose Road, Southampton, 1994
H48VNH	Volvo B10M-60	Jonckheere Deauville	C51FT	1990	Buddens, Romsey, 1992
J704CWT	Volvo B10M-60	Plaxton Première 350	C48FT	1992	Wallace Arnold, 1995
J408AWF	Volvo B10M-60	Van Hool Alizée	C50F	1992	Tellings-Golden Miller, 1998
K665NGB	Mercedes-Benz 609D	Made-to-Measure	C24F	1992	Blythswood demonstrator, 1993
L883STR	Ford Transit VE6	Ford	M14	1994	
M849ABX	Ford Transit VE6	Ford	M14	1995	
M71BPX	Ford Transit VE6	Ford	M14	1995	
N372VRW	Peugeot Boxer	Devon Conversions	M12	1995	Peugeot Talbot demo, 1996
P385ARY	Iveco EuroMini CC95.18	Indcar	C35F	1996	
R219AOR	Iveco TurboDaily 59-12	Marshall C31	B25F	1997	

Previous Registrations:

BPO109W	PJT515W, POR1	HJI8686	G340KWE	SJI4431	MEL562P
F554TLW	F204HGN, RIB5084	NSU513	ENF567Y, XTW359, GNF466Y		

Livery:- White, red, orange and yellow

Formerly in the Tellings-Golden Miller fleet, J408AWF is now with Home James. This Van Hool Alizée-bodied Volvo B10M is seen in the vicinity of London Victoria Coach Station while performing duplication for National Express. *Colin Lloyd*

HORSEMAN

Horseman Coaches Ltd, Whitley Wood Depot, Whitley Wood Road, Reading

FKX291T	Bedford YRQ	Plaxton Supreme IV	C38F	1979	Smith, Reading, 1989
TVH135X	Ford R1014	Plaxton Supreme V	C35F	1982	Abbeyways, Huddersfield, 1983
D781VMO	DAF SB2300DHS585	Plaxton Paramount 3200 II	C53F	1986	
D782VMO	DAF SB2300DHS585	Plaxton Paramount 3200 II	C53F	1986	
D783VMO	DAF SB2300DHS585	Plaxton Paramount 3200 II	C53F	1986	
D784VMO	DAF SB2300DHS585	Plaxton Paramount 3200 II	C53F	1986	
D785VMO	DAF SB2300DHS585	Plaxton Paramount 3200 II	C53F	1986	
D578MVR	Leyland Tiger TRCTL11/3RZ	Plaxton Paramount 3200 III	C53F	1987	Shearings, 1992
D579MVR	Leyland Tiger TRCTL11/3RZ	Plaxton Paramount 3200 III	C53F	1987	Shearings, 1992
D582MVR	Leyland Tiger TRCTL11/3RZ	Plaxton Paramount 3200 III	C53F	1987	Shearings, 1992
D237YRX	DAF SB2305DHS585	Van Hool Alizée	C53FT	1987	
D238YRX	DAF SB2305DHS585	Van Hool Alizée	C53FT	1987	
E682UNE	Leyland Tiger TRCTL11/3RZ	Plaxton Paramount 3200 III	C53F	1988	Shearings, 1992
E683UNE	Leyland Tiger TRCTL11/3RZ	Plaxton Paramount 3200 III	C53F	1988	Shearings, 1992
E684UNE	Leyland Tiger TRCTL11/3RZ	Plaxton Paramount 3200 III	C53F	1988	Shearings, 1992
E685UNE	Leyland Tiger TRCTL11/3RZ	Plaxton Paramount 3200 III	C53F	1988	Shearings, 1992
E687UNE	Leyland Tiger TRCTL11/3RZ	Plaxton Paramount 3200 III	C53F	1988	Shearings, 1992
E694UNE	Leyland Tiger TRCTL11/3RZ	Plaxton Paramount 3200 III	C53F	1988	Shearings, 1992
E695UNE	Leyland Tiger TRCTL11/3RZ	Plaxton Paramount 3200 III	C53F	1988	Shearings, 1992
E696UNE	Leyland Tiger TRCTL11/3RZ	Plaxton Paramount 3200 III	C53F	1988	Shearings, 1992
E697UNE	Leyland Tiger TRCTL11/3RZ	Plaxton Paramount 3200 III	C53F	1988	Shearings, 1992
E698UNE	Leyland Tiger TRCTL11/3RZ	Plaxton Paramount 3200 III	C53F	1988	Shearings, 1992
F633OHD	DAF SB2305DHS585	Duple 340	C57F	1988	
F634OHD	DAF SB2305DHS585	Duple 340	C57F	1988	
F635OHD	DAF SB2305DHS585	Duple 340	C53F	1988	
F636OHD	DAF SB2305DHS585	Duple 340	C57F	1989	
F638OHD	DAF SB2305DHS585	Duple 340	C57F	1989	
F845YJX	DAF SBR2305DHS570	Van Hool Astrobel	CH57/14CT	1989	Thomas, Clydach Vale, 1992
H224TCP	DAF SB2305DHS585	Duple 340	C51F	1990	
H225TCP	DAF SB2305DHS585	Duple 340	C57F	1990	
H226TCP	DAF SB2305DHS585	Duple 340	C57F	1990	
H227TCP	DAF SB2305DHS585	Duple 340	C57F	1990	
H228TCP	DAF SB2305DHS585	Duple 340	C57F	1990	
H229TCP	DAF SBR3000DKZ570	Plaxton Paramount 4000 III	CH55/19CT	1990	
K1HCL	Mercedes-Benz O303	Plaxton Paramount 3500 III	C51F	1992	
K2HCL	Mercedes-Benz O303	Plaxton Paramount 3500 III	C51F	1992	
L201BPL	Toyota Coaster HDB30R	Caetano Optimo II	C21F	1993	
L202BPL	Toyota Coaster HDB30R	Caetano Optimo II	C21F	1993	
L203BPL	Toyota Coaster HDB30R	Caetano Optimo II	C21F	1993	
L205BPL	Toyota Coaster HDB30R	Caetano Optimo II	C21F	1993	
L206BPL	Toyota Coaster HDB30R	Caetano Optimo II	C21F	1993	
L207BPL	Toyota Coaster HDB30R	Caetano Optimo II	C21F	1993	
L208BPL	Toyota Coaster HDB30R	Caetano Optimo II	C21F	1993	
L210BPL	Toyota Coaster HDB30R	Caetano Optimo II	C21F	1993	
L211BPL	Toyota Coaster HDB30R	Caetano Optimo II	C21F	1993	
L212BPL	Toyota Coaster HDB30R	Caetano Optimo II	C21F	1993	
L213BPL	Toyota Coaster HDB30R	Caetano Optimo II	C21F	1993	
L214BPL	Toyota Coaster HDB30R	Caetano Optimo II	C21F	1993	
L215BPL	Toyota Coaster HDB30R	Caetano Optimo II	C21F	1993	
L350MKU	Volvo B10M-60	Plaxton Excalibur	C49F	1994	
L351MKU	Volvo B10M-60	Plaxton Excalibur	C49F	1994	
M653SBL	Toyota Coaster HZB50R	Caetano Optimo III	C21F	1995	
M654SBL	Toyota Coaster HZB50R	Caetano Optimo III	C21F	1995	
M655SBL	Toyota Coaster HZB50R	Caetano Optimo III	C21F	1995	
M656SBL	Toyota Coaster HZB50R	Caetano Optimo III	C21F	1995	
M657SBL	Toyota Coaster HZB50R	Caetano Optimo III	C21F	1995	
M658SBL	Volvo B10M-62	Plaxton Excalibur	C53F	1995	
M659SBL	Volvo B10M-62	Plaxton Excalibur	C53F	1995	
N660VJB	Volvo B10M-62	Plaxton Excalibur	C53F	1995	
N661VJB	Volvo B10M-62	Plaxton Excalibur	C53F	1995	
N662VJB	Volvo B10M-62	Plaxton Excalibur	C53F	1995	

N663VJB	Volvo B10M-62	Plaxton Excalibur	C53F	1995	
N664VJB	Volvo B10M-62	Plaxton Excalibur	C53F	1995	
N665VJB	Volvo B10M-62	Plaxton Excalibur	C53F	1995	
N669VJB	Toyota Coaster HZB50R	Caetano Optimo III	C21F	1995	
N670VJB	Toyota Coaster HZB50R	Caetano Optimo III	C21F	1995	
N671VJB	Toyota Coaster HZB50R	Caetano Optimo III	C21F	1996	
N672VJB	Toyota Coaster HZB50R	Caetano Optimo III	C21F	1996	
N673VJB	Toyota Coaster HZB50R	Caetano Optimo III	C21F	1996	
P492LLU	Mercedes-Benz Sprinter 312D	Devon Conversions	M8	1996	Alamo Rental, W Drayton, 1998
P493LLU	Mercedes-Benz Sprinter 312D	Devon Conversions	M8	1996	Alamo Rental, W Drayton, 1998
P494LLU	Mercedes-Benz Sprinter 312D	Devon Conversions	M8	1996	Alamo Rental, W Drayton, 1998
P336CDF	Ford Transti VE6	Ford	M8	1996	Alamo Rental, W Drayton, 1998
P167ANR	Dennis Javelin 12SDA2155	Caetano Algarve II	C57F	1996	
P168ANR	Dennis Javelin 12SDA2155	Caetano Algarve II	C57F	1996	
R204STF	Dennis Javelin	UVG S320	C69F	1997	
R791WOY	Mercedes-Benz Sprinter 312D	Autobus Classique	M8	1997	
R792WOY	Mercedes-Benz Sprinter 312D	Autobus Classique	M8	1997	
R793WOY	Mercedes-Benz Sprinter 312D	Autobus Classique	M8	1997	
R794WOY	Mercedes-Benz Sprinter 312D	Autobus Classique	M8	1997	
R795WOY	Mercedes-Benz Sprinter 312D	Autobus Classique	M8	1997	
R796WOY	Mercedes-Benz Sprinter 312D	Autobus Classique	M8	1997	
R797WOY	Mercedes-Benz Sprinter 312D	Autobus Classique	M8	1997	
S431SLF	Mercedes-Benz Sprinter 312D	Autobus Classique	M8	1998	
S432SLF	Mercedes-Benz Sprinter 312D	Autobus Classique	M8	1998	
S433SLF	Mercedes-Benz Sprinter 312D	Autobus Classique	M8	1998	
S434SLF	Mercedes-Benz Sprinter 312D	Autobus Classique	M8	1998	
S435SLF	Mercedes-Benz Sprinter 312D	Autobus Classique	M8	1998	

Livery:- White and multicoloured graphics. White, yellow and red (National Car Rentals) P492-4LLU, R791-7WOY, s431-5SLF; blue and yellow (Windsor Crown Carriages) L205BPL, L206BPL.

Depots:- Reading (Whitley Wood Road) and Theale (Old Bath Road)

Opposite, top:- **DAF chassis were chosen by Horseman for several years with several body styles being applied. Illustrating the pair of Van Hools in the fleet is D237YRX which carries a banner advising passengers that Horseman won the Coach Operator of the Year title in 1994.**
Opposite, bottom:- **R204STF is the sole UVG coach in the Horseman fleet and joined the company in 1997. It is seen here in corporate livery and is notable for its 69-seat capacity.**

Horseman of Reading operate a large number of Toyota Coaster minicoaches. Most are contracted to work on behalf of major clients and display appropriate liveries and lettering. L214BPL is one of several that work at Heathrow Airport and carries lettering for both the Heathrow Park Thistle Hotel and the Eurodollar car rental chain who use adjacent premises to the west of Heathrow.
Andrew Jarosz

I O W TOURS

R Cox, T Witty & E Law, 3 New Road, Lake, Sandown, Isle of Wight, PO36 9JN.

M247TAK	Scania K93CRB	Van Hool Alizée	C57F	1995
N687AHL	Scania K113TRB	Irizar Century 12.37	C51FT	1996
N688AHL	Scania K93CRB	Berkhof Excellence 1000L	C55F	1995
P97GHE	Scania K113CRB	Van Hool Alizée	C53F	1996

Livery:- Two-tone blue

Vehicles are located at the following hotels:- St Anthony's Hotel, Hill Street, Sandown; Channel View Hotel, Royal Street, Sandown and Jesmond-dene Hotel, Culver Parade, Sandown

I.O.W. Tours is operated by a group of hotel owners. The coaches are primarily employed conveying hotel guests. The entire fleet is based on Scania chassis. In the case of N688AHL, it is a K93CRB which carries a Berkhof Excellence 1000L body. All four vehicles have South Yorkshire registrations, indicating that they were obtained from the Scania sales centre at Worksop. *Don Vincent*

ISLAND COACH SERVICES

R J Long, Spithead Business Centre, Newport Road, Lake, Isle of Wight, PO40 9PP

UCW162X	Volvo B10M-61	Jonckheere Bermuda	C53F	1982	?, 1997
YNN33Y	Volvo B10M-61	LAG Galaxy	C53F	1983	Thompson, Uxbridge, 1995
HAV1Y	Volvo B10M-61	LAG Galaxy	C49FT	1983	Rothwells Super Travel, 1997
AAX311A	Leyland Tiger TRCTL11/3R	Duple Laser	C48F	1983	Rhondda (Parfitts), 1997
A501HUT	Bedford YNT	Duple Laser	C53F	1984	McPate, Kirkby in Ashfield, 1995
B373NAB	MAN SR280	MAN	C49FT	1985	Wightline, Newport, 1998
C31SNH	Mercedes-Benz L608D	Frank Guy	C21F	1986	Carmel, Northlew, 1994
YXI2841	Mercedes-Benz O303/15RHD	Mercedes-Benz	C49FT	1988	Derwent, Swalwell, 1988
HSK843	MAN 16.290 HOCLR	Jonckheere Deauville P5999C49FT		1989	Supreme, Hadleigh, 1998

Previous Registrations:

AAX311A	SDW912Y	HSK843	F918YNV	YXI2841	F378MUT
B373NAB	B160FHR, 800AVJ	UCW162X	ENV829X,		

Livery:- White and blue

Island Coach Services operate this Volvo B10M from the company's base on the Isle of Wight. A 53-seater, YNN33Y was bodied by LAG with the Galaxy model of coachwork. *Don Vincent*

JACOBS

Jacobs International Coaches Ltd, 1 Deer Park Industrial Estate, Knowle Lane, Horton Heath, Hampshire

VTK254	Bedford YRT	Duple Dominant	C53F	1974	Moore, Windsor, 1987
8177KP	Bristol LHS6L	Plaxton Supreme III	C35F	1978	Oakley Coaches, 1998
FGN891X	Mercedes-Benz L508D	Reeve Burgess	C19F	1982	Thorne, Horley, 1989
UCT838	Volvo B10M-61	Duple Dominant IV	C57F	1982	Corp, Fairoak, 1986
A604TGO	Mercedes-Benz L608D	Reeve Burgess	C21F	1983	Grayline, Witney, 1988
A484JRU	Ford Transit 190	Robin Hood	B16F	1984	
B995CUS	Mercedes-Benz L307D	Reeve Burgess	M12	1985	Corp, Fairoak, 1986
D212MKK	Scania K92CRS	East Lancashire	H55/37F	1987	Oakley Coaches, 1996
D213MKK	Scania K92CRS	East Lancashire	H55/37F	1987	Oakley Coaches, 1996
E205OEL	Ford Transit VE6	Dormobile	B16F	1988	
F350OOR	Ford Transit VE6	Ford	M14	1988	private owner, 1992
PAZ3270	Mercedes-Benz 609D	Robin Hood	C19F	1988	Angela, Lowford, 1997
F950HTT	Mercedes-Benz 609D	Devon Conversions	C21F	1988	Dartline, Totnes, 1997
F419YFX	Ford Transit VE6	Bristol Street	M2L	1989	
F610VLJ	Ford Transit VE6	Bristol Street	M3L	1989	
498ANX	Volvo B10M-60	Van Hool Alizée	C49FT	1989	
F451XFX	Ford Transit VE6	Ford	M14	1989	
F481ENH	Mercedes-Benz 811D	Reeve Burgess Beaver	C25F	1989	Redline, Penwortham, 1994
G75BRU	Ford Transit VE6	Bristol Street	M2L	1989	
G425BJT	Ford Transit VE6	Bristol Street	M14	1989	private owner, 1991
G483BJT	Ford Transit VE6	Bristol Street	M2L	1989	
G495BJT	Ford Transit VE6	Bristol Street	M2L	1989	
G730CFX	Ford Transit VE6	Bristol Street	M2L	1989	
G740CFX	Ford Transit VE6	Bristol Street	M3L	1989	
G660DLJ	Ford Transit VE6	Bristol Street	M6L	1990	
G378EJT	Ford Transit VE6	Bristol Street	M6L	1990	

Leger Travel of Doncaster is a major tour operator but hires in vehicles from all over the country. Coaches dedicated to Leger Travel work display that company's white and two tone blue colours. Jacobs P382ARY is such a vehicle. It is one of two unusual Iveco EuroRiders operated by the Hampshire company and fitted with Beulas coachwork.

The oldest vehicle in the Jacobs fleet is VTK254. Dating from 1974, this long lasting Bedford YRT carries a Duple Dominant body. Unusually the Duple body of this coach has survived without a major rebuild, even the chrome strips beneath the windows, a notorious area for corrosion, are still in place. *David Donati collection*

H673KPR	Ford Transit VE6	Bristol Street	M3L	1991	
H905LVX	Ford Transit VE6	Bristol Street	M14	1991	Bristol Street demo, 1991
K126XRU	Ford Transit VE6	Ford	M11	1993	private owner, 1995
K127XRU	Ford Transit VE6	Ford	M11	1993	private owner, 1995
L499BEL	Ford Transit VE6	Bristol Street	M3L	1993	
L730BPR	Ford Transit VE6	Bristol Street	M7L	1994	
L295CJT	Ford Transit VE6	Bristol Street	M14	1994	
YHR702	Volvo B10M-62	Van Hool Alizée	C49F	1994	
832DDV	Volvo B10M-62	Van Hool Alizée	C49FT	1995	
N107ECR	Ford Transit VE6	Bristol Street	M14	1996	
N590TAY	Iveco EuroRider 391.12.35	Beulas Stergo E35	C49FT	1996	
P382ARY	Iveco EuroRider 391.12.35	Beulas Stergo E35	C49FT	1996	
P286LOW	Ford Transit VE6	Bristol Street	M2L	1997	
P291LOW	Ford Transit VE6	Bristol Street	M5L	1997	

Previous Registrations:

498ANX	F28TMP	PAZ3270	2439TR
832DDV	M213UYD	UCT838	KRV878Y
8177KP	YUS35S	VTK254	BMB116M
F481ENH	F24DVV, A20CLC	YHR702	M119TYB

Livery:- White with multicoloured stripes

JOHN PIKE

J S Pike, Scott Close, Walworth Industrial Estate, Andover, Hampshire, SP10 5NU

CRU301L	Bristol VRT/SL2/6G	Eastern Coach Works	H43/33F	1972	Hampshire Bus, 1988
IUI5035	Bristol VRT/SL3/6LXB	Eastern Coach Works	H43/31F	1980	Stagecoach South, 1997
IUI5036	Bristol VRT/SL3/680(6LXB)	Eastern Coach Works	H43/31F	1981	Stagecoach South, 1997
IUI5037	Bristol VRT/SL3/6LXB	Eastern Coach Works	H43/31F	1979	Stagecoach South, 1997
YPJ501Y	Leyland Olympian ONTL11/2R	Eastern Coach Works	CH45/29F	1983	The Bee Line, 1991
A158OOT	Mercedes-Benz L608D	Robin Hood	C25F	1983	
HIL6802	Iveco 79-14	Robin Hood	C31F	1986	
D708VRX	Ford Transit	Pike	M4L	1986	McLardy, Andover, 1990
5300RU	Volvo B10M-61	Duple	C57F	1987	Harry Shaw, Coventry, 1995
PIL2249	Volvo B10M-61	Plaxton Paramount 3500 III	C53F	1988	Stevens, Bristol, 1993
IUI5045	Mercedes-Benz 609D	Pike	C25FL	1988	van, 1997
F55TPR	Ford Transit VE6	Ford	M8	1988	
F365YFX	Ford Transit VE6	Ford	M8	1989	Edwards, Kings Somborne, 1990
A11UFB	Mercedes-Benz 407D	Mercedes-Benz	M10L	1992	van, 1995
HIL3670	Volvo B10M-60	Plaxton Paramount 3500 III	C53F	1990	Capitol, Cwmbran, 1996
J174PKJ	Ford Transit VE6	Pike	M10L	1992	van, 1995
K853YTG	Ford Transit VE6	Ford	M10L	1993	van, 1996
L941URL	Ford Transit VE6	Pike	M12	1994	van, 1996
M771BHU	Ford Transit VE6	Ford	M14	1994	Naish & May, South' ton, 1996
M505NCG	Volvo B10M-62	Plaxton Première 320	C49FT	1995	Excelsior, Bournemouth, 1997
N521TRU	Volvo B10M-62	Plaxton Première 320	C49FT	1996	Excelsior, Bournemouth, 1997

Previous Registrations:

5300RU	D33FRW, 92DNX	IUI5035	JWV256W
A11UFB	?	IUI5036	JWV266W
PIL2249	E281OMG, HIL3670, E281OMG	IUI5037	EAP978V
HIL3670	G63RGG	IUI5045	E367GHD
HIL6802	C293AOR	M505NCG	A8EXC

Livery:- Grey, maroon and black

Displaying the branding John Pike Voyages is HIL3670. This Volvo B10M is fitted with Plaxton Paramount coachwork. It was originally in the large fleet of Park's of Hamilton, a major source of modern coaches for other operators as Park's retain a very young coach fleet. HIL3670 came to John Pike via Welsh operator Capitol of Cwmbran.
Andrew Jarosz

LUCKETT

H Luckett & Co Ltd, Broad Cut, Wallington, Fareham, PO16 8TB

2105	A12HLC	Toyota Coaster HDB30R	Caetano Optimo II	C21F	1992
2106	TSU648	Toyota Coaster HZB50R	Caetano Optimo III	C21F	1996
2107	P881MTR	Toyota Coaster HZB50R	Caetano Optimo III	C21F	1997
3303	A6LTG	Mercedes-Benz 814D	Reeve Burgess Beaver	C33F	1990	Hatt's, Foxham, 1998
3505	A13HLC	Dennis Javelin 10SDA2119	Berkhof E'llence 1000 Midi	C35F	1993
3801	P483GTF	Dennis Javelin (10m)	Berkhof Axial	C38FT	1997
4908	A17HLC	Scania K113CRB	Irizar Century 12.35	C49FT	1995
4909	A19HLC	Scania K113CRB	Irizar Century 12.35	C49FT	1995
4910	N855DKU	Scania K113CRB	Irizar Century 12.35	C49FT	1996
4912	A16HLC	Scania K113CRB	Van Hool Alizée	C49FT	1995	Slattery's, Kentish Town, 1996
4913	A18HLC	Scania K113CRB	Irizar Century 12.35	C49FT	1994	Holmeswood Coaches, 1996
4914	P120GHE	Scania K113CRB	Irizar Century 12.35	C49FT	1997
4915	P130GHE	Scania K113CRB	Irizar Century 12.35	C49FT	1997
4916	P140GHE	Scania K113CRB	Irizar Century 12.35	C49FT	1997
4917	A20HLC	Scania K113CRB	Irizar Century 12.35	C49FT	1994	Harry Shaw, Coventry, 1997
4918	A10HLC	Scania K113TRB	Irizar Century 12.37	C49FT	1995	Abbeyways, Halifax, 1997
4919	R2HLC	Dennis Javelin	Berkhof Axial	C49FT	1998
4920	R4HLC	Dennis Javelin	Berkhof Axial	C49FT	1998
5102	8589EL	Scania K113CRB	Berkhof Excellence 2000	C51F	1992
5326	SJI8132	Dennis Javelin 12SDA1916	Plaxton Paramount 3200 III	C53F	1989	Plaxton demonstrator, 1990
5330	SJI8131	Dennis Javelin 12SDA2101	Berkhof Excellence 1000	C53FT	1991
5337	666VMX	Dennis Javelin 11SDL1905	Duple 320	C53F	1988	Fowler, Holbeach Drove, 1995
5338	P668GJB	Dennis Javelin	Berkhof Axial	C53F	1997
5339	R10HLC	Dennis Javelin	Berkhof Excellence 1000L	C53F	1997

Lucketts have an unusual fleet numbering scheme. The first two digits of the number indicate the seating capacity of the coach. In the case of Dennis Javelin 5339, R10HLC it is a 53 seater and one of three Javelins in the fleet to carry Belgian built Berkhof Excellence 1000 coachwork. *Colin Lloyd*

Lucketts 5330, SJI8131, is a Dennis Javelin with Berkhof Excellence 1000 bodywork it is seen in Millbank while visiting London. Lucketts have undergone a major restructuring over the last two years resulting in a much younger fleet, a new image and livery and the award of Coach Operator of the Year 1998. *Colin Lloyd*

Spanish coachbuilder Irizar have made major inroads into the British coach market in recent years. Exclusively, Irizar coachwork is being imported into the UK on Scania chassis. Lucketts 5507, R6HLC is an 1998 Irizar Century mounted on the latest Scania chassis, the L94IB. Two further Scanias are anticipated in the near future. *David Heath*

Small capacity quality midicoaches are increasing in popularity as coach operators cater for smaller groups such as office team activities. Lucketts operate P483GTF in 38-seat form as 3801 and the Berkhof Axial-bodied coach is seen passing through Parliament Square, London. *Colin Lloyd*

5340	A18LTG	Volvo B10M-60	Jonckheere Deauville P599	C53F	1990	Q Drive, Battersea, 1998
5341	A19LTG	Volvo B10M-60	Jonckheere Deauville P599	C53F	1990	Q Drive, Battersea, 1998
5342	A20LTG	Volvo B10M-60	Jonckheere Deauville P599	C53F	1990	Q Drive, Battersea, 1998
5504	A14LLT	Scania K93CRB	Van Hool Alizée	C55F	1992	Pemico, S Bermondsey, 1997
5505	A15LLT	Scania K93CRB	Van Hool Alizée	C55F	1992	Pemico, S Bermondsey, 1997
5506	R5HLC	Scania L94IB	Irizar Intercentury 12.32	C55F	1998	
5507	R6HLC	Scania L94IB	Irizar Intercentury 12.32	C55F	1998	
7301	8686DN	Leyland Olympian ONTL11/3R	Eastern Coach Works	CH45/28F	1983	Skills, Nottingham, 1995
7302	A7HLC	Scania K113TRA	Van Hool Astrobel	CH57/16CT	1993	Harry Shaw, Coventry, 1996

Previous Registrations:

666VMX	E500RFL	A17HLC	M330VET
8589EL	J95UBL	A18HLC	L5HWD, L861LBV
8686DN	YPJ505Y	A18LTG	G976LRP
A6LTG	G256NCK, MIL1854, G714XPM	A19HLC	M320VET
A7HLC	K21GVC, 3KOV, K151NDU	A19LTG	G977LRP
A10HLC	M21UVH	A20HLC	L5URE
A12HLC	K466PNR	A20LTG	G978LRP
A13HLC	E440BMO	SJI8131	J261HBP
A14LLT	J218XKY	SJI8132	G960WNR
A15LLT	J219XKY	TSU648	N944RBC
A16HLC	M326VET		

Livery: White, blue, grey and orange; white and blue (Leger Travel) 4908/17; blue (Travelsphere) 4912.

C534BHY, latterly with Badgerline, is one of two Ford Transits that operate for M-Travel on their Isle of Wight services. The vehicles carry a mainly red livery. *Phillip Stephenson*

McLeans N383EAK is one of a pair of Plaxton coaches purchased in 1996 and is seen at the operator's base in Oxfordshire. As indicated by the plate, the company operate school services in the area. Interestingly, the 1998 intake of coaches are all small capacity vehicles. *Andrew Jarosz*

M TRAVEL

Redbeam Ltd
Comer Mill, Forest Road, Newport, Isle of Wight, PO30 5LY

	Reg	Chassis	Body	Type	Year	History
	C476TAY	Ford Transit 190	Robin Hood	B16F	1985	Midland Fox, 1994
w	C534BHY	Ford Transit 190	Dormobile	B16F	1986	Badgerline, 1994
	E271HDL	Iveco Daily 49.10	Robin Hood City Nippy	B23F	1987	Southern Vectis, 1997
	E274HDL	Iveco Daily 49.10	Robin Hood City Nippy	B23F	1987	Southern Vectis, 1998
	E275HDL	Iveco Daily 49.10	Robin Hood City Nippy	B23F	1987	Southern Vectis, 1997
	E276HDL	Iveco Daily 49.10	Robin Hood City Nippy	B23F	1987	Southern Vectis, 1997
	F995XOV	Iveco Daily 49.10	Carlyle Dailybus 2	B25F	1989	Essex Buses, 1998

Livery:- Red

McLEANS

McLeans Coaches & Taxis Ltd, 5 Two Rivers Industrial Estate, Station Lane, Witney, OX8 6BH

Reg	Chassis	Body	Type	Year	History
C652XDF	Mercedes-Benz L608D	Alexander AM	B20F	1986	Cheltenham & District, 1996
HIL6649	Mercedes-Benz 709D	Jubilee	C20F	1987	Star Cars, Witney, 1996
F274JWL	Mercedes-Benz 811D	Reeve Burgess Beaver	C33F	1988	
F850NJO	Mercedes-Benz 811D	Reeve Burgess Beaver	C33F	1989	
K208SFP	Toyota Coaster HDB30R	Caetano Optimo II	C21F	1992	Chauffeurs, Birmingham, 1997
N383EAK	Volvo B10M-62	Plaxton Premiére 350	C49FT	1996	
N384EAK	Volvo B10M-62	Plaxton Premiére 350	C49FT	1996	
P774BJF	Volvo B10M-62	Caetano Algarve II	C49FT	1996	
P775BJF	Volvo B10M-62	Caetano Algarve II	C49FT	1996	
P776BJF	MAN 11.190	Caetano Algarve II	C35F	1996	
P778BJF	Volvo B10M-62	Caetano Algarve II	C49FT	1997	
R192LBC	Volvo B10M-62	Caetano Algarve II	C49FT	1998	
R193LBC	Toyota Coaster BB50R	Caetano Optimo IV	C21F	1998	
	Mercedes-Benz Vario O814	Plaxton Cheetah	C32F	1998	On order
	Mercedes-Benz Vario O814	Plaxton Cheetah	C32F	1998	On order

Previous Registrations:
HIL6649   D603KWT

Livery:- white

MARCHWOOD MOTORWAYS

Marchwood Motorways (Southampton) Ltd, 200 Salisbury Road, Totton,
Southampton, SO4 3PF

JUO983	Bristol LL6B	Eastern Coach Works	B39F	1948	Marchwood, Haverfordwest, '81
CEL105T	Bedford YMT	Plaxton Supreme IV	C53F	1979	Swallow, Bristol, 1986
BHO442V	Leyland Leopard PSU5C/4R	Duple Dominant II	C55F	1980	
UFX630X	Leyland Tiger TRCTL11/3R	Duple Dominant IV	C57F	1981	
225ASV	Bova FLD12.250	Bova Futura	C57F	1986	
SIB3272	Leyland Olympian ONLXCT/2R	East Lancashire	DPH47/29F	1986	Southampton Citybus, 1996
SIB3273	Leyland Olympian ONLXCT/2R	East Lancashire	DPH47/29F	1986	Southampton Citybus, 1996
D647ETR	Iveco Daily 49.10	Robin Hood City Nippy	B19F	1987	
D648ETR	Iveco Daily 49.10	Robin Hood City Nippy	B19F	1987	
670DHO	LAG G355Z	LAG Panoramic	C49FT	1989	
F247RJX	DAF SB2305DHS585	Duple 340	C57F	1989	
F248RJX	DAF SB2305DHS585	Duple 340	C57F	1989	
G364FOP	Iveco Daily 49.10	Carlyle Dailybus 2	B25F	1990	Strathclyde, 1991
H712KPR	Ford Transit VE6	Bristol Street	M14	1991	
L381RYC	Bova FHD12.340	Bova Futura	C51FT	1994	
L382RYC	Bova FHD12.270	Bova Futura	C57F	1994	
M844LFP	Toyota Coaster HZB50R	Caetano Optimo III	C21F	1995	
M845LFP	Toyota Coaster HZB50R	Caetano Optimo III	C18F	1995	
M846LFP	MAN 11.190	Caetano Algarve II	C35F	1995	
M104BPX	Ford Transit VE6	Ford	M12	1995	
N593DOR	Ford Transit VE6	Passenger Vehicle Bodies	M14L	1995	
N36FWU	DAF DE33WSSB3000	Van Hool Alizée	C51FT	1996	
N37FWU	DAF DE33WSSB3000	Van Hool Alizée	C51FT	1996	
N38FWU	DAF DE33WSSB3000	Van Hool Alizée	C51FT	1996	
N39FWU	DAF DE33WSSB3000	Van Hool Alizée	C51FT	1996	
N41FWU	DAF DE33WSSB3000	Van Hool Alizée	C51FT	1996	
N42FWU	DAF DE33WSSB3000	Van Hool Alizée	C51FT	1996	
P124RWR	DAF DE33WSSB3000	Ikarus Blue Danube	C55F	1997	
P125RWR	DAF DE33WSSB3000	Ikarus Blue Danube	C55F	1997	
P126RWR	DAF DE33WSSB3000	Ikarus Blue Danube	C55F	1997	
R63GNW	DAF DE33WSSB3000	Ikarus Blue Danube	C53F	1998	
R64GNW	DAF DE33WSSB3000	Van Hool Alizée	C51F	1998	
R65GNW	DAF DE33WSSB3000	Van Hool Alizée	C51F	1998	

Opposite:- **Marchwood Motorways operate several Solent Blueline services under a franchise arrangement. While the majority of the buses are now Dennis Darts, four DAF buses are operated, two with Optare Delta bodywork. The other pair are represented by Ikarus Citybus L509EHD. Also of DAF manufacture is N42FWU which is fitted with Van Hool Alizée bodywork.** *Les Peters.*

LAG Panoramics looked particularly modern when delivered in 1989. The deep windscreen is the main feature as shown on Marchwood's only remaining example, 670DHO.
Robert Edworthy

Toyota Coaster, M846LFP is seen parked in the Marchwood depot and is one of two operated by the company. The Toyota has been primarily imported into Britain by Salvador Caetano UK, although several other sales franchises also exist. Four variants of the model have been built, M846LFP being a mark III. Confusingly, though, mark IV models are available in two widths but are indistinct on paper other than by seating capacity.

Solent Blueline franchise vehicles:

263	N301FOR	Iveco TurboDaily 59-12	Mellor	B29F	1995
264	N302FOR	Iveco TurboDaily 59-12	Mellor	B29F	1995
265	N303FOR	Iveco TurboDaily 59-12	Mellor	B29F	1996
266	N304FOR	Iveco TurboDaily 59-12	Mellor	B29F	1996
267	P190PBP	Iveco TurboDaily 59-12	Mellor	B27F	1997
268	P191PBP	Iveco TurboDaily 59-12	Mellor	B27F	1997
291	F731OOT	Iveco Daily 49.10	Robin Hood City Nippy	B23F	1988
293	H975EOR	Iveco Daily 49.10	Phoenix	B23F	1991
502	F246RJX	DAF SB220LC550	Optare Delta	B47F	1989
503	J45GCX	DAF SB220LC550	Optare Delta	B49F	1992
504	L509EHD	DAF SB220LC550	Ikarus Citibus	C48F	1993
505	L510EHD	DAF SB220LC550	Ikarus Citibus	C48F	1993

551-565			Dennis Dart SLF			UVG UrbanStar		N44F	1997
551	R551UOT	554	R554UOT	558	R558UOT	561	R561UOT	564	R564UOT
552	R552UOT	556	R556UOT	559	R559UOT	562	R562UOT	565	R565UOT
553	R553UOT	557	R557UOT	560	R560UOT	563	R563UOT		

Previous Registrations:

225ASV	C337VRY		SIB3272	C287BBP
670DHO	F630SRP		SIB3273	C288BBP

Livery:- Silver and red; two-tone blue and yellow (Solent Blueline).

Named vehicles:- 505 *County of Hampshire;* 553 *Pride of Southampton.*

The South Central Bus Handbook

MERVYNS COACHES

M CL & J Annetts and L Porter, The New Coach House, Basingstoke Road, Innersdown, Hampshire.

HOD75	Bedford OB	Duple Vista	C29F	1949	Porter, Dummer, 1982
XKR469	Bedford YLQ	Plaxton Supreme IV	C35F	1980	Smith, Buntingford, 1988
741UKL	Bedford YMP	Plaxton Paramount 3200	C45F	1984	Olivine, Hounslow, 1989
A462ODY	Bedford YNT	Plaxton Paramount 3200 E	C53F	1984	Rambler, Hastings, 1997

Previous Registrations:

741UKL	B566HRM	HOD75	From new
A462ODY	A627YWF, ODY395	XRR469	CDK850V

Livery:- Cream and brown

HOD75 in the Mervyns Coaches fleet is a Duple Vista-bodied Bedford OB. While the normal vehicle on the Winchester service is normally one of the other vehicles, HOD75 is seen operating the 1998 New Year's Day service. The attractive vehicle may also be found on the service at other bank holiday times. *Byron Gage*

NEWNHAM COACHES

AS Bone & Sons Ltd, Hillside Service Station, London Road, Hook, Hampshire, RG27 9EG

HKE680L	Bristol VRT/SL3/6G	Eastern Coach Works	H43/29F	1973	The Bee Line, 1992
NOB323M	Daimler Fleetline CRG6LX	Park Royal	H43/33F	1973	West Midlands, 1987
PCR305M	Leyland Atlantean AN68/1R	East Lancashire	H45/31F	1974	Southampton Citybus, 1996
RFM894M	Leyland National 1151/1R		B49F	1974	Crosville Cymru, 1991
YDL671T	Bristol VRT/SL3/6LXB	Eastern Coach Works	H43/31F	1979	Southern Vectis, 1995
YDL674T	Bristol VRT/SL3/6LXB	Eastern Coach Works	H43/31F	1979	Southern Vectis, 1995

Livery:- Blue and cream

Newnham Coaches operate school contract services using a variety of service buses. Unfortunately, we are unable to illustrate this fleet in this edition as no suitable picture of this operator's vehicles is available. However, representing the minibus operation of Priory of Gosport is Mercedes-Benz E986NMK which has bus bodywork with high-back seating. *David Donati collection*

OAKLEY COACHES

M W Jones, 1 Clerken Green, Andover Road, Oakley,
Basingstoke, Hampshire, RG23 7HB

FDC411V	Leyland Leopard PSU3E/4R	Plaxton Supreme IV Exp	DP55F	1980	Kingston-upon-Hull, 1995
FDC412V	Leyland Leopard PSU3E/4R	Plaxton Supreme IV Exp	DP55F	1980	Kingston-upon-Hull, 1995
OPE613W	Bedford YMQ	Duple Dominant	C33F	1981	Gale, Haslemere, 1984
GDZ8449	Scania K112CRS	Plaxton Paramount 3500	C49FT	1984	Carterton Coaches, 1995
LIL2174	Scania K112CRS	Plaxton Paramount 3500	C53F	1984	Carterton Coaches, 1995
OIW5198	Scania K112CRS	Plaxton Paramount 3500	C53F	1985	Snell, Newton Abbott, 1994
B919NPC	Bedford YMP	Lex	B37F	1985	Tillingbourne, Cranleigh, 1994
B630DDW	Bedford YNT	Plaxton Paramount 3200 II	C53F	1985	CTC, Cardiff, 1988
B635DDW	Bedford YNT	Plaxton Paramount 3200 II	C53F	1985	CTC, Cardiff, 1988
C805FMC	Leyland Tiger TRCTL11/3RZ	Duple 340	C53F	1986	Frames Rickard, Brentford, 1989
C355SVV	Scania K92CRB	Jonckheere TransCity	B47D	1986	Cairngorm Chairlift, 1995
D21NWO	Leyland Tiger TRCTL11/3RZ	Duple 320	C51F	1987	Bebb, Llantwit Fardre, 1989
D22NWO	Leyland Tiger TRCTL11/3RZ	Duple 320	C55F	1987	Bebb, Llantwit Fardre, 1989
F816TMD	Mercedes-Benz 609D	Reeve Burgess Beaver	C23F	1989	
H13BED	Scania K93CRB	Plaxton Paramount 3200 III	C53F	1990	Chambers, Stevenage, 1996
BED2T	Leyland Swift ST2R44C97T5	Reeve Burgess Harrier	C37F	1991	Welcombe, Stratford, 1995
B4OAK	Leyland Swift ST2R44C97T5	Reeve Burgess Harrier	C37F	1991	Cropper, Kirkstall, 1996
B7BED	Leyland Swift ST2R44C97T5	Reeve Burgess Harrier	C37F	1991	Dereham Coachways, 1996

Previous Registrations:

B4OAK	J532BWU	GDZ8449	A489POD	LIL2174	B122HTM
B7BED	J786TDC	H13BED	H802RWJ, H6CRC, H199MSX	OIW5198	B970HTY
BED2T	H489LRW				

Depots:- Beach Arms Service Station (Oakley Buses)

Oakley Coaches operate tendered services on behalf of Hampshire County Council. Seen on route 28 to Alton is BED2T, a Leyland Swift with Reeve Burgess Harrier coachwork. It is one of three such vehicles in the fleet all of which have been re-registered. The operator also uses the fleetnames Porters Coaches and Gibsons. *Les Peters*

PEARCES

C & M Pearce, 39 Abingdon Road, Dorchester-on-Thames, Oxfordshire OX9 8JZ

JUD597W	Ford R1014	Plaxton Supreme IV Exp	C45F	1980	House, Watlington, 1987
H634HBW	Toyota Hiace	Toyota	M8	1990	
J100OFC	Toyota Coaster HDB30R	Caetano Optimo II	C18F	1991	
K100OMP	Iveco 315-8-17	Lorraine	C30F	1992	
K200OMP	Iveco 315-8-17	Lorraine	C30F	1992	
L11VWL	Plaxton 425	Lorraine	C53F	1993	
M300MFC	Toyota Coaster HZB50R	Caetano Optimo III	C21F	1994	
M968RWL	Bova FLC12.280	Bova Futura Club	C53F	1995	
N1VWL	Mercedes-Benz 711D	Plaxton Beaver	C25F	1995	
N129MBW	Scania K113CRB	Van Hool Alizée	C F	1996	
N649KWL	Dennis Javelin 12SDA2159	Plaxton Premiere 350	C53F	1996	
P677CUD	Toyota Coaster HZB50R	Caetano Optimo III	C21F	1997	
R329VJO	Dennis Javelin	Neoplan Transliner	C53F	1998	
R902GJO	Dennis Javelin (10m)	Plaxton Premiere 320	C39F	1998	

Previous Registrations:

M300MFC	M489HBC	NIVWL	N108BHL

Livery: White, yellow and brown

Depot: Tower Road, Berinsfield

Representing the varied fleet of Oxfordshire operator Pearces is one of their latest vehicles, R329VJO, a Neoplan Transliner. *Robert Edworthy*

PRINCESS SUMMERBEE

JHG Barfoot, Princess Garage, Botley Road, West End,
Southampton, SO3 3HA

406AOT	Leyland Leopard PSU3E/4R	Duple Dominant	C53F	1973	Southend, 1988
HDL232V	Ford R1014	Plaxton Supreme IV	C31F	1980	Safford's, Little Gransden, 1988
991FOT	Volvo B58-61	Plaxton Supreme IV	C51F	1980	Chiltern Queens, Woodcote, 1994
HSV336	DAF MB200DKTL600	Jonckheere Bermuda	C53F	1981	Lucketts, Fareham, 1990
489AOU	Volvo B10M-61	Duple Goldliner IV	C50F	1982	Coliseum, West End, 1989
A314NMJ	Ford Transit 190	Mellor	M6L	1983	Reynolds, Perivale, 1984
TIB8562	Scania K112CRS	Jonckheere Jubilee P50	C51FT	1984	Scanoaches, North Acton, 1994
549KYA	Van Hool T815	Van Hool Alizée	C53F	1984	Gaelicbus, Ballachulish, 1993
479COT	Van Hool TD824	Van Hool Astromega	CH55/20DT	1984	Time Travel, Thornton H, 1992
PJI6394	Scania K112CRS	Jonckheere Jubilee P599	C53F	1985	Beestons, Hadley, 1995
C592VUT	DAF SB2300DHS585	Smit Orion	C53F	1986	South Coast, Southampton, '97
C119BRV	Iveco Daily 49.10	Robin Hood City Nippy	B19F	1986	Eastleigh Com.Serv, 1997
KIW5922	DAF SB2300DHS585	Caetano Algarve	C51F	1987	Acton Holidays, Acton, 1996
987FOU	Quest J	Jonckheere Piccolo P35	C37F	1987	J&D Euro, Harrow Weald, 1998
F177XAV	Iveco Daily 49.10	Passenger Vehicle Bodies	M12L	1988	van, 1995
F215AVH	Iveco Daily 49.10	Robin Hood City Nippy	B9FL	1989	Kirklees MBC 1998
282GOT	Scania K113CRB	Berkhof Excellence	C49FT	1990	Appleby (Halcyon), 1998
SAZ4959	Ford Transit VE6	Ford	M14	1997	private owner, 1997

Previous Registrations:-

282GOT	G402PRH, 485DKH	HDL232V	CEB137V, 282GOT
406AOT	YWW359S	HSV336	DPO909W
479COT	A242UTC, VJR248, A243WGT	KIW5922	D336MHB
489AOU	JBK222X	PJI6394	B701EOF
549KYA	A780VLG	SAZ4959	From new
987FOU	D322VVV, 5189RU, D196YHK	TIB8562	A118XNH
991FOT	LUA244V		

Livery:- White, red and orange

TIB8562 from the Princess Summerbee fleet is a Scania with Jonckheere bodywork.one of four vehicles carrying that coach builders products albeit each differing markedly from each other.
David Donati

GKL827N is primarily used by Priory for school contract duties in the Portsmouth area. The vehicle was once Maidstone and District number 5827. *Philip Lamb*

Photographed at Chessington is PSU951, one of a pair of Plaxton Paramount 4000-bodied DAF coaches in the Priory fleet. It was new to hills of Tredegar and is one of the predominantly DAF-powered vehicles on the fleet. *David Heath*

PRIORY OF GOSPORT

Cyril Cowdrey Ltd, Quay Lane, Priory Road, Hardway, Gosport, Hampshire, PO12 4LJ
Southern Coaches Ltd, Everymans Garage, Maudlin, Chichester, PO18 0PB

Reg	Chassis	Body	Type	Year	History
GKL827N	Bristol VRT/SL2/6G	Eastern Coach Works	H43/31F	1974	Warrens, Ticehurst, 1993
OKE141P	Leyland Leopard PSU3C/4R	Duple Dominant	C47F	1976	Hom, Flimwell, 1996
NTT575W	Volvo B58-56	Plaxton Supreme IV Exp	C53F	1981	Seward, Dalwood, 1997
SMY621X	Bova EL26/581	Bova Europa	C52F	1982	Marchwood Motorways, 1998
CAY211Y	Bova EL26/581	Bova Europa	C53F	1983	Williams, Brecon, 1995
CAY212Y	Bova EL26/581	Bova Europa	C53F	1983	Williams, Brecon, 1995
RJI8726	DAF MB200DKFL600	Plaxton Paramount 3200	C50FT	1983	Heaton, Mayford, 1996
ERE235Y	Ford Transit 190	?	M10L	1983	Autistic Childrens Home, 1995
RJI1647	Bova FHD12.280	Bova Futura	C49FT	1984	Heaton, Mayford, 1997
DDZ1639	DAF SB2300DHS585	Jonckheere Jubilee P99	CH57/21CT	1986	Diamond-Glantawe, 1996
MBZ7136	Bova FHD12.280	Bova Futura	C53F	1985	Dolphin, Poole, 1998
C606WTP	Ford Transit 190	Carlyle	B16F	1985	Southern Vectis, 1997
C381NHJ	Scania K112TRS	Berkhof Emperor	CH55/21CT	1986	APT, Rayleigh, 1994
894FUY	Bova FHD12.290	Bova Futura	C49FT	1986	
D514NDA	Freight Rover Sherpa	Carlyle	B18F	1986	Streamline, Bath, 1996
D119VFV	DAF SB2300DHTD585	Plaxton Paramount 3200 II	C53F	1986	Street, Chivenor, 1997
D254OOJ	Freight Rover Sherpa	Carlyle	B18F	1987	Phil Anslow, Pontypool, 1995
D52TLV	Freight Rover Sherpa	Carlyle	B20F	1987	
PSU951	DAF SBR3000DKSB570	Plaxton Paramount 4000 III	CH55/19CT	1988	Baker, Weston-s-Mare, 1996
RJI8610	DAF SBR3000DKZ570	Plaxton Paramount 4000 III	CH55/19CT	1988	Baker, Weston-s-Mare, 1996
E986NMK	Mercedes-Benz 609D	Reeve Burgess	C25F	1988	
E357AMR	Mercedes-Benz 307D	Reeve Burgess	M12	1988	Heaton, Mayford, 1997
IIL8746	Bova FHD12.290	Bova Futura	C49FT	1988	Parnham, Ludgershall, 1995
E739JAY	DAF MB230DKFL615	Caetano Algarve	C53F	1988	Swallow, Bristol, , 1997
E492CPE	DAF MB230LB615	Caetano Algarve	C53F	1988	Heaton, Mayford, 1997
752FUV	Toyota Coaster HB31R	Caetano Optimo	C20F	1988	Rover, Horsley, 1996
GFO366	Bova FHD12.290	Bova Futura	C49FT	1988	Clapton Coaches, 1994
G423WFP	Bova FHD12.290	Bova Futura	C55F	1990	Moseley demonstrator, 1994
J461JRV	Bova FHD12.290	Bova Futura	C57F	1992	
K807EET	Bova FHD12.290	Bova Futura	C49FT	1993	Bailey, Biddisham, 1997
L680MET	Mercedes-Benz 711D	Plaxton Beaver	B25F	1993	Clapton Coaches, 1997
L120OWF	Bova FLD12.270	Bova Futura	C53F	1994	
M477UYA	Bova FLD12.270	Bova Futura	C53F	1994	
M199UYB	Bova FHD12.340	Bova Futura	C53FT	1994	
M212UYD	Bova FHD12.340	Bova Futura	C53F	1995	
M214UYD	Bova FLD12.270	Bova Futura	C53F	1995	
N709CYC	Bova FHD12.340	Bova Futura	C49FT	1996	
P933KYC	Bova FHD12.300	Bova Futura	C53F	1996	
R636VYB	Bova FHD10.340	Bova Futura	C36FT	1997	
R204WYD	Bova FLD12.270	Bova Futura	C57F	1998	

Previous Registrations:

Reg	Previous		Reg	Previous
752FUV	E240NFA		IIL8746	E278HRY
894FUY	D264NOD		L680MET	L680MET, DSK660
C381NHJ	C591, 827APT		MBZ7136	B62OMB
C606WTP	C262SDL, WXI6291		PSU951	E482SHB
DDZ1639	B500CBD		RJI1647	A667EMY
E739JAY	E739JAY, 927DAF		RJI8610	E640KCX
E492CPE	E178KNH, HIL5682		RJI8726	EDH540Y, OJI4362, UJW538Y
GFO366	F26EKR		SMY621X	SMY621X, 225ASV

Livery: White, yellow and brown.

READING BUSES

Reading Transport Ltd, Great Knollys Street, Reading, RG1 7HH

11-17						Leyland Olympian ONLXB/1RH* Optare			H42/26D	1988	*15/6 are ONLXCT/1RH	
11	E911DRD	13	E913DRD	15	E915DRD			16	E916DRD	17	E917DRD
12	E912DRD	14	E914DRD								

68	YJB68T	Leyland Titan TNLXB2RRSp	Park Royal	H44/25D	1979
69	YJB69T	Leyland Titan TNLXB2RRSp	Park Royal	H44/25D	1979

70-74						Leyland Titan TNLXB2RR	Leyland		H44/26D	1983	
70	SBL70Y	71	RMO71Y	72	RMO72Y			73	RMO73Y	74	RMO74Y

75-79						Leyland Titan TNLXC1RF	Leyland		DPH39/27F	1983	
75	RMO75Y	76	RMO76Y	77	RMO77Y			78	RMO78Y	79	RMO79Y

82	D82UTF	Leyland Olympian ONLXCT/1RH Eastern Coach Works	DPH39/25F	1986
83	D83UTF	Leyland Olympian ONLXCT/1RH Eastern Coach Works	DPH39/25F	1986
84	D84UTF	Leyland Olympian ONLXCT/1RH Eastern Coach Works	DPH39/25F	1986
85	F85MJH	Leyland Olympian ONLXCT/1RH Optare	DPH39/25F	1988
86	F86MJH	Leyland Olympian ONLXCT/1RH Optare	DPH39/25F	1988
87	F87MJH	Leyland Olympian ONLXCT/1RH Optare	DPH39/25F	1988

Reading Buses have been a keen user of Optare designed products with all the models represented in the fleet. Minibus operation moved from the MCW MetroRider to the Optare product as production moved to Leeds. Representing the type here is 626, M930TYG, which was previously a type demonstrator. *Colin Lloyd*

Commuting services from the Reading area into London are operated as Goldline. Pictured near Wokingham fire station in May 1998 is L529EHD, a DAF SB2700 with Van Hool bodywork. *Keith Grimes*

162-183

				MCW Metrobus DR102/8*		MCW		H43/27D	1979-81 *166-183 are DR102/16	

162	WRD160T	168	CJH168V	172	CJH172V	176	HCF176W	180	HCF180W
164	CJH164V	169	CJH169V	173	HCF173W	177	HCF177W	181	HCF181W
165	CJH165V	170	CJH170V	174	HCF174W	178	HCF178W	182	HCF182W
166	CJH166V	171	CJH171V	175	HCF175W	179	HCF179W	183	HCF183W

185-193

MCW Metrobus DR102/25*   MCW   H45/28D   1982   *189-93 are DR102/30

185	LMO185X	187	LMO187X	189	LMO189X	191	LMO191X	193	LMO193X
186	LMO186X	188	LMO188X	190	LMO190X	192	LMO192X		

201-210

Mercedes-Benz 811D   Optare StarRider   B26F   1988-89 The Bee Line, 1992

201	F531NRD	203	F533NRD	205	F535NRD	207	F361SDP	209	F363SDP
202	F532NRD	204	F534NRD	206	F360SDP	208	F362SDP	210	F364SDP

214	D939KNW	Volkswagen LT55	Optare City Pacer	B25F	1986	
215	E236VUD	Volkswagen LT55	Optare City Pacer	B25F	1987	Lancaster, 1992
217	H847UUA	Volkswagen LT55	Optare City Pacer	C25F	1991	Bebbs, Llantwit Fardre, 1995
218	D898NUA	Volkswagen LT55	Optare City Pacer	DP21F	1987	Blackpool, 1996
219	E557GFR	Volkswagen LT55	Optare City Pacer	B21F	1987	Blackpool, 1996
220	BUS5X	Scania K113CRB	Van Hool Alizée	C49FT	1989	
221	E558GFR	Volkswagen LT55	Optare City Pacer	B21F	1987	Blackpool, 1996
222	D560YCW	Volkswagen LT55	Optare City Pacer	B21F	1987	Blackpool, 1996
224	E999UYG	Volkswagen LT55	Optare City Pacer	DP25F	1988	Hants & Dorset, 1997
225	E996UYG	Volkswagen LT55	Optare City Pacer	DP25F	1988	Hants & Dorset, 1997
234	J786KHD	DAF SB2700HS585	Van Hool Alizée	C51F	1992	Chesterfield, 1995
235	J788KHD	DAF SB2700HS585	Van Hool Alizée	C51F	1992	Hallmark, Luton, 1996
236	J799KHD	DAF SB2700HS585	Van Hool Alizéc	C51F	1992	Jones, Eccles, 1992
237	L529EHD	DAF SB2700HS585	Van Hool Alizée	C51FT	1994	RDJ International, Torquay, 1998
251	K505RJX	DAF SB2700HS585	Van Hool Alizée	C55F	1992	
261	G608SGU	Leyland Tiger TRCL10/3ARZA	Plaxton Paramount 3200 III	C57F	1990	Selkent, 1993
262	G100VMM	Leyland Tiger TRCL10/3ARZA	Plaxton Paramount 3200 III	C57F	1990	East London, 1993
271	L671RUA	Bova FLC12.280	Bova Futura Club	C53F	1994	Bova demonstrator, 1994

Having previously run a fleet of Bristol VRT double deck buses, Reading Buses turned to the MCW Metrobus for large orders in the late 1970s and early 1980s. Dating from 1981 is 73, HCF173W, seen carrying the cream, maroon and turquoise livery. *Mark Lyons*

272	M272SBT	Bova FLC12.280	Bova Futura Club	C53F	1995	
273	N501MWW	Bova FLC12.280	Bova Futura Club	C53F	1996	Optare demonstrator, 1997
274	R466GUA	Bova FLC12.280	Bova Futura Club	C53F	1998	Optare demonstrator, 1998
314	NDR155M	Leyland National 1151/1R/0402 (Volvo)		B49F	1974	The Bee Line, 1992
333	GPC731N	Leyland National 11351/1R (Volvo)		B49F	1974	The Bee Line, 1992
339	GPJ895N	Leyland National 11351/1R (Volvo)		B49F	1975	The Bee Line, 1992
340	GPJ896N	Leyland National 11351/1R (Volvo)		B49F	1975	The Bee Line, 1992
343	KPA355P	Leyland National 11351/1R		B49F	1975	The Bee Line, 1992
344	FNS162T	Leyland National 11351A/1R (Volvo)		B52F	1979	Choice Travel, Willenhall, 1992
345	KRE281P	Leyland National 11351/1R (Volvo)		B52F	1976	PMT, 1993
346	KRE283P	Leyland National 11351/1R (Volvo)		B52F	1976	PMT, 1993
357	NPJ483R	Leyland National 11351A/1R (Volvo)		B49F	1977	The Bee Line, 1992
382	LPF603P	Leyland National 11351/1R/SC (Volvo)		B49F	1976	The Bee Line, 1992

455-469		MCW Metrobus DR102/63		MCW		H45/30F	1987-88 London Buses, 1991

455	E454SON	458	E458SON	461	E247KCF	464	E464SON	467	E467SON
456	E456SON	459	E459SON	462	E462SON	465	E465SON	468	E468SON
457	E457SON	460	E460SON	463	E463SON	466	E466SON	469	E469SON

501-510		DAF SB220LC550	Optare Delta	B49F*	1989	*508 is B44F

501	G501XBL	503	G503XBL	505	G505XBL	507	G507XBL	509	G509XBL
502	G502XBL	504	G504XBL	506	G506XBL	508	G508XBL	510	G510XBL

511-520		DAF DE02LTSB220	Optare Delta	B47F	1995-96

511	M511PDP	513	M513PDP	515	N515YTF	517	N517YTF	519	N519YTF
512	M512PDP	514	N514YTF	516	N516YTF	518	N518YTF	520	N520YTF

Seen departing Reading rail station on service 34 is Reading Buses 501, G501XBL. It is one of ten Optare Deltas purchased in 1989. A further batch of similar vehicles entered the fleet in 1995/6. Despite being ten years old, the design of the body, which is only available on the DAF chassis, remains modern looking. *Malc McDonald*

601-606

		MCW MetroRider MF154/8		MCW		B31F	1988	
601	E601HTF	603	E603HTF	604	E604HTF	605	E605HTF	606	E606HTF
602	E602HTF							

607-613

		Optare MetroRider MR07		Optare		B25F	1991	
607	J607SJB	609	J609SJB	611	J611SJB	612	J612SJB	613	H613NJB
608	J608SJB	610	J610SJB					

614-623

		Optare MetroRider MR17		Optare		B25F	1994	
614	M614NRD	616	L616LJM	618	L618LJM	620	L620LJM	622	M622PDP
615	L615LJM	617	L617LJM	619	L619LJM	621	M621PDP	623	M623PDP

624	N624ATF	Optare MetroRider MR17 (CNG)	Optare	B25F	1996	
625	M23UUA	Optare MetroRider MR17	Optare	B29F	1995	Optare demonstrator, 1995
626	M930TYG	Optare MetroRider MR17	Optare	B27F	1995	Optare demonstrator, 1995
627	R627SJM	Optare MetroRider MR17	Optare	B25F	1997	
628	R628SJM	Optare MetroRider MR17	Optare	B25F	1997	
629	R629SJM	Optare MetroRider MR17	Optare	B25F	1997	
661	J965JNL	Optare MetroRider MR03	Optare	B28F	1991	Metrobus, Orpington, 1996
662	J966JNL	Optare MetroRider MR03	Optare	B28F	1991	Metrobus, Orpington, 1996
701	MRD1	DAF DB250WB505	Optare Spectra	H43/28F	1992	
702	K702BBL	DAF DB250WB505	Optare Spectra	H46/28F	1992	
703	K703BBL	DAF DB250WB505	Optare Spectra	H46/28F	1992	
704	K170FYG	DAF DB250WB505	Optare Spectra	H46/28F	1992	Optare demonstrator, 1993
705	L705FRD	DAF DB250RS505	Optare Spectra	H46/28F	1994	
706	L706FRD	DAF DB250RS505	Optare Spectra	H46/28F	1994	
707	L707LJM	DAF DB250RS505	Optare Spectra	H46/28F	1994	
751	L751FRD	DAF DB250RS505	Optare Spectra	DPH37/25F	1993	
752	L752FRD	DAF DB250RS505	Optare Spectra	DPH37/25F	1993	
781	F771OJH	Volvo B10M-62	Jonckheere Jubilee P50	C55F	1989	The Bee Line, 1992
784	F774OJH	Volvo B10M-62	Jonckheere Jubilee P50	C55F	1989	The Bee Line, 1992
785	F755OJH	Volvo B10M-62	Jonckheere Jubilee P50	C55F	1989	The Bee Line, 1992

The Newbury operations of Q Drive's Bee Line business were taken over by Reading Buses in 1992. Maintained as a separate unit, the Newbury vehicles carry a green band instead of the standard Reading turquoise. Number 803, K803DCF is one of 14 Optare Vecta bodied MAN products in the fleet.
British Bus Publishing

801	K801DCF	MAN 11.180		Optare Vecta	B40F	1993			
802	K802DCF	MAN 11.180		Optare Vecta	B40F	1993			

803-813 MAN 11.190 Optare Vecta B40F 1993-96

803	K803DCF	806	L806FRD	808	L808FRD	810	M810PDP	812	N812XJH
804	K804DCF	807	L807FRD	809	M809PDP	811	M811PDP	813	N813XJH
805	K805DCF								

814	M957VWY	MAN 11.190	Optare Vecta	B40F	1995	Optare demonstrator, 1995

901-924 Optare L1150 Optare Excel B39F 1997

901	P901EGM	906	P906EGM	911	P911GJM	916	R916SJM	921	P921SJH
902	P902EGM	907	P907EGM	912	P912GJM	917	R917SJH	922	P922SJH
903	P903EGM	908	P908EGM	913	P913GJM	918	R918SJH	923	P923SJH
904	P904EGM	909	P909EGM	914	P914GJM	919	R919SJH	924	P924SJH
905	P905EGM	910	P910EGM	915	P915GJM	920	R920SJH		

Depots:- Newbury (201-10, 333/9/40-3-6/57/82/614/21-4/801/3) and Reading (remainder).

Livery:- Cream, maroon and turquoise (Reading Buses); cream, maroon and green (Newbury Buses); blue and cream (Goldline) 234/7

Opposite, top:- **The Optare Spectra was built on DAF DB250 bodywork and provides an attractive modern design. The first Reading example, 701, was shown at the 1992 Coach and Bus show and carries the cherished index mark MRD1. The vehicle Is seen on local service in Reading The latest low-floor version of the model was the first of the type in the UK, though this variant has yet to enter service with Reading.**
Opposite, bottom:- **The latest single-deck low floor bus from the Optare builder is the Excel. The integral vehicle brings style influences similar to those seen in The Netherlands. From the Reading batch 908, P908EGM, is seen in the town.**

READING MAINLINE

The Greater Reading Omnibus Co Ltd, PO Box 147, Reading, RG3 2XY

Owned by Reading Transport Ltd from May 1998

1	ALM34B	AEC Routemaster R2RH	Park Royal	H36/28R	1964	Southend, 1994
2	WLT993	AEC Routemaster R2RH	Park Royal	H36/28R	1962	Southend, 1994
3	XVS319	AEC Routemaster R2RH	Park Royal	H36/28R	1961	Southend, 1994
4	ALM11B	AEC Routemaster R2RH	Park Royal	H36/28R	1964	Southend, 1994
5	WLT937	AEC Routemaster R2RH	Park Royal	H36/28R	1961	Southend, 1994
6	WLT577	AEC Routemaster R2RH	Park Royal	H36/28R	1961	Southend, 1994
7	VLT44	AEC Routemaster R2RH	Park Royal	H36/28R	1959	Southend, 1994
8	YTS973A	AEC Routemaster R2RH	Park Royal	H36/28R	1962	Blue Triangle, Rainham, 1994
9	WLT790	AEC Routemaster R2RH	Park Royal	H36/28R	1961	non PSV, 1994
10	WYJ857	AEC Routemaster R2RH	Park Royal	H36/28R	1960	Southend, 1994
11	AST416A	AEC Routemaster R2RH	Park Royal	H36/28R	1960	Strathtay, 1994
12	AST415A	AEC Routemaster R2RH	Park Royal	H36/28R	1959	Strathtay, 1994
13	WTS186A	AEC Routemaster R2RH	Park Royal	H36/28R	1962	Strathtay, 1994
14	WLT316	AEC Routemaster R2RH	Park Royal	H36/28R	1960	Strathtay, 1994
15	WVS423	AEC Routemaster R2RH	Park Royal	H36/28R	1962	preservation, 1994
16	WLT621	AEC Routemaster R2RH	Park Royal	H36/28R	1961	Shaftesbury & District, 1994
17	859DYE	AEC Routemaster 2R2RH	Park Royal	H36/28R	1964	non PSV, 1994
18	PVS828	AEC Routemaster R2RH	Park Royal	H36/28R	1962	London General, 1995
19	XVS839	AEC Routemaster R2RH	Park Royal	H36/28R	1960	South London, 1995
20	XVS830	AEC Routemaster R2RH	Park Royal	H36/28R	1960	CentreWest, 1995
21	CUV201C	AEC Routemaster R2RH	Park Royal	H36/28R	1965	London United, 1995
22	XYJ440	AEC Routemaster R2RH	Park Royal	H36/28R	1961	London Central, 1995
23	JFO256	AEC Routemaster R2RH	Park Royal	H36/28R	1959	London United, 1995
24	MFF580	AEC Routemaster R2RH	Park Royal	H36/28R	1961	London United, 1995
25	ALD990B	AEC Routemaster R2RH	Park Royal	H36/28R	1964	East Yorkshire, 1995

Reading Mainline 7, VLT44, is seen on service in Reading. Recently, the operation has been acquired by Reading Buses, though the initial plans are to continue to run with the Routemasters. *Ralph Stevens*

Reading Mainline obtained Routemasters from a number of operators who have discontinued this type of operation. No.35, 640DYE was purchased from Blackpool in 1997. It is seen on route C outside Reading rail station. All the Reading Mainline routes are lettered rather than numbered. *M E Lyons*

26	NRH803A	AEC Routemaster R2RH	Park Royal	H36/28R	1962	East Yorkshire, 1995
27	WTS102A	AEC Routemaster R2RH	Park Royal	H36/28R	1961	Strathtay, 1994
28	XSL220A	AEC Routemaster R2RH	Park Royal	H36/28R	1959	Strathtay, 1994
29	ALD948B	AEC Routemaster 2R2RH	Park Royal	H36/28R	1964	CentreWest, 1995
30	ALM37B	AEC Routemaster R2RH	Park Royal	H36/28R	1962	preservation, 1994
31	WLT938	AEC Routemaster R2RH	Park Royal	H36/28R	1961	on loan from preservation
32	LDS280A	AEC Routemaster R2RH	Park Royal	H36/28R	1959	BTS Coaches, 1997
33	ALD989B	AEC Routemaster R2RH	Park Royal	H36/28R	1964	Blackpool, 1997
34	357CLT	AEC Routemaster R2RH	Park Royal	H36/28R	1962	Blackpool, 1997
35	640DYE	AEC Routemaster R2RH	Park Royal	H36/28R	1963	Blackpool, 1997
36	735DYE	AEC Routemaster R2RH	Park Royal	H36/28R	1963	Blackpool, 1997
37	650DYE	AEC Routemaster R2RH	Park Royal	H36/28R	1963	Blackpool, 1997
38	627DYE	AEC Routemaster R2RH	Park Royal	H36/28R	1963	Blackpool, 1997
39	583CLT	AEC Routemaster R2RH	Park Royal	H36/28R	1963	Blackpool, 1997
40	WLT848	AEC Routemaster R2RH	Park Royal	H36/28R	1961	Blackpool, 1997
41	WLT879	AEC Routemaster R2RH	Park Royal	H36/28R	1961	Blackpool, 1997
42	ALM71B	AEC Routemaster R2RH	Park Royal	H36/28R	1964	Blackpool, 1997
43	ALM89B	AEC Routemaster R2RH	Park Royal	H36/28R	1964	Blackpool, 1997
44	ALD966B	AEC Routemaster 2R2RH	Park Royal	H36/28R	1964	Blackpool, 1997

Previous Registrations:

AST415A	VLT45	WTS102A	WLT917
AST416A	VLT191	WTS186A	143CLT
JFO256	VLT23, LGH31T	WVS423	WLT999
LDS280A	VLT104	WYJ857	VLT172
MFF580	WLT931	XSL220A	VLT26
NRH803A	WLT871	XVS319	WLT949
PVS828	18CLT	XVS830	VLT180
XVS839	VLT244	XYJ440	WLT838
WLT316	WLT316, WTS333A	YTS973A	17CLT

Livery: Red and cream

SEAVIEW SERVICES

A & MA Robinson, Seafield Garage, College Farm, Faulkner Lane, Sandown,
Isle of Wight, PO36 9AZ

1	ODL678	Volvo B10M-61	Jonckheere Jubilee P50	C53F	1985	Skills, Nottingham, 1991
2	XDL696	Bedford YNT	Plaxton Paramount 3200	C57F	1983	Moss, Sandown, 1994
3	PDL230	Volvo B58-61	Van Hool Alizée	C52F	1982	Harris, Armadale, 1986
4	KDZ8761	Leyland Tiger TRCTL11/3R	Plaxton Paramount 3500	C53F	1984	Southern Vectis, 1992
5	LDZ3474	Leyland Tiger TRCTL11/3R	Plaxton Paramount 3500	C51F	1984	Southern Vectis, 1992
7	PDL298	Bedford YMT	Duple Dominant II	C53F	1980	Smiths, Liss, 1988
8	TDL856	Volvo B10M-61	Plaxton Paramount 3200 II	C57F	1986	O'Connor, Hanwell, 1989
9	WXI6291	Leyland Tiger TRCTL11/3ARZ	Plaxton Paramount 3500 III	C53F	1988	Southern Vectis, 1997
13	C316TDL	Leyland Tiger TRCTL11/3RH	Plaxton Paramount 3500 II	C49F	1986	Southern Vectis, 1997
	G144ULG	Volvo B10M-60	Jonckheere Jubilee P599	C51FT	1990	Barratts, Nantwich, 1998
	H901EDL	Kässbohrer Setra S215HD	Kässbohrer	C49F	1991	Southern Vectis, 1997

Previous Registrations:

C316TDL	C316TDL, 390CDL	PDL230	CGA198X
G144ULG	G653ONH, B3BCL,	PDL298	KPC403W
H901EDL	H901EDL, WDL142	TDL856	C590GMC
KDZ8761	A588RFR, 390CDL	WXI6291	W321JDL
LDZ3474	A781WHB, VDL263	XDL696	A374BDL
ODL678	B41KAL		

Livery:- Two-tone green and red

Seaview services for many years operated a bus route from Ryde through the picturesque village of Sandown which gave the company its name. The two-tone green and red livery survives but the company now only operates coach services. No2, XDL696 is a Bedford YNT which has been based on the isle of Wight from new having previously been in the fleet of Moss, Sandown. *Don Vincent*

SOLENT BLUE LINE

Musterphantom Ltd, 168-170 High Street, Southampton, SO1 0BY

123	DBV23W	Bristol VRT/SL3/6LXB	Eastern Coach Works	H43/31F	1980	Midland Red (G&G), 1995

149-165
Bristol VRT/SL3/501(6LXB) — Eastern Coach Works — H43/31F — 1979 — Hampshire Bus, 1987

149	LHG449T	152	LHG452T	156	LHG456T	160	TRN160V	163	TRN163V
150	LHG450T	154	LHG454T	157	LHG457T	161	TRN161V	164w	TRN164V
151	LHG451T	155	LHG455T	159	LHG459T	162	TRN162V	165	TRN165V

166	YDL676T	Bristol VRT/SL3/6LXB	Eastern Coach Works	H43/31F	1980	Southern Vectis, 1996
167	FDL678V	Bristol VRT/SL3/6LXB	Eastern Coach Works	H43/31F	1980	Southern Vectis, 1996
168	FDL680V	Bristol VRT/SL3/6LXB	Eastern Coach Works	H43/31F	1980	Southern Vectis, 1996
169	FDL677V	Bristol VRT/SL3/6LXB	Eastern Coach Works	H43/31F	1980	Southern Vectis, 1996

231-235
Iveco Daily 49.10 — Car Chair — B28F — 1992

231w	J231KDL	232	J232KDL	233	J233KDL	234	J234KDL	235	J235KDL

241	M241XPO	Iveco TurboDaily 59-12	English Car Chair	B29F	1994
242	M242XPO	Iveco TurboDaily 59-12	English Car Chair	B29F	1994
243	M243XPO	Iveco TurboDaily 59-12	English Car Chair	B29F	1994
244	M244XPO	Iveco TurboDaily 59-12	English Car Chair	B29F	1994

245-260
Iveco TurboDaily 59-12 — Mellor — B29F — 1995

245	M245BPO	249	M249BPO	252	M252BPO	255	N255ECR	258	N258ECR
246	M246BPO	250	M250BPO	253	N253ECR	256	N256ECR	259	N259FOR
247	M247BPO	251	M251BPO	254	N254ECR	257	N257ECR	260	N260FOR
248	M248BPO								

262	F862LCUL	MCW MetroRider MF158/15	MCW	B31F	1988	Arriva Kent & Thameside, 1998
263	F863LCUL	MCW MetroRider MF158/15	MCW	B31F	1988	Arriva Kent & Thameside, 1998
526	L526YDL	Volvo B10B	Alexander Strider	B51F	1994	
527	L527YDL	Volvo B10B	Alexander Strider	B51F	1994	
528	L528YDL	Volvo B10B	Alexander Strider	B51F	1994	
529	L227THP	Volvo B10B	Alexander Strider	B51F	1993	Volvo demonstrator, 1994

694-705
Leyland Olympian ONLXB/1R — Eastern Coach Works — H45/30F — 1983-84 — *695 is DPH41/32F
694-700 Southern Vectis 1989-92; 701-5 Hampshire Bus, 1987

694	WDL694Y	697	A697DDL	700	A700DDL	702	A202MEL	704	A204MEL
695	A695FDL	699	A699DDL	701	A201MEL	703	A203MEL	705	A205MEL

The first minibuses for Solent Blue Line not to have been built in the locality were a batch of Mellor- bodied Iveco models supplied in 1995. Representing the Rochdale builder is 259, N259FOR.
Philip Lamb

706	F706RDL	Leyland Olympian ONCL10/1RZ	Leyland	DPH39/29F	1989			
707	F707RDL	Leyland Olympian ONCL10/1RZ	Leyland	DPH39/29F	1989			
708	F708SDL	Leyland Olympian ONCL10/1RZ	Leyland	DPH39/29F	1989			
709	F709SDL	Leyland Olympian ONCL10/1RZ	Leyland	DPH39/29F	1989			

721-734

Leyland Olympian ON2R50C13Z5 Leyland — H47/31F* — 1989-91 — *721/2 are DPH39/29F

721	G721WDL	728	H728DDL	731	H731DDL	733	H733DDL	734	H734DDL
722	G722WDL	729	H729DDL	732	H732DDL				

735	M735BBP	Volvo Olympian YN2RC16Z5	East Lancashire	DPH41/29F	1995	
736	M736BBP	Volvo Olympian YN2RV18Z4	East Lancashire	DPH41/29F	1995	
737	R737XRV	Volvo Olympian	Northern Coutries Palatine I	DPH41/29F	1998	
738	R738XRV	Volvo Olympian	Northern Coutries Palatine I	DPH41/29F	1998	
739	R739XRV	Volvo Olympian	Northern Coutries Palatine I	DPH41/29F	1998	
741	R741XRV	Volvo Olympian	Northern Coutries Palatine I	DPH41/29F	1998	
817	F817URN	Leyland Olympian ONCL10/1RZ	Leyland	H47/31F	1988	Leyland demonstrator, 1990

Ancilliary vehicles:-

220	C220XRU	Ford Transit 190	Robin Hood	B16F	1985	Southern Vectis, 1989
221	C221XRU	Ford Transit 190	Robin Hood	van	1985	Southern Vectis, 1987
226	C226XRU	Ford Transit 190	Robin Hood	van	1985	Southern Vectis, 1987

Previous Registrations:

A295FDL   A702DDL, WDL142   F817URN   BMN88G

Named vehicles:-
149 *Southampton Mencap*; 150 *Wendy Knight*; 154 *TS Astrid*; 155 *Jose Nicholls*; 160 *Eileen Howlett*; 161 *British Diabetic Association*; 162 *Action for Animals*; 163 *Romsey Lions*; 164 *Mary Hall*; 526 *City of Southampton*; 527 *Borough of Eastleigh*; 528 *City of Winchester*, 529 *Leukaemia Busters*; 707 *Venturers Search & Rescue*; 709 *WessCancer Trust*; 721 *Southampton - Le Harve Twinning Society*; 722 *Training Corps*.

Livery:- Yellow and two-tone blue.

Depots:- Eastleigh (Barton Park) and Hythe (Berkeley Garage).

Opposite,top:- **The Bristol VRs inhereted from Hampshire Bus were high-bridge models that originated with Ribble. From that batch, 155, LHG455T, is shown here.** *Andy Jarosz*
Opposite, bottom:- **Four Alexander Strider-bodied Volvo buses joined the fleet in 1994, though one had previously been used by the chassis manufacturer for demonstration work. Also pictured working service 19 is 528, L528YDL.** *Malc McDonald*

Solent Blue Line and parent company Southern Vectis both purchased Volvo Olympians in 1998. They carry the Palatine I version of the Northern Counties body and have high-backed seats fitted. Seen in Southampton bound for Eastleigh on service 48 is 741. R741XRV.
Dave Heath

SOLENT HOLIDAYS

J M & P R Skew, Brookside Garage, Crow Lane, Crow, Hampshire, BH24 3EA

ALJ568A	Mercedes-Benz O303/15R	Mercedes-Benz	C53F	1983	Redwing, Purley, 1988
RIA1445	Mercedes-Benz O303/15R	Mercedes-Benz	C53F	1983	Redwing, Purley, 1988
NIW6503	Kässbohrer Setra S215HR	Kässbohrer Rational	C53F	1984	Kings Coaches, Stanway, 1993
RIW8799	Kässbohrer Setra S210HD	Kässbohrer	C35FT	1985	Luckett, Fareham, 1997
MIW5799	Scania K112CRS	Van Hool Alizée	C53F	1986	Wing, Sleaford, 1992
F22VFX	Ford Transit VE6	Ford	M14	1988	
OIW5798	Scania K113CRB	Van Hool Alizée	C55F	1989	Kentishman, Swanley, 1993
G774EPF	Mercedes-Benz 408D	Crystals	M15	1990	Aspden, Blackburn, 1994
SIW1934	Scania K113CRB	Van Hool Alizée	C49F	1995	Fargo Coachlines, Rayne, 1997
M214TNO	Ford Transit VE6	Ford	M14	1995	Economy Hire, 1996
N698AHL	Scania K113TRB	Irizar Century 12.37	C49FT	1996	

Previous Registrations:

ALJ568A	PUL91Y	RIA1445	PUL102Y, ALJ993A
MIW5799	D231OET, MFU383, D352XJL	RIW8799	B34AAG, 74DRH, RIA1445
NIW6503	A70FPH	SIW1934	M309VET
OIW5798	CIB3683		

Livery: White and blue

The Van Hool Alizée family has been mounted on a variety of chassis or deployed as an integral vehicle, with exports from Belgium to most parts of the globe. In the case of Solent Holidays' OIW5798, the Scania K113CRB chassis was use. The Alizée body has, after many years of production, recently undergone a major re-styling and is now known as the Alizée T9. *David Donati*

SOUTHERN VECTIS

Southern Vectis Omnibus Co, Nelson Road, Newport, Isle of Wight, PO30 1RD

202	KDL202W	Bristol LHS6L	Eastern Coach Works	DP31F	1980
203	KDL203W	Bristol LHS6L	Eastern Coach Works	DP31F	1980
236	J236KDL	Iveco Daily 49.10	Car Chair	B23F	1992
237	J237KDL	Iveco Daily 49.10	Car Chair	B23F	1992
238	J238KDL	Iveco Daily 49.10	Car Chair	B23F	1992

240-247

Iveco TurboDaily 59-12   Mellor   DP23F   1996-97

| 240 | N240PDL | 242 | N242PDL | 244 | P244VDL | 246 | P246VDL | 247 | P247VDL |
| 241 | N241PDL | 243 | N243PDL | 245 | P245VDL | | | | |

| 261 | N261FOR | Iveco TurboDaily 59-12 | Mellor | B23F | 1995 | Solent Blue Line, 1996 |
| 262 | N262FOR | Iveco TurboDaily 59-12 | Mellor | B23F | 1995 | Solent Blue Line, 1996 |

283-287

Iveco Daily 49.10   Robin Hood City Nippy   B23F   1989

| 283 | F283SDL | 284 | F284SDL | 285 | F285SDL | 286 | F286SDL | 287 | F287SDL |

288	G565YTR	Iveco Daily 49.10	Phoenix	B23F	1990	Phoenix demonstrator, 1990
289	H289DDL	Iveco Daily 49.10	Phoenix	B23F	1990	Phoenix demonstrator, 1990
314	TJI8784	Leyland Tiger TRCTL11/3RH	Plaxton Paramount 3500 II	C49F	1986	
315	473CDL	Leyland Tiger TRCTL11/3RH	Plaxton Paramount 3500 II	C49F	1986	
320	TJI7520	Leyland Tiger TRCTL11/3ARZ	Plaxton Paramount 3500 III	C53F	1988	
505	UFX505S	Bristol VRT/SL3/6LXB	Eastern Coach Works	CO43/31F	1977	Hants & Dorset, 1979
506	UFX506S	Bristol VRT/SL3/6LXB	Eastern Coach Works	CO43/31F	1977	Hants & Dorset, 1979

679-685

Bristol VRT/SL3/6LXB   Eastern Coach Works   H43/31F   1980-81

| 679 | FDL679V | 682 | FDL682V | 683 | DPX683W | 684 | DPX684W | 685 | DPX685W |
| 681 | FDL681V | | | | | | | | |

686-698

Leyland Olympian ONLXB/1R   Eastern Coach Works   DPH40/30F   1982-84

686	RDL686X	689	RDL689X	691	RDL691X	693	WDL693Y	696	WDL696Y
687	RDL687X	690	RDL690X	692	WDL692Y	695	WDL695Y	698	A698DDL
688	RDL688X								

710	F710SDL	Leyland Olympian ONCL10/1RZ	Leyland	DPH41/29F	1989
711	F711SDL	Leyland Olympian ONCL10/1RZ	Leyland	DPH41/29F	1989
712	F712SDL	Leyland Olympian ONCL10/1RZ	Leyland	DPH41/29F	1989

713-727

Leyland Olympian ON2R50C13Z5   Leyland   DPH41/29F   1989-90

713	G713WDL	716	G716WDL	719	G719WDL	724	G724XDL	726	G726XDL
714	G714WDL	717	G717WDL	720	G720WDL	725	G725XDL	727	G727XDL
715	G715WDL	718	G718WDL	723	G723XDL				

735-743

Leyland Olympian ON2R50C13Z5   Northern Counties   DPH41/29F   1993

| 735 | K735ODL | 737 | K737ODL | 739 | K739ODL | 741 | K741ODL | 743 | K743ODL |
| 736 | K736ODL | 738 | K738ODL | 740 | K740ODL | 742 | K742ODL | | |

744-751

Volvo Olympian YN2R50C18Z4   Northern Counties   DPH41/29F   1995

| 744 | M745HDL | 746 | M746HDL | 749 | M749HDL | 750 | M750HDL | 751 | M751HDL |
| 745 | M745HDL | 748 | M748HDL | | | | | | |

752-759   Volvo Olympian   Northern Counties Palatine I DPH41/29F   1998

752	R752GDL	754	R754GDL	756	R756GDL	758	R758GDL	759	R759GDL
753	R753GDL	755	R755GDL	757	R757GDL				

810-815   Dennis Dart 8.5SDL3052   UVG Urban Star   DP33F   1996

810	N810PDL	812	N812PDL	813	N813PDL	814	N814PDL	815	N815PDL
811	N811PDL								

864	F86TDL	Leyland Tiger TRCTL11/3R	Marshall Campaigner	DP53F	1983	MoD, 1995
903	WDL142	Volvo B10M-62	Plaxton Excalibur	C53F	1996	Horseman, Reading, 1997
904	WDL748	Volvo B10M-62	Plaxton Excalibur	C53F	1996	Horseman, Reading, 1997

Heritage vehicles

500	MDL955	Bristol Lodekka LD6G	Eastern Coach Works	O33/27R	1956	preservation, 1993
501	MDL952	Bristol Lodekka LD6G	Eastern Coach Works	O33/27R	1956	
502	CDL899	Bristol K5G	Eastern Coach Works	O30/26R	1939	
507	MDL953	Bristol Lodekka LD6G	Eastern Coach Works	O33/27R	1956	Connells, Aylesbury, 1994
628	SDL638J	Bristol VRT/SL/6G	Eastern Coach Works	H39/31F	1971	
863	TDL563K	Bristol RELL6G	Eastern Coach Works	B53F	1971	

Ancilliary vehicles

009	NDL490G	Bristol VRT/SL/6G	Eastern Coach Works	H-/-F	1969
	C265SDL	Ford Transit 190	Carlyle	van	1985
	C268SDL	Ford Transit 190	Carlyle	van	1985

Previous Registrations:

473CDL	C315TDL	VDL613S	UFX855S, 473CDL
TJI7520	E320JDL	WDL142	N667VJB
TJI8784	C314TDL, WDL748	WDL748	N668VJB

Opposite:- **Southern Vectis are the decendents of the National Bus Company subsidiary that operated on the Isle of Wight. A traditional livery has been adopted shown here on Bristol LHS 202, KDL202W; Volvo Olympian 749, M749HDL and** *(below)* **Dennis Dart 815, N815PDL. This latter vehicle carries the less-common UVG bodywork.** *Glyn Matthews*

STAGECOACH OXFORD

Thames Transit Ltd, Horspath Road, Cowley, Oxfordshire, OX4 2RY

1	L723JUD	Volvo B10M-60	Jonckheere Deauville 45	C49FT	1994	
2	L724JUD	Volvo B10M-60	Jonckheere Deauville 45	C49FT	1994	
3	3063VC	Volvo B10M-60	Plaxton Paramount 3500 III	C49FT	1990	Stagecoach Midland Red, 1997
5	L212GJO	Volvo B10M-60	Jonckheere Deauville 45	C49FT	1993	
6	9258VC	Volvo B10M-60	Plaxton Paramount 3500 III	C49FT	1990	Stagecoach Midland Red, 1997
8	N41MJO	Volvo B10M-62	Berkhof Excellence 1000LD	C51FT	1996	
9	M103XBW	Volvo B10M-62	Berkhof Excellence 1000LD	C51FT	1995	
10	H639UWR	Volvo B10M-60	Plaxton Paramount 3500 III	C48FT	1991	Wallace Arnold, 1994
11	H640UWR	Volvo B10M-60	Plaxton Paramount 3500 III	C48FT	1991	Wallace Arnold, 1994
12	N42MJO	Volvo B10M-62	Berkhof Excellence 1000LD	C51FT	1996	
14	N43MJO	Volvo B10M-62	Berkhof Excellence 1000LD	C51FT	1996	
15	H641UWR	Volvo B10M-60	Plaxton Paramount 3500 III	C48FT	1991	Wallace Arnold, 1994
16	M104XBW	Volvo B10M-62	Berkhof Excellence 1000LD	C51FT	1995	
17	H650UWR	Volvo B10M-60	Plaxton Paramount 3500 III	C48FT	1991	Wallace Arnold, 1994
18	L155LBW	Volvo B10M-62	Jonckheere Deauville 45	C49FT	1994	
19	N45MJO	Volvo B10M-62	Berkhof Excellence 1000LD	C51FT	1996	
20	J420HDS	Volvo B10M-60	Plaxton Excalibur	C44FT	1992	Stagecoach Busways, 1997
21	L159LBW	Volvo B10M-62	Jonckheere Deauville 45	C49FT	1994	
22	J456FSR	Volvo B10M-62	Plaxton Expressliner	C46FT	1992	Bluebird Buses, 1997
23	N46MJO	Volvo B10M-62	Berkhof Excellence 1000LD	C51FT	1996	
24	J424HDS	Volvo B10M-60	Plaxton Excalibur	C44FT	1992	Stagecoach Busways, 1997
25	M105XBW	Volvo B10M-62	Berkhof Excellence 1000LD	C51FT	1995	
26	M106XBW	Volvo B10M-62	Berkhof Excellence 1000LD	C51FT	1995	
28	M107XBW	Volvo B10M-62	Berkhof Excellence 1000LD	C42FT	1995	
29	L156LBW	Volvo B10M-62	Jonckheere Deauville 45	C49FT	1994	
30	L157LBW	Volvo B10M-62	Jonckheere Deauville 45	C49FT	1994	
31	L158LBW	Volvo B10M-62	Jonckheere Deauville 45	C49FT	1994	
32	N47MJO	Volvo B10M-62	Berkhof Excellence 1000LD	C51FT	1996	
33	N48MJO	Volvo B10M-62	Berkhof Excellence 1000LD	C51FT	1996	
122	D122PTT	Ford Transit VE6	Mellor	B16F	1987	
132	D132PTT	Ford Transit VE6	Mellor	B16F	1987	
247	L247FDV	Iveco Daily 49-12 - Hybrid	Mellor	B13D	1994	
248	L248FDV	Iveco Daily 49-12 - Hybrid	Mellor	B13D	1994	
308	E829ATT	Mercedes-Benz 709D	Reeve Burgess Beaver	DP25F	1988	

309-324

Mercedes-Benz 709D   Reeve Burgess Beaver   DP25F   1988

309	E309BWL	312	F312EJO	318	F318EJO	322	F322EJO	324	F324EJO
311	F311EJO	314	F314EJO						

326-346

Mercedes-Benz 709D   Reeve Burgess Beaver   B25F   1989

326	F776FDV	329	F766FDV	332	F769FDV	339	F409KOD	345	F403KOD
327	F764FDV	330	F767FDV	333	F770FDV	344	F402KOD	346	F746FDV
328	F765FDV	331	F768FDV						

350-354

Mercedes-Benz 709D   Carlyle   B29F   1990

350	G950TDV	351	G951TDV	352	G952TDV	353	G843UDV	354	G954TDV

Opposite:- **Stagecoach Oxford have been the beneficiary of a major fleet upgrade since being purchased from Thames Transit. The early delivery of Volvo Olympians have seen them move to manchester in exchange for single-decks, while the dual-doored Darts have found a more suitable home in London, newer examples now seen in town. The latest double-deck arrivals are dual-doored Olympians represented here by 522, R422XFC and** *(upper picture)* **Alexander-bodied Dart 839, P677NOJ which came into Stagecoach from Volvo where its was a demonstrator.** *Colin Lloyd*

The Oxford to London Express - Oxford Tube - that Stagecoach Oxford operate will be enhanced further this next year as new vehicle arrive. However, pending their arrival new lettering to improve passenger awareness to this 24-hour service has been applied to the current vehicles. Seen in the new red and gold livery is 10, H639UWR. *Colin Lloyd*

355-366

						Mercedes-Benz 811D		Carlyle		B33F		1990			

355	G831UDV	358	G834UDV	361	G837UDV	363	G839UDV	365	G841UDV
356	G832UDV	359w	G835UDV	362	G838UDV	364	G840UDV	366	G842UDV
357	G833UDV	360	G836UDV						

367	H109HDV	Mercedes-Benz 811D	Marshall C19	B29F	1991	Docklands Transit, 1997

371-383

		Mercedes-Benz Vario 0 814	Alexander ALX100	B29F	1998	On order

371	S371DFC	374	S374DFC	377	S377DFC	380	S380DFC	382	S382DFC
372	S372DFC	375	S375DFC	378	S378DFC	381	S381DFC	383	S383DFC
373	S373DFC	376	S376DFC	379	S379DFC				

399	H790GTA	Mercedes-Benz 811D	Marshall C19	B29F	1991	Docklands Transit, 1997
500	SVK627G	Leyland Atlantean PDR1/1R	Alexander J	O44/30F	1969	Stagecoach Busways, 1998

514-526

		Volvo Olympian	Alexander RL	H51/32D	1998

514	R414XFC	517	R417XFC	520	R420XFC	523	R423XFC	525	R425XFC
515	R415XFC	518	R418XFC	521	R421XFC	524	R424XFC	526	R426XFC
516	R416XFC	519	R419XFC	522	R422XFC				

700-708

		Dennis Dart 9.8SDL3054	Plaxton Pointer	B37D	1995

700	M59VJO	702	M93WBW	704	M95WBW	706	M96WBW	708	M98WBW
701	M101WBW	703	M94WBW	705	M96WBW	707	M97WBW		

709-714

		Dennis Dart 9.8SDL3054	Alexander Dash	B40F	1995-96	Stagecoach Selkent, 1998

709	N609KGF	711	N611LGC	712	N612LGC	713	N613LGC	714	N614LGC
710	N610KGF								

Now in Stagecoach corporate livery is Oxford 361, G837UDV, a Mercedes-Benz 811 with Carlyle bodywork. The vehicle is seen entering the city centre on a bus and bicycle only lane. *Terry Blackman*

| 715 | NDZ3015 | Dennis Dart 9SDL3016 | Wright Handy-bus | B35F | 1993 | Stagecoach East London, 1998 |
| 716 | NDZ3016 | Dennis Dart 9SDL3016 | Wright Handy-bus | B35F | 1993 | Stagecoach East London, 1998 |

725-730		Dennis Dart 9.8SDL3054	Alexander Dash	B40F	1995-96	Stagecoach Selkent, 1998
725	P625PGP	727	P627PGP	728	P628PGP	729	P629PGP	730	P630PGP
726	P626PGP								

746-750		Dennis Dart 9SDL3016	Wright Handy-bus	B35F	1993	Stagecoach East London, 1998
746	NDZ3146	747	NDZ3147	748	NDZ3148	749	NDZ3149	750	NDZ3150

751	N51KBW	Dennis Dart 9.8SDL3054	Plaxton Pointer	B37D	1996
752	N52KBW	Dennis Dart 9.8SDL3054	Plaxton Pointer	B37D	1996
753	N53KBW	Dennis Dart 9.8SDL3054	Plaxton Pointer	B37D	1996
754	N54KBW	Dennis Dart 9.8SDL3054	Plaxton Pointer	B37D	1996

756-764		Dennis Dart 9.8SDL3054	Plaxton Pointer	B40F	1996
756	N56KBW	758	N58KBW	761	N61KBW	763	N63KBW	764	N64KBW
757	N57KBW	759	N59KBW	762	N62KBW				

771-788		Dennis Dart 9.8SDL3054	Plaxton Pointer	B37D	1995
771	M61VJO	774	M74VJO	776	M76VJO	779	M79VJO	787	N47EJO
772	M62VJO	775	M75VJO	778	M78VJO	784	M84WBW	788	N48EJO

793	R63UFC	Dennis Dart		Plaxton Pointer	B40F	1997
794	R64UFC	Dennis Dart		Plaxton Pointer	B40F	1997
795	R65UFC	Dennis Dart		Plaxton Pointer	B40F	1997

Stagecoach Oxford took delivery of nine of the final order for Volvo B10M buses, and are looking forward to receiving the first of the MAN low-floor buses in the Autumn. Shown in the city is 907, R907XFC which carries lettering for the Bus Points awards now offered to passengers in return for loyalty to the Stagecoach service.

801-829

Dennis Dart SLF — Alexander ALX200 — N37F — 1998

801	R801YUD	807	R807YUD	813	R813YUD	819	R819YUD	825	R825YUD
802	R802YUD	808	R808YUD	814	R814YUD	820	R720YUD	826	R826YUD
803	R803YUD	809	R809YUD	815	R815YUD	821	R821YUD	827	R827YUD
804	R804YUD	810	R810YUD	816	R816YUD	822	R822YUD	828	R828YUD
805	R805YUD	811	R811YUD	817	R817YUD	823	R823YUD	829	R829YUD
806	R706YUD	812	R812YUD	818	R818YUD	824	R824YUD		

831-844

Volvo B6BLE — Alexander ALX200 — N40F — 1997 — Stagecoach Manchester, 1998

831	P321JND	834	P324JND	837	P327JND	840	P330JND	842	P332JND
832	P322JND	835	P325JND	838	P328JND	841	P331JND	844	P334JND
833	P323JND	836	P326JND	839	P677NOJ				

901	N901PFC	Dennis Lance 11SDA3113	Plaxton Verde	B49F	1996
902	N902PFC	Dennis Lance 11SDA3113	Plaxton Verde	B49F	1996
903	N903PFC	Dennis Lance 11SDA3113	Plaxton Verde	B49F	1996

904-912

Volvo B10M-55 — Plaxton Paladin — B48F — 1998

904	R904XFC	906	R906XFC	908	R908XFC	910	R910XFC	912	R912XFC
905	R905XFC	907	R907XFC	909	R909XFC	911	R911XFC		

913-941

MAN 18.220 — Alexander ALX200 — N-F — 1998 — On order

913	S913CFC	919	S919CFC	925	S925CFC	931	S931CFC	937	S937CFC
914	S914CFC	920	S920CFC	926	S926CFC	932	S932CFC	938	S938CFC
915	S915CFC	921	S921CFC	927	S927CFC	933	S933CFC	939	S939CFC
916	S916CFC	922	S922CFC	928	S928CFC	934	S934CFC	940	S940CFC
917	S917CFC	923	S923CFC	929	S929CFC	935	S935CFC	941	S941CFC
918	S918CFC	924	S924CFC	930	S930CFC	936	S936CFC		

1801w	L801HJO	Optare MetroRider MREL	Optare	B18F	1993	On loan from Southern Electric
1802w	L802HJO	Optare MetroRider MREL	Optare	B18F	1993	On loan from Southern Electric
1803w	L803HJO	Optare MetroRider MREL	Optare	B18F	1993	On loan from Southern Electric
1804w	L804HJO	Optare MetroRider MREL	Optare	B18F	1993	On loan from Southern Electric

Ancilliary vehicles

98	LSV670	Leyland Tiger TRCTL11/3RZ	Plaxton Paramount 3500 II	C53F	1987	
103	D103PTT	Ford Transit VE6	Mellor	B16F	1987	
137	D137PTT	Ford Transit VE6	Mellor	B16F	1987	
789	D789NDV	Ford Transit 190D	Mellor	B16F	1987	
3318	AFJ738T	Bristol LH6L	Plaxton Supreme III Express	C43F	1979	Devon General, 1996

Previous Registrations:

3063VC	G543LWU	J424HDS	J424HDS, KSU464
9258VC	G554LWU	LSV670	C129KJO
J420HDS	J420HDS, KSU462		

Allocations:-

Chipping Norton

| Lance | 901 | 902 | 903 |

Oxford (Horspath Road, Cowley) - Stagecoach Oxford - Oxford Tube

Transit	122							
Iveco Hybrid	247	248						
Mercedes-Benz	308	309	312	314	318	322	323	324
	326	327	328	329	330	331	333	339
	350	355	356	357	358	360	363	364
	365	366	367	399				
Volvo Coach	1	2	3	5	6	8	9	10
	11	12	14	15	16	17	18	19
	20	21	22	23	24	25	26	28
	29	30	31	32	33			
Dart	700	701	702	703	704	705	706	707
	708	709	710	711	712	713	714	715
	716	725	726	727	728	729	730	746
	747	748	749	750	751	752	753	754
	756	757	758	759	760	761	762	763
	764	771	772	773	774	775	776	777
	778	779	780	781	782	783	784	785
	786	787	788	793	794	795	801	802
	803	804	805	806	807	808	809	810
	811	812	813	814	815	816	817	818
	819	820	821	822	823	824	825	826
	827	828	829					
Volvo B6	831	832	833	834	835	836	837	838
	839	840	841	842	843	844		
Volvo B10B	904	905	906	907	908	909	910	911
	912							
Olympian	514	515	516	517	518	519	520	521
	522	523	524	525	526			

Witney (Corn Street) - Stagecoach Oxford

Transit	132							
Mercedes-Benz	311	332	344	345	346	351	352	353
	354	361	362					

Unallocated

| MetroRider | 1801 | 1802 | 1803 | 1804 |
| Mercedes-Benz | 359 | | | |

Livery:- Stagecoach corporate white, orange, red and blue.

STAGECOACH SOUTH

Stagecoach (South) Ltd, Lewes Enterprise Centre, 112 Malling Street,
Lewes, East Sussex, BN7 2RB

1-24		Dennis Dart SLF		Alexander ALX200		N37F		1997-98		
1	R701DNJ	6	R706DNJ	11	R711DNJ	16	R816HCD	21	R821HCD
2	R702DNJ	7	R707DNJ	12	R812HCD	17	R817HCD	22	R822HCD
3	R703DNJ	8	R708DNJ	13	R813HCD	18	R818HCD	23	R823HCD
4	R704DNJ	9	R709DNJ	14	R814HCD	19	R819HCD	24	R824HCD
5	R705DNJ	10	R710DNJ	15	R815HCD				

100-118		Leyland National 11351A/1R				B52F		1979		
100	AYJ100T	107	AYJ107T	110	ENJ910V	112	ENJ912V	114	ENJ914V
102	AYJ102T	109	ENJ909V	111	ENJ911V				

119-126		Leyland National 2 NL116L11/1R				B52F		1980	124 fitted with TL11 engine	
119	GYJ919V	121	GYJ921V	123	HFG923V	125	OUF262W	126	SYC852
120	GYJ920V	122	GYJ922V	124	JNJ194V				

127	FDV830V	Leyland National 2 NL116L11/1R	B52F	1980
128	FDV831V	Leyland National 2 NL116L11/1R	B52F	1980

129-138		Leyland National 2 NL116AL11/1R				B49F*		1982	*129 is B45F 130 is fitted with TL11 engine	
129	HUF603X	131	HUF625X	133	HUF639X	135	HUF604X	137	HUF592X
130	HUF579X	132	PMT199X	134	HUF451X	136	HUF593X	138	HUF626X

139	FDV829V	Leyland National 2 NL116L11/1R	B48F	1980	
140	CPO98W	Leyland National 2 NL106L11/1R	B41F	1980	Portsmouth, 1990
142	CPO100W	Leyland National 2 NL106L11/1R	DP40F	1980	Portsmouth, 1990
143	ERV115W	Leyland National 2 NL106AL11/1R	B41F	1981	Portsmouth, 1990
144	ERV116W	Leyland National 2 NL106AL11/1R	B41F	1981	Portsmouth, 1990
145	ERV117W	Leyland National 2 NL106AL11/1R	B41F	1981	Portsmouth, 1990
146	ERV118W	Leyland National 2 NL106AL11/1R	B41F	1981	Portsmouth, 1990
147	BCW827V	Leyland National 2 NL106L11/1R	B44F	1980	Ribble, 1994
148	UFG48S	Leyland National 11351A/2R	B52F	1977	
149	JCK849W	Leyland National 2 NL106AL11/1R	B44F	1981	Ribble, 1994
150	PEX620W	Leyland National 2 NL116L11/1R	B49F	1981	Stagecoach Cambus, 1997
151	PEX621W	Leyland National 2 NL116L11/1R	B49F	1981	Stagecoach Cambus, 1997
159	YRN816V	Leyland National 2 NL106L11/1R	B44F	1980	Ribble, 1994
160	YRN821V	Leyland National 2 NL106L11/1R	B44F	1980	Ribble, 1994
163w	PCD73R	Leyland National 11351A/1R	B49F	1976	
169	WYJ169S	Leyland National 11351A/2R(DAF)	B48F	1978	
173	YCD73T	Leyland National 11351A/2R	B52F	1978	
174	YCD74T	Leyland National 11351A/2R	B48F	1978	
176	YCD76T	Leyland National 11351A/2R	B48F	1978	
177	YCD77T	Leyland National 11351A/2R	B48F	1978	
179	PCD79R	Leyland National 11351A/1R	B49F	1977	
180	PCD80R	Leyland National 11351A/1R	B49F	1977	
182	YCD82T	Leyland National 11351A/2R	B48F	1978	
191	AYJ91T	Leyland National 11351A/1R	B52F	1979	
192	AYJ92T	Leyland National 11351A/1R	B52F	1979	
195	AYJ95T	Leyland National 11351A/1R	B52F	1979	
196	RJT146R	Leyland National 11351A/1R	B49F	1977	
197	AYJ97T	Leyland National 11351A/1R	B52F	1979	

The South Central Bus Handbook

Stagecoach South operate along the south coast from Hampshire to Kent with one fleet serving the various operations. The latest vehicles in the fleet are further Dennis Dart SLF, with additional Volvo Olympians due later in the year. Pictured here is a Leyland example, 215, H815CBP. *David Longbottom*

201-206

Leyland Olympian ON2R56G13Z4 Alexander RL H51/36F 1988

201	F601MSL	203	F603MSL	204	F604MSL	205	F605MSL	206	F606MSL
202	F602MSL								

207-214

Leyland Olympian ON2R56G13Z4 Alexander RL DPH51/31F 1989

207	G807RTS	209	G809RTS	211	G211SSL	213	G213SSL	214	G214SSL
208	G808RTS	210	G210SSL	212	G212SSL				

215-219

Leyland Olympian ON2R56G13Z4 Alexander RL H51/34F 1990

215	H815CBP	216	H816CBP	217	H817CBP	218	H818CBP	219	H819CBP

220	J720GAP	Leyland Olympian ON2R56G13Z4 Alexander RL	DPH47/27F	1992
221	J721GAP	Leyland Olympian ON2R56G13Z4 Alexander RL	DPH47/27F	1992
222	J722GAP	Leyland Olympian ON2R56G13Z4 Alexander RL	DPH47/27F	1992
223	J623GCR	Leyland Olympian ON2R56G13Z4 Alexander RL	H47/30F	1991
224	J624GCR	Leyland Olympian ON2R56G13Z4 Alexander RL	H47/30F	1991

225-234

Leyland Olympian ON2R56G13Z4 Alexander RL H51/34F 1990

225	G705TCD	227	G707TCD	229	G709TCD	231	G701TCD	233	G703TCD
226	G706TCD	228	G708TCD	230	G710TCD	232	G702TCD	234	G704TCD

235-240

Leyland Olympian ON2R50G13Z4 Alexander RL DPH43/27F 1992

235	K235NHC	237	K237NHC	238	K238NHC	239	K239NHC	240	K240NHC
236	K236NHC								

241-250

Volvo Olympian YN2RV18Z4 Northern Counties Palatine DPH43/25F 1993

241	L241SDY	243	L243SDY	245	L245SDY	247	L247SDY	249	L249SDY
242	L242SDY	244	L244SDY	246	L246SDY	248	L248SDY	250	L250SDY

The final order for Volvo B10M buses placed with Northern Counties were built at Plaxton's Scarborough facility, though they are to the same Paladin design as the earlier deliveries. The new arrivals are based at Aldershot, Hastings and Winchester, where 654, R654HCD is seen.
Roger Marshall.

254	K714ASC	Leyland Olympian ON2R50G13Z4 Alexander RL		H47/32F	1992	Fife Scottish, 1994
255	K715ASC	Leyland Olympian ON2R50G13Z4 Alexander RL		H47/32F	1992	Fife Scottish, 1994
256	K716ASC	Leyland Olympian ON2R50G13Z4 Alexander RL		H47/32F	1992	Fife Scottish, 1994
257	K717ASC	Leyland Olympian ON2R50G13Z4 Alexander RL		H47/32F	1992	Fife Scottish, 1994

260-290   Volvo Olympian   Alexander RL   H51/36F*   1996-97   *260-3 are H51/32F
*288-90 are DPH47/32F

260	P260WPN	265	P265VPN	276	P276VPN	282	P282VPN	287	P287VPN
261	P261WPN	266	P266VPN	277	P277VPN	283	P283VPN	288	P288VPN
262	P262WPN	267	P267VPN	278	P278VPN	284	P284VPN	289	P289VPN
263	P263WPN	268	P268VPN	279	P279VPN	285	P285VPN	290	P290VPN
264	P264VPN	269	P269VPN	281	P281VPN	286	P286VPN		

291-301   Volvo Olympian   Alexander RL   H51/36F   1998

| 291 | R291HCD | 293 | R293HCD | 295 | R295HCD | 297 | R297HCD | 299 | R299HCD |
| 292 | R292HCD | 294 | R294HCD | 296 | R296HCD | 298 | R298HCD | 301 | R301HCD |

341-359   Volvo Olympian YN2RC16V3   Alexander RL   DPH47/28F   1996

341	N341MPN	345	N345MPN	349	N349MPN	353	N353MPN	357	N357MPN
342	N342MPN	346	N346MPN	350	N350MPN	354	N354MPN	358	N358MPN
343	N343MPN	347	N347MPN	351	N351MPN	355	N355MPN	359	N359MPN
344	N344MPN	348	N348MPN	352	N352MPN	356	N356MPN		

Opposite, top:- **Stagecoach South inherited a large number of elderly Bristol VRs, and to aid early replacment a large number of Leyland Titans were transferred from the London companies as new vehicles arrived there. One of those now based at Portsmouth is 7248, KYV348X.**
Opposite, bottom:- **The latest Dennis Darts started the fleet numbering system again at 1. These carry additional lettering to promote the easy-access of the low floor. Pictured at Winchester is 16, R816HCD.**

360-380 Volvo Olympian YN2RC16V3 Alexander RL H47/32F 1995

360	N360LPN	365	N365LPN	369	N369LPN	373	N373LPN	377	N377LPN
361	N361LPN	366	N366LPN	370	N370LPN	374	N374LPN	378	N378LPN
362	N362LPN	367	N367LPN	371	N371LPN	375	N375LPN	379	N379LPN
363	N363LPN	368	N368LPN	372	N372LPN	376	N376LPN	380	N380LPN
364	N364LPN								

381-399 Volvo Olympian YN2RC16V3 Alexander RL DPH47/28F 1995-96

381	N381LPN	385	N385LPN	389	N389LPN	393	N393LPN	397	N397LPN
382	N382LPN	386	N386LPN	390	N390LPN	394	N394LPN	398	N398LPN
383	N383LPN	387	N387LPN	391	N391LPN	395	N395LPN	399	N399LPN
384	N384LPN	388	N388LPN	392	N392LPN	396	N396LPN		

400	400DCD	Volvo B6-9.9M	Alexander Dash	DP35F	1994
401	401DCD	Volvo B6-9.9M	Alexander Dash	DP35F	1994
402	402DCD	Volvo B6-9.9M	Alexander Dash	DP35F	1994
403	403DCD	Volvo B6-9.9M	Alexander Dash	DP31F	1994

451-455 Dennis Dart Alexander Dash DP40F 1996

451	N451PAP	452	N452PAP	453	N453PAP	454	N454PAP	455	N455PAP

456-467 Dennis Dart Alexander Dash B40F 1996

456	N456PAP	459	N459PAP	462	N462PAP	464	N464PAP	466	N466PAP
457	N457PAP	460	N460PAP	463	N463PAP	465	N465PAP	467	N467PAP
458	N458PAP	461	N461PAP						

471-486 Dennis Dart 9.8SDL3054 Alexander Dash B36F 1995 Stagecoach East London, 1998

471	N311AMC	475	N315AMC	481	N321AMC	483	N323AMC	485	N325AMC
472	N312AMC	476	N316AMC	482	N322AMC	484	N324AMC	486	N326AMC
474	N314AMC								

491-497 Dennis Dart 9.8SDL3054 Alexander Dash B40F 1995 Stagecoach Selkent, 1998

491	N601KGF	493	N603KGF	495	N605KGF	496	N606KGF	497	N607KGF
492	N602KGF	494	N604KGF						

501-580 Dennis Dart 9.8SDL3017 Alexander Dash B41F* 1991-92 *535-80 are B40F

501	J501GCD	517	J517GCD	533	J533GCD	549	J549GCD	565	K565NHC
502	J502GCD	518	J518GCD	534	J534GCD	550	J550GCD	566	K566NHC
503	J503GCD	519	J519GCD	535	J535GCD	551	J551GCD	567	K567NHC
504	J504GCD	520	J520GCD	536	J536GCD	552	J552GCD	568	K568NHC
505	J505GCD	521	J521GCD	537	J537GCD	553	K553NHC	569	K569NHC
506	J506GCD	522	J522GCD	538	J538GCD	554	K554NHC	570	K570NHC
507	J507GCD	523	J523GCD	539	J539GCD	555	K655NHC	571	K571NHC
508	J508GCD	524	J524GCD	540	J540GCD	556	K556NHC	572	K572NHC
509	J509GCD	525	J525GCD	541	J541GCD	557	K557NHC	573	K573NHC
510	J510GCD	526	J526GCD	542	J542GCD	558	K558NHC	574	K574NHC
511	J511GCD	527	J527GCD	543	J543GCD	559	K559NHC	575	K575NHC
512	J512GCD	528	J528GCD	544	J544GCD	560	K660NHC	576	K576NHC
513	J513GCD	529	J529GCD	545	J545GCD	561	K561NHC	577	K577NHC
514	J514GCD	530	J530GCD	546	J546GCD	562	K562NHC	578	K578NHC
515	J515GCD	531	J531GCD	547	J547GCD	563	K563NHC	579	K579NHC
516	J516GCD	532	J532GCD	548	J548GCD	564	K564NHC	580	K580NHC

581	J701YRM	Dennis Dart 9.8DL3017	Alexander Dash	B41F	1991	Cumberland, 1992
582	J702YRM	Dennis Dart 9.8DL3017	Alexander Dash	B41F	1991	Cumberland, 1992
583	J703YRM	Dennis Dart 9.8DL3017	Alexander Dash	B41F	1992	Cumberland, 1992

584-588 Dennis Dart 9.8DL3017 Alexander Dash B40F 1992

584	K584ODY	585	K585ODY	586	K586ODY	587	K587ODY	588	K588ODY

As well as Leyland Titans, single-door Dennis Darts are being replaced in the capital by dual-doored version from Oxford. Several of the single-door models are now entering service with Stagecoach South where they are replacing Leyland Nationals. Pictured in Guildford is Aldershot-based 475, N315AMC seen here shortly after entering service. *David Heath*

601-605

Volvo B10M-55 — Northern Counties Paladin — DP49F — 1994

601	L601VCD	602	L602VCD	603	L603VCD	604	404DCD	605	405DCD

606-635

Volvo B10M-55 — Alexander PS — DP48F — 1994

606	406DCD	612	412DCD	618	L618TDY	624	L624TDY	630	L630TDY
607	407DCD	613	413DCD	619	419DCD	625	L625TDY	631	L631TDY
608	408DCD	614	414DCD	620	420DCD	626	L626TDY	632	L632TDY
609	L609TDY	615	M615APN	621	421DCD	627	L627TDY	633	L633TDY
610	410DCD	616	L616TDY	622	422DCD	628	L628TDY	634	L634TDY
611	411DCD	617	L617TDY	623	423DCD	629	L629TDY	635	L635TDY

636-645

Volvo B10M-55 — Alexander PS — DP48F — 1995

636	M636BCD	638	M638BCD	640	N640LPN	642	N642LPN	644	N644LPN
637	M637BCD	639	M639BCD	641	N641LPN	643	N643LPN	645	N645LPN

646	R646HCD	Volvo B10M-55	Plaxton Paladin	B48F	1998
647	R647HCD	Volvo B10M-55	Plaxton Paladin	B48F	1998
648	R648HCD	Volvo B10M-55	Plaxton Paladin	B48F	1998
649	R649HCD	Volvo B10M-55	Plaxton Paladin	B48F	1998
650	M650BCD	Volvo B10M-55	Alexander PS	DP48F	1995
651	M651BCD	Volvo B10M-55	Alexander PS	DP48F	1995
652	M652BCD	Volvo B10M-55	Alexander PS	DP48F	1995
653	R653HCD	Volvo B10M-55	Plaxton Paladin	B48F	1998
654	R654HCD	Volvo B10M-55	Plaxton Paladin	B48F	1998
655	415DCD	Volvo B10M-55	Alexander PS	DP48F	1994	Ribble, 1994
656	416DCD	Volvo B10M-55	Alexander PS	DP48F	1994	Ribble, 1994
657	417DCD	Volvo B10M-55	Alexander PS	DP48F	1994	Ribble, 1994
658	418DCD	Volvo B10M-55	Alexander PS	DP48F	1994	Ribble, 1994
659	K789DAO	Volvo B10M-55	Alexander PS	DP48F	1993	Cumberland, 1994
660	K790DAO	Volvo B10M-55	Alexander PS	DP48F	1993	Cumberland, 1994
661	K791DAO	Volvo B10M-55	Alexander PS	DP48F	1993	Cumberland, 1994

662-670

Volvo B10M-55 — Northern Counties Paladin — DP47F — 1995

662	M662ECD	664	M664ECD	667	M667ECD	669	M669ECD	**670** M670ECD
663	M663ECD	665	M665ECD	668	M668ECD			

671	M311YSC	Volvo B10M-55	Alexander PS	DP48F	1995	Fife Scottish, 1995
672	M312YSC	Volvo B10M-55	Alexander PS	DP48F	1995	Fife Scottish, 1995
673	M313YSC	Volvo B10M-55	Alexander PS	DP48F	1995	Fife Scottish, 1995

674-680

Volvo B10M-55 — Plaxton Paladin — B48F — 1998

674	R674HCD	676	R676HCD	678	R678HCD	679	R679HCD	**680** R680HCD
675	R675HCD	677	R677HCD					

686	EAP986V	Bristol VRT/SL3/6LXB	Eastern Coach Works	H43/31F	1980	
688	EAP988V	Bristol VRT/SL3/6LXB	Eastern Coach Works	H43/31F	1980	
759	BKE859T	Bristol VRT/SL3/6LXB	Eastern Coach Works	H43/31F	1979	Hastings & District, 1989

841-850

Mercedes-Benz 709D — Alexander Sprint — B23F* — 1990 — *841-3 are DP25F

841	G71APO	844	G974ARV	847	G977ARV	849	H679BTP	**850** H680BTP
843	G73APO	845	G975ARV	848	G978ARV			

853-888

Mercedes-Benz 709D — Alexander Sprint — B25F — 1993

853	K853ODY	861	K861ODY	868	K868ODY	875	K875ODY	**882** L882SDY
854	K854ODY	862	K862ODY	869	K869ODY	876	K876ODY	**883** L883SDY
855	K855ODY	863	K863ODY	870	K870ODY	877	K877ODY	**884** L884SDY
856	K856ODY	864	K864ODY	871	K871ODY	878	K878ODY	**885** L885SDY
857	K857ODY	865	K865ODY	872	K872ODY	879	K879ODY	**886** L886SDY
858	K858ODY	866	K866ODY	873	K873ODY	880	K880ODY	**887** L887SDY
859	K859ODY	867	K867ODY	874	K874ODY	881	L881SDY	**888** L188SDY
860	K860ODY							

889-904

Mercedes-Benz 709D — Alexander Sprint — B25F* — 1995 — *894-904 are B23F

889	M889ECD	892	N192LPN	895	N195LPN	898	N198LPN	**902** N202LPN
890	M890ECD	893	N193LPN	896	N196LPN	899	N199LPN	**903** N203LPN
891	N191LPN	894	N194LPN	897	N197LPN	901	N201LPN	**904** N204LPN

905-977

Mercedes-Benz 709D — Alexander Sprint — B25F* — 1996 — *924-77 are B23F

905	N905NAP	920	N920NAP	935	N935NAP	950	N950NAP	**964** N964NAP
906	N906NAP	921	N921NAP	936	N936NAP	951	N951NAP	**965** N965NAP
907	N907NAP	922	N922NAP	937	N937NAP	952	N952NAP	**966** N966NAP
908	N908NAP	923	N923NAP	938	N938NAP	953	N953NAP	**967** N967NAP
909	N909NAP	924	N924NAP	939	N939NAP	954	N954NAP	**968** N968NAP
910	N910NAP	925	N925NAP	940	N940NAP	955	N955NAP	**969** N969NAP
911	N911NAP	926	N926NAP	941	N941NAP	956	N956NAP	**970** N970NAP
912	N912NAP	927	N927NAP	942	N942NAP	957	N957NAP	**971** N971NAP
913	N913NAP	928	N928NAP	943	N943NAP	958	N958NAP	**972** N972NAP
914	N914NAP	929	N929NAP	944	N944NAP	959	N959NAP	**973** N973NAP
915	N915NAP	930	N930NAP	945	N945NAP	960	N960NAP	**974** N974NAP
916	N916NAP	931	N931NAP	946	N946NAP	961	N961NAP	**975** N975NAP
917	N917NAP	932	N932NAP	947	N947NAP	962	N962NAP	**976** N976NAP
918	N918NAP	933	N933NAP	948	N948NAP	963	N963NAP	**977** N977NAP
919	N919NAP	934	N934NAP	949	N949NAP			

1105	M105CCD	Dennis Javelin 11SDL2133	Plaxton Premiere Interurban	DP47F	1995
1106	M106CCD	Dennis Javelin 11SDL2133	Plaxton Premiere Interurban	DP47F	1995
1108	M108CCD	Dennis Javelin 11SDL2133	Plaxton Premiere Interurban	DP47F	1995

1188w	NFN88R	Leyland National 11351A/1R		DP48F	1977	East Kent, 1993
1201w	HPK503N	Leyland National 11351/1R		B49F	1975	Alder Valley, 1992
1203	HPK505N	Leyland National 11351/1R		B49F	1975	Alder Valley, 1992
1218	KPA369P	Leyland National 11351/1R		B49F	1975	Alder Valley, 1992
1223	KPA374P	Leyland National 11351/1R		B49F	1975	Alder Valley, 1992
1228	KPA379P	Leyland National 11351/1R		B49F	1975	Alder Valley, 1992
1247	LPF605P	Leyland National 11351/1R/SC		B49F	1976	Alder Valley, 1992
1344	PJJ344S	Leyland National 10351A/1R		B41F	1977	East Kent, 1993

1401	J401LKO	DAF SB220LC550	Optare Delta	B49F	1991	East Kent, 1993
1402	J402LKO	DAF SB220LC550	Optare Delta	B49F	1991	East Kent, 1993
1403	J403LKO	DAF SB220LC550	Optare Delta	B49F	1991	East Kent, 1993

1404-1408		Dennis Lance SLF	Berkhof 2000	N40F	1994	
1404	M404OKM	**1405** M405OKM	**1406** M406OKM	**1407** M407OKM	**1408** M408OKM	

1546	GFN546N	Leyland National 10351/1R		B40F	1975	East Kent, 1993
1898w	JJG898P	Leyland National 11351A/1R		B49F	1976	East Kent, 1993

2136	N136MPN	OCC Omni	OCC	B21F	1995	Sussex Bus, 1996
2220	M220DWV	Mercedes-Benz 811D	Plaxton Beaver	B29F	1995	Richardson Travel, 1997
2586	XIA586	Leyland National 11351A/1R (Urban Bus)		B62F	1977	Sussex Bus, 1996
2612	OUF863W	Leyland Leopard PSU3F/4R	Willowbrook Warrior (1990)	B48F	1981	Sussex Bus, 1996
2651	F651RBP	Iveco Daily 49.10	Robin Hood City Nippy	B25F	1989	Sussex Bus, 1996
2682	RUF970M	Leyland Leopard PSU3B/4R	Willowbrook Warrior (1990)	B49F	1973	Sussex Bus, 1996
2857	XIA857	Leyland National 11351A/1R		B48F	1976	Sussex Bus, 1996
2978w	JYJ269N	Leyland Leopard PSU3B/4R	Willowbrook Warrior (1988)	B53F	1975	Sussex Bus, 1996
2992	JNJ718V	Leyland Leopard PSU3E/4R	Willowbrook Warrior (1990)	DP60F	1979	Sussex Bus, 1996

5001	472YMF	DAF SB220LC550	Optare Delta	B40D	1992	On loan from East London
5002	YLJ332	DAF SB220LC550	Optare Delta	B40D	1992	On loan from East London
5003	NFX667	Dennis Dart 9.8SDL3017	Alexander Dash	DP32F	1992	On loan from East London
5004	XYK976	Dennis Dart 9.8SDL3017	Alexander Dash	DP32F	1992	On loan from East London

7201	KYV511X	Leyland Titan TNLXB2RR	Leyland	H44/24F	1982	Stagecoach Selkent, 1995
7203	A823SUL	Leyland Titan TNLXB2RR	Leyland	H44/26F	1983	Stagecoach Selkent, 1995
7204	OHV744Y	Leyland Titan TNLXB2RR	Leyland	H44/27F	1983	Stagecoach East London, 1997
7205	KYN305X	Leyland Titan TNLXB2RR	Leyland	H44/24F	1981	Stagecoach Selkent, 1995
7207	OHV697Y	Leyland Titan TNLXB2RR	Leyland	H44/24F	1983	Stagecoach East London, 1997
7208	OHV688Y	Leyland Titan TNLXB2RR	Leyland	H44/24F	1983	Stagecoach East London, 1997
7209	OHV769Y	Leyland Titan TNLXB2RR	Leyland	H44/27F	1983	Stagecoach East London, 1997
7211	NUW611Y	Leyland Titan TNLXB2RR	Leyland	H44/24F	1982	Stagecoach Selkent, 1995
7214	OHV784Y	Leyland Titan TNLXB2RR	Leyland	H44/27F	1983	Stagecoach East London, 1997
7215	CUL215V	Leyland Titan TNLXB2RRSp	Park Royal	H44/26F	1980	Stagecoach Selkent, 1995
7220	KYV420X	Leyland Titan TNLXB2RR	Leyland	H44/24F	1982	Stagecoach Selkent, 1995
7221	OHV761Y	Leyland Titan TNLXB2RR	Leyland	H44/27F	1983	Stagecoach East London, 1997
7223	KYV523X	Leyland Titan TNLXB2RR	Leyland	H44/26F	1982	Stagecoach Selkent, 1995
7224	OHV724Y	Leyland Titan TNLXB2RR	Leyland	H44/27F	1983	Stagecoach East London, 1997
7225	CUL225V	Leyland Titan TNLXB2RRSp	Park Royal	H44/24F	1980	Stagecoach Selkent, 1995
7229	EYE229V	Leyland Titan TNLXB2RRSp	Park Royal	H44/26F	1980	Stagecoach Selkent, 1995
7231	OHV731Y	Leyland Titan TNLXB2RR	Leyland	H44/27F	1983	Stagecoach East London, 1997
7233	EYE233V	Leyland Titan TNLXB2RRSp	Park Royal	H44/26F	1980	Stagecoach Selkent, 1995
7235	NUW645Y	Leyland Titan TNLXB2RR	Leyland	H44/27F	1982	Stagecoach East London, 1997
7237	EYE237V	Leyland Titan TNLXB2RRSp	Park Royal	H44/26F	1980	Stagecoach Selkent, 1995
7240	EYE240V	Leyland Titan TNLXB2RRSp	Park Royal	H44/26F	1980	Stagecoach Selkent, 1995
7242	KYV442X	Leyland Titan TNLXB2RR	Leyland	H44/24F	1982	Stagecoach Selkent, 1995
7243	OHV743Y	Leyland Titan TNLXB2RR	Leyland	H44/27F	1983	Stagecoach East London, 1997
7244	EYE244V	Leyland Titan TNLXB2RRSp	Park Royal	H44/26F	1980	Stagecoach Selkent, 1995
7245	KYV345X	Leyland Titan TNTL112RR	Leyland	H44/26F	1981	Stagecoach Selkent, 1995
7247	NUW647Y	Leyland Titan TNLXB2RR	Leyland	H44/27F	1982	Stagecoach Selkent, 1995
7248	KYV348X	Leyland Titan TNLXB2RR	Leyland	H44/24F	1981	Stagecoach Selkent, 1995
7250	EYE250V	Leyland Titan TNLXB2RRSp	Park Royal	H44/26F	1980	Stagecoach Selkent, 1995
7251	KYV451X	Leyland Titan TNLXB2RR	Leyland	H44/24F	1982	Stagecoach Selkent, 1995
7259	OHV759Y	Leyland Titan TNLXB2RR	Leyland	H44/27F	1983	Stagecoach East London, 1997
7261	KYV361X	Leyland Titan TNLXB2RR	Leyland	H44/24F	1981	Stagecoach Selkent, 1995
7263	NUW663Y	Leyland Titan TNLXB2RR	Leyland	H44/27F	1982	Stagecoach East London, 1997
7268	CUL168V	Leyland Titan TNLXB2RRSp	Park Royal	H44/24F	1980	Stagecoach Selkent, 1995
7269	CUL169V	Leyland Titan TNLXB2RRSp	Park Royal	H44/26F	1980	Stagecoach Selkent, 1995
7270	NUW670Y	Leyland Titan TNLXB2RR	Leyland	H44/27F	1982	Stagecoach East London, 1997
7271	NUW671Y	Leyland Titan TNLXB2RR	Leyland	H44/27F	1982	Stagecoach Selkent, 1997
7272	NUW672Y	Leyland Titan TNLXB2RR	Leyland	H44/27F	1982	Stagecoach East London, 1997
7274	KYV474X	Leyland Titan TNLXB2RR	Leyland	H44/24F	1982	Stagecoach Selkent, 1995
7279	CUL79V	Leyland Titan TNLXB2RRSp	Park Royal	H44/26F	1980	Stagecoach Selkent, 1995
7280	CUL180V	Leyland Titan TNLXB2RRSp	Park Royal	H44/24F	1980	Stagecoach Selkent, 1995
7281	B121WUV	Leyland Titan TNLXB2RR	Leyland	H44/29F	1984	Stagecoach Selkent, 1997
7284	B124WUV	Leyland Titan TNLXB2RR	Leyland	H44/29F	1984	Stagecoach Selkent, 1997
7285	B125WUV	Leyland Titan TNLXB2RR	Leyland	H44/29F	1984	Stagecoach Selkent, 1997
7287	KYN487X	Leyland Titan TNLXB2RR	Leyland	H44/24F	1982	Stagecoach Selkent, 1995
7288	KYN288X	Leyland Titan TNLXB2RR	Leyland	H44/24F	1981	Stagecoach Selkent, 1995

The Leyland Titan was noted for its sophistication from its inception, thus the model was more expensive than its Olympian stable-mate. As a result it attracted fewer customers. Now the vehicles are being moved out of London and converted to single-door. The completed vehicle type is represented in 2794, NUW594Y, which latterly worked for Stagecoach Selkent. *David Heath*

7290	CUL190V	Leyland Titan TNLXB2RRSp	Park Royal	H44/24F	1980	Stagecoach Selkent, 1995
7294	NUW594Y	Leyland Titan TNLXB2RR	Leyland	H44/24F	1982	Stagecoach Selkent, 1995
7296	NUW596Y	Leyland Titan TNLXB2RR	Leyland	H44/24F	1982	Stagecoach Selkent, 1995
7297	KYV397X	Leyland Titan TNLXB2RR	Leyland	H44/24F	1982	Stagecoach Selkent, 1995
7298	CUL198V	Leyland Titan TNLXB2RRSp	Park Royal	H44/26F	1980	Stagecoach Selkent, 1995

7301-7309

		Volvo Citybus B10M-50	Northern Counties	DPH43/33F	1989

7301	F301MYJ	7303	F303MYJ	7305	F305MYJ	7307	F307MYJ	7309	F309MYJ
7302	F302MYJ	7304	F304MYJ	7306	F306MYJ	7308	F308MYJ		

7353	JWV253W	Bristol VRT/SL3/6LXB	Eastern Coach Works	DPH43/31F	1980
7355w	JWV255W	Bristol VRT/SL3/6LXB	Eastern Coach Works	H43/31F	1980
7369	JWV269W	Bristol VRT/SL3/680(6LXB)	Eastern Coach Works	H43/31F	1981
7373	EAP973V	Bristol VRT/SL3/6LXB	Eastern Coach Works	H43/31F	1979

7435-7450

		Bristol VRT/SL3/6LXB	Eastern Coach Works	H43/31F	1979-81

7435	FDV839V	7446	LFJ874W	7448	LFJ870W	7449	LFJ875W	7450	LFJ880W
7438	KRU838W								

7620	HKE690L	Bristol VRT/SL2/6LXB	Eastern Coach Works	O43/34F	1973	Hastings & District, 1989
7621	UWV621S	Bristol VRT/SL3/6LXB	Eastern Coach Works	CO43/31F	1978	
7622	CBV2S	Bristol VRT/SL3/501(6LXB)	Eastern Coach Works	O43/31F	1977	On loan from Cumberland.
7623	UWV623S	Bristol VRT/SL3/6LXB	Eastern Coach Works	CO43/31F	1978	

The South Central Bus Handbook

Open-top buses have been an attraction to the English sea-side tripper since buses first ran. Stagecoach South has a considerable length of coastline, and Hastings and Eastbourne continue the tradition with two Bristol VRs each. Seen here is 7621, UWV621S. *David Longbottom*

7650-7685

Bristol VRT/SL3/6LXB   Eastern Coach Works   H43/31F   1980-81 East Kent, 1993
7655 was rebodied 1983

7650	XJJ650V	7658	XJJ658V	7664	XJJ664V	7671	BJG671V	7679	CJJ679W
7651	XJJ651V	7659	XJJ659V	7665	XJJ665V	7672	BJG672V	7680	SKL680X
7652	XJJ652V	7660	XJJ660V	7667	XJJ667V	7673	BJG673V	7681	SKL681X
7653	XJJ653V	7661	XJJ661V	7668	XJJ668V	7674	BJG674V	7682	SKL682X
7654	XJJ654V	7662	XJJ662V	7669	XJJ669V	7675	BJG675V	7683	SKL683X
7655	XJJ655V	7663	XJJ663V	7670	XJJ670V	7677	CJJ677W	7685	SKL685X
7657	XJJ657V							

7746-7755

MCW Metrobus Mk2 DR132/11   MCW   H46/31F   1988   East Kent, 1993

7746	E746SKR	7748	E748SKR	7750	E750SKR	7752	E752SKR	7754	E754UKR
7747	E747SKR	7749	E749SKR	7751	E751SKR	7753	E753SKR	7755	E755UKR

7761-7767

MCW Metrobus Mk2 DR132/15   MCW   DPH43/27F   1989   East Kent, 1993

7761	F761EKM	7763	F763EKM	7765	F765EKM	7766	F766EKM	7767	F767EKM
7762	F762EKM	7764	F764EKM					

7771-7775

MCW Metrobus Mk2 DR132/14   MCW   H46/31F   1989   East Kent, 1993

7771	F771EKM	7772	F772EKM	7773	F773EKM	7774	F774EKM	7775	F775EKM

7781	F781KKP	Scania N113DRB	Alexander RH	H47/33F	1989	East Kent, 1993
7782	F782KKP	Scania N113DRB	Alexander RH	H47/33F	1989	East Kent, 1993

7801-7810

Leyland Olympian ON2R56C16Z4 Northern Counties   H51/34F   1990   East Kent, 1993

7801	H801BKK	7803	H803BKK	7805	H805BKK	7807	H807BKK	7809	H809BKK
7802	H802BKK	7804	H804BKK	7806	H806BKK	7808	H808BKK	7810	H810BKK

7811	J811NKK	Leyland Olympian ON2R50C13Z4	Northern Counties	H47/30F	1992	East Kent, 1993
7812	J812NKK	Leyland Olympian ON2R50C13Z4	Northern Counties	H47/30F	1992	East Kent, 1993
7813	J813NKK	Leyland Olympian ON2R50C13Z4	Northern Counties	H47/30F	1992	East Kent, 1993
7814	J814NKK	Leyland Olympian ON2R50C13Z4	Northern Counties	H47/30F	1992	East Kent, 1993

7821-7830

Leyland Olympian ON2R50C13Z4 Northern Counties — H47/30F — 1993 — 7821-5 East Kent, 1993

7821	K821TKP	7823	K823TKP	7825	K825TKP	7827	L827BKK	7829	L829BKK
7822	K822TKP	7824	K824TKP	7826	L826BKK	7828	L828BKK	7830	L830BKK

7961-7985

Bristol VRT/SL3/6LXB — Eastern Coach Works — H43/31F — 1978-81 — Alder Valley, 1992

7961	GGM81W	7972	WJM832T	7979	CJH119V	7982	CJH142V	7985	CJH145V
7969	WJM829T	7977	CJH117V	7980	CJH120V				

8211	D211VEV	Scania K112CRB	Berkhof Esprite 350	C40DT	1987	East Kent, 1993
8243	SIB8243	Volvo B10M-60	Plaxton Paramount 3500 III	C49FT	1991	East Kent, 1993

8404-8410

Volvo B10M-62 — Plaxton Première 350 — C53F* — 1995 — *8410 convertible to C49FT; 8404-6 are C51FT

8404	M404BFG	8406	M406BFG	8408	M408BFG	8409	M409BFG	8410	M410BFG
8405	M405BFG	8407	M407BFG						

8503	IIL3503	Volvo B10M-61	Van Hool Alizée	C49FT	1988	Bluebird Buses, 1995
8505	IIL3505	Volvo B10M-61	Van Hool Alizée	C49FT	1988	Bluebird Buses, 1995
8618	WVT618	Volvo B10M-61	Plaxton Paramount 3500 III	C50F	1987	Bluebird Buses, 1995
8856	J856NKK	Scania K93CRB	Plaxton Paramount 3500 III	C49FT	1992	East Kent, 1993
8909	J909NKP	Volvo B10M-60	Plaxton Expressliner	C49FT	1992	East Kent, 1993
8910	K910TKP	Volvo B10M-60	Plaxton Expressliner 2	C49FT	1993	East Kent, 1993

8911-8918

Volvo B10M-62 — Plaxton Expressliner 2 — C49FT — 1994-95

8911	M911WJK	8913	M913WJK	8915	M915WJK	8917	M917WJK	8918	M918WJK
8912	M912WJK	8914	M914WJK	8916	M916WJK				

8996	PFN873	Bova FHD12.280	Bova Futura	C49FT	1986	East Kent, 1993

Special event vehicles: (traditional liveries)

0135	CD7045	Leyland G7	Short	O27/24R	1922	
0409	409DCD	Leyland Titan PD3/4	Northern Counties	FCO39/30F	1964	
0424	424DCD	Leyland Titan PD3/4	Northern Counties	FCO39/30F	1964	
0813	UF4813	Leyland Titan TD1	Brush	O27/24R	1929	
0946	MFN946F	AEC Regent V 3D3RA	Park Royal	H40/32F	1967	Hastings & District, 1989

Named Vehicles:-

8404 Spirit of Margate; 8405 Spirit of Sandgate; 8406 Spirit of Seabrook; 8503 Spirit of Margate; 8505 Spirit of Ramsgate; 8856 Spirit of Leeds Castle; 8910 Spirit of Hythe; 8911 Spirit of Sandwich; 8912 Spirit of Dover; 8913 Spirit of Canterbury; 8914 Spirit of Folkestone; 8915 Spirit of Walmer; 8916 Spirit of Deal; 8917 Spirit of Whitfield; 8918 Spirit of Ashford.

The number of Bristol VR buses operating with the Stagecoach South operations is reducing following further deliveries of new Volvo Olympians. Later in 1998 a further batch of the type is expected, so the hour-glass on 7961, GGM81W, seen here at Winchester is running out.
Andrew Jarosz

Previous Registrations:-

400DCD	M490BFG		HUF451X	RUF434X, XLD244
401DCD	M401BFG		HUF579X	RUF430X, 400DCD
402DCD	M402BFG		HUF592X	RUF437X, 407DCD
403DCD	M403BFG		HUF593X	RUF436X, 406DCD
404DCD	L604VCD		HUF603X	RUF429X, 415DCD
405DCD	L605VCD		HUF604X	RUF435X, 405DCD
406DCD	L606TDY		HUF625X	RUF431X, 411DCD
407DCD	L607TDY		HUF626X	RUF438X, 410DCD
408DCD	L608TDY		HUF639X	RUF433X, 420DCD
409DCD	from new		IIL3503	E625UNE, TXI2426, E936XSB
410DCD	M610APN		IIL3505	E623UNE, XIA257, E942XSB
411DCD	M611APN		JNJ194V	HFG924V, DSV943
412DCD	M612APN		JNJ718V	OMA506V, TCS157, CSU992
413DCD	M613APN		JYJ269N	HWY718N, CSU934, CSU978
414DCD	M614APN		NFX667	K716PCN
415DCD	L345KCK		OUF262W	JWV125W, LYJ145
416DCD	L346KCK		OUF863W	PWT278W, XSU612
417DCD	L347KCK		PFN873	C996FKM
418DCD	L348KCK		RUF970M	OKG158M, XSU682
419DCD	L619TDY		SIB8243	H826AHS
420DCD	L620TDY		SYC852	JWV126W
421DCD	L621TDY		WVT618	D202LWX
422DCD	L622TDY		XIA586	RYG773R
423DCD	L623TDY		XIA857	PKP548R, XIA256
424DCD	424DCD, AOR158B		XYK976	K719PCN
472YMF	J713CYG		YLJ332	J715CYG

Allocations:-

Aldershot (Halimote Road) - Hants & Surrey - South West Trains ⋘

Outstations - Alton; Haslemere and Petersfield

Mercedes-Benz	865	866	867	868	869	870	871	872
	873	874	875	876	877	878	879	880
	905	906	907	908	909	910	911	912
	913	914						
Dart	472	474	475	482	483	522	523	529
	534	570	571	572	575	576	577	584
	585	586	587	588	5004⋘			
National	109	150	1218	1223	1238			
Volvo PS	618	635	646	647	656	657		
Bristol VR	686	759	7650	7654	7665	7667	7969	7972
	7979	7980	7982	7985				
Olympian	223	236	239	351	352	353	391	392

Andover (Livingstone Road) - Hampshire Bus

Mercedes-Benz	854	855	856	857	858	859	860	
Dart	542	544	545	547	548	581		
National	107	174	191	192	196			
Volvo NC	601	602	603	604	605			
Volvo PS	606	607	608	615	616	617	626	627
	631	655	658					
Olympian	213	214	257	293	294	295		

Ashford (Brunswick Road) - East Kent

Mercedes-Benz	844	845	849	850	894	895	896	897
	898	922	923	945	946	947	948	949
	950	951	952					
National	182	1344						
Volvo PS	644	645	679	680				
Bristol VR	7652	7660	7673	7674				
Titan	7285							
Olympian	285	377	378	7806				

Basingstoke (Bus Station) - Hampshire Bus

Mercedes-Benz	853							
Dart	459	460	461	462	471	481	526	527
	531	532	533	535	546	549	550	573
	574	578	582					
Volvo PS/NC	643	651	652	662	663	664	665	667
	668	669	670					
Bristol VR	749	7369	7438	7446	7448	7449	7450	7680
	7965	7977						
Olympian	201	202	203	204	207	208	224	268
	269	276	277	279	288	289	290	366
	367	379	380	393	394			

Chichester (Southgate) - Sussex Coastline - Sussex Bus ▲

Iveco	2651▲							
Omni	2136▲							
Mercedes-Benz	891▲	892▲	893	917	918	919	920	921
	2220▲							
Dart	541	553	554	555	580			
Leopard	2612▲	2682▲	2992▲					
National 1	1203	2586▲	2857▲					
National 2	120	121	122	123	125	128▲	133	134
	137							
Volvo PS	626	628	629					
Olympian	209	217	220	221	222	225	228	232
	278	281	282	341				

Dover (Russell Street) - East Kent - National Express🚌

Mercedes-Benz	953	954	955	956	957	959	960	961
	962	963	964	965	967			
Volvo Coach	8503🚌	8505🚌						
Volvo Expressliner	8909	8910	8911	8912	8913	8914	8915	8916
	8917	8918						
Volvo PS	633	639	640	641	642	676	677	678
Bristol VR	7653	7655	7658	7659	7661	7663	7664	
Olympian	386	387	389	390	7826	7827	7828	

Eastbourne (Cavendish Place) - South Coast Buses

Outstations - Lewes; Uckfield and Seaford

Mercedes-Benz	881	882	883	884	885	886	887	888
	889	890						
Dart	451	452	453	454	455	456	494	495
	496	497						
National 1	110	112	114	148	169	173	176	177
	179	1115						
National 2	146	160						
Volvo PS	609	612	613	614	619	620	636	637
	638	650	671	672	673			
Bristol VR	7621	7622						
Volvo B10M DD	7301	7302	7303	7304	7305	7306	7307	7308
	7309							
Olympian	241	242	356	357	358	359	373	374
	388							

1998 has seen many of the remaining Leyland Nationals in Stagecoach fleets being replaced, while several remain with the South operations. Pictured in Hastings, in immaculate condition, is South Coast Buses' 107, AYJ107T. *Terry Blackman*

Folkestone (Kent Road, Cheriton) - East Kent

Outstation - New Romney

Mercedes-Benz	958	966	968	969	970	971	972	
	973	974	975	976				
Dart	457	458	476					
Javelin Interurban	1106							
National	195							
Titan	7209	7271	7270	7272				
Olympian	286	287	296	297	298	375	376	
	7811	7812	7813	7814	7821	7822	7823	7829

Hastings (Beaufort Road, Silverhill, St Leonards) - South Coast Buses

Dart	464	465	466	467	501	502	503	504
	505	506	507	508	509	510	511	512
	513	514	516	517	518	519	520	521
	579	583						
National 2	136	140	142	143	144	145	147	159
Volvo B10M	653	674	675					
Bristol VR	7620	7623						
Titan	7203	7205	7215	7223	7233	7237	7240	7244
	7250	7268	7274	7279	7280	7287	7288	7290
Olympian	382	383	384	385				

The coaches allocated to the two East Kent divisions retain special liveries for the East Kent Coaches operations. This cream and dark red livery is seen on Plaxton-bodied Volvo 8407, M407BFG, from the 1995 delivery. Coaches for the group being delivered in 1998 will have Jonckheere bodywork, where appropriate, in National Express livery. *Terry Blackman*

Herne Bay (High Street) - East Kent - Canterbury Park & Ride[P]

Outstation - Canterbury

Mercedes-Benz	847	848	863	935	936	937	938	939
	940	941	942	943	944			
DAF Delta	1401[P]	1402[P]	1403[P]					
Javelin Interurban	1105	1108						
Lance	1404[P]	1405[P]	1406[P]	1407[P]	1408[P]			
Scania coach	8211							
Titan	7208	7224	7235	7247	7281	7284		
Scania	7781	7782						
Olympian	226	227	230	254	255	256	283	284
	360	361	362	363	364	365	368	369
	370	371	372	7801	7802	7803	7804	
	7805	7807	7808	7809	7810			

Portsmouth (Langstone Point) - Sussex Coastline

Mercedes-Benz	841	843						
Dart	551	552						
Volvo PS	621	622	623	624				
Bristol VR	688	7657						
Titan	7201	7204	7207	7211	7214	7220	7221	7225
	7229	7231	7242	7243	7245	7248	7251	7259
	7261	7263	7269	7294	7296	7297	7298	
Olympian	215	216	218	219	229	231	233	234
	235	240	342	395	396	397	398	399
	7824	7825	7830					

Thanet (Margate Road, Westwood) - East Kent - National Express(

Outstation - Deal

Mercedes-Benz	899	901	902	903	904	925	926	927
	928	929	930	931	932	933	934	977
Dart SLF	18	19	21	22	23	24		
Volvo PS	632	634	659	660	661			
Volvo Coach	8243ï	8404ï	8405ï	8406ï	8407ï	8408ï	8409ï	8410ï
	8618							
Scania	8856							
Bova	8996							
Bristol VR	7669	7671	7681	7682	7683			
Metrobus	7746	7747	7748	7749	7750	7751	7752	7753
	7754	7755	7761	7762	7763	7764	7765	7766
	7767	7771	7772	7773	7774	7775		
Olympian	264	265	266	267	299	301	354	355
	381							

Winchester (The Broadway) - Hampshire Bus - South West Trains ⋙ – Park & Ride P

Outstations - Alton; Bishops Waltham and Petersfield

Mercedes-Benz	861	915	916	924				
Dart SLF	12	13	14	15	16	17		
Dart	484	485	486	524	528	530	536	
	537	538	539	540	543	568	569	5003⋙
Volvo B6	400P	401	402P	403P				
Volvo PS	648	649	654					
National	1247							
DAF-Delta	5001⋙	5002⋙						
Bristol VR	7353	7373	7435	7651	7668	7677	7961	
Olympian	205	206	210	211	212	246	247	248
	249	250	260	261	262	263	291	292

Worthing (Library Place) - Sussex Coastline

Outstations - Henfield and Littlehampton

Mercedes-Benz	862	864						
Dart SLF	1	2	3	4	5	6	7	8
	9	10	11					
Dart	491	492	493	556	557	558	559	560
	561	562	563	564	565	566	567	
National 2	119	124	126	127	129	130	131	132
	135	138	139	151				
Volvo PS	610	611	630					
Olympian	237	238	243	244	245	343	344	345
	346	347	348	349	350			

Unallocated

National	102	163	1188	1201	1898
Leopard	2978				
Bristol VR	7355				

TAPPINS

Tappins Coaches, Holiday House, Station Road, Didcot, Oxfordshire, OX11 7LZ

770EWL	Leyland National 1151/1R/0401		B52F	1973	South Wales, 1986
BFS14L	Leyland Atlantean AN68/1R	Alexander AL	O45/33F	1973	Lothian, 1990
BFS34L	Leyland Atlantean AN68/1R	Alexander AL	O45/33F	1973	Lothian, 1990
BFS48L	Leyland Atlantean AN68/1R	Alexander AL	O45/33F	1973	Lothian, 1990
BFS49L	Leyland Atlantean AN68/1R	Alexander AL	O45/33F	1973	Lothian, 1990
BFS50L	Leyland Atlantean AN68/1R	Alexander AL	O45/33F	1973	Lothian, 1990
OSF939M	Leyland Atlantean AN68/1R	Alexander AL	O45/33F	1974	Lothian, 1991
653GBU	Leyland National 2 NL116AL11/1R		B52F	1982	AERE, Harwell, 1991
461XPB	Volvo B10M-61	Plaxton Viewmaster IV	C53F	1982	
500EFC	Volvo B10M-61	Plaxton Viewmaster IV	C53F	1982	
B161FWJ	Volvo B10M-61	Plaxton Paramount 3500	C53F	1985	
B163FWJ	Volvo B10M-61	Plaxton Paramount 3500	C53F	1985	
C323UFP	Volvo B10M-61	Plaxton Paramount 3500 II	C53F	1986	
C324UFP	Volvo B10M-61	Plaxton Paramount 3500 II	C53F	1986	
C325UFP	Volvo B10M-61	Plaxton Paramount 3500 II	C53F	1986	
YUE338	Volvo B10M-61	Plaxton Paramount 3500 II	C49FT	1986	
KBZ7145	Ford Transit 190	Carlyle	B16F	1986	The Bee Line, 1994
D73HRU	Volvo B10M-61	Plaxton Paramount 3500 III	C53F	1987	
D74HRU	Volvo B10M-61	Plaxton Paramount 3500 III	C53F	1987	
D75HRU	Volvo B10M-61	Plaxton Paramount 3500 III	C53F	1987	
E471SON	MCW Metrobus DR102/63	MCW	H45/30F	1988	London Buses, 1992

Opposite, and below:- **Tappins is a family operation based at Didcot in Oxfordshire. Many of the modern vehicles are used on contracts for foreign tourists as well as local contract work. In Oxford, the company operate open-top tours using Lothian Transport vehicles. Pictured below is Plaxton Paramount 3500, G511LWU.** *Robert Edworthy*

E260PEL	Volvo B10M-61	Plaxton Paramount 3500 III	C53F	1988	
IIL1832	Neoplan N122/3	Neoplan Skyliner	CH57/18DT	1988	Voyager, Selby, 1992
F400DUG	Volvo B10M-60	Plaxton Paramount 3500 III	C48F	1989	Wallace Arnold, 1993
F165XLJ	Volvo B10M-60	Plaxton Paramount 3500 III	C53F	1989	
F166XLJ	Volvo B10M-60	Plaxton Paramount 3500 III	C53F	1989	
G417VAY	Volvo B10M-60	Plaxton Paramount 3500 III	C53F	1990	
G418VAY	Volvo B10M-60	Plaxton Paramount 3500 III	C53F	1990	
G419VAY	Volvo B10M-60	Plaxton Paramount 3500 III	C53F	1990	
G504LWU	Volvo B10M-60	Plaxton Paramount 3500 III	C50F	1990	Wallace Arnold, 1993
G505LWU	Volvo B10M-60	Plaxton Paramount 3500 III	C50F	1990	Wallace Arnold, 1993
G506LWU	Volvo B10M-60	Plaxton Paramount 3500 III	C50F	1990	Wallace Arnold, 1993
G507LWU	Volvo B10M-60	Plaxton Paramount 3500 III	C50F	1990	Wallace Arnold, 1993
G508LWU	Volvo B10M-60	Plaxton Paramount 3500 III	C50F	1990	Wallace Arnold, 1993
G509LWU	Volvo B10M-60	Plaxton Paramount 3500 III	C50F	1990	Wallace Arnold, 1993
G510LWU	Volvo B10M-60	Plaxton Paramount 3500 III	C50F	1990	Wallace Arnold, 1993
G511LWU	Volvo B10M-60	Plaxton Paramount 3500 III	C50F	1990	Wallace Arnold, 1993
G512LWU	Volvo B10M-60	Plaxton Paramount 3500 III	C50F	1990	Wallace Arnold, 1993
G513LWU	Volvo B10M-60	Plaxton Paramount 3500 III	C50F	1990	Wallace Arnold, 1993
H261GRY	Volvo B10M-60	Plaxton Paramount 3500 III	C53F	1991	
H262GRY	Volvo B10M-60	Plaxton Paramount 3500 III	C53F	1991	
K301GDT	Volvo B10M-60	Van Hool Alizée	C53F	1993	
K302GDT	Volvo B10M-60	Van Hool Alizée	C53F	1993	
L540XJU	Mazda E2200	Howletts	M8	1993	
N171LHU	Volvo B10M-62	Van Hool Alizée	C53F	1996	
N172LHU	Volvo B10M-62	Van Hool Alizée	C53F	1996	
N173LHU	Volvo B10M-62	Van Hool Alizée	C53F	1996	
N174LHU	Volvo B10M-62	Van Hool Alizée	C53F	1996	
N175LHU	Volvo B10M-62	Van Hool Alizée	C53F	1996	
N176LHU	Volvo B10M-62	Van Hool Alizée	C53F	1996	
N177LHU	Volvo B10M-62	Van Hool Alizée	C53F	1996	
N178LHU	Volvo B10M-62	Van Hool Alizée	C53F	1996	
N179LHU	Volvo B10M-62	Van Hool Alizée	C53F	1996	
N180LHU	Volvo B10M-62	Van Hool Alizée	C53F	1996	
P414HRB	Toyota Coaster BB50R	Caetano Optimo IV	C21F	1997	
P415HRB	Toyota Coaster BB50R	Caetano Optimo IV	C21F	1997	

Previous Registrations:

461XPB	NBL904X	770EWL	NWN720M	KBZ7145	D826UTF
500EFC	NBL905X	IIL1832	E480YWJ	YUE338	C326UFP
653GBU	WBW735X				

Depots:- Station Road, Didcot and Collett Road Southmead Ind Est, Didcot.

Livery:- Orange, black and white

Pictured at Chessington during 1998 is Tappins' Neoplan Skyliner IIL1832, currently the only double-deck coach in the fleet.
David Heath

TRAVEL TAYLOR

Taylor's of Sutton Scotney Ltd, The Garage, Sutton Scotney, Hampshire, SO21 3JL

VPF285S	Bristol VRT/SL3/6LXB	Eastern Coach Works	H43/31F	1978	Oakley Coaches, 1996
HWJ921W	Bristol VRT/SL3/501	Eastern Coach Works	H43/31F	1980	RoadCar, 1995
HWJ926W	Bristol VRT/SL3/501	Eastern Coach Works	H43/31F	1980	RoadCar, 1995
HWJ927W	Bristol VRT/SL3/501	Eastern Coach Works	H43/31F	1980	RoadCar, 1995
HUD493W	Bristol VRT/SL3/6LXB	Eastern Coach Works	H43/27D	1980	City of Oxford, 1993
HUD497W	Bristol VRT/SL3/6LXB	Eastern Coach Works	H43/27D	1980	City of Oxford, 1993
KJO504W	Bristol VRT/SL3/6LXB	Eastern Coach Works	H43/27D	1980	City of Oxford, 1994
KJO510W	Bristol VRT/SL3/6LXB	Eastern Coach Works	H43/27D	1980	City of Oxford, 1993
SVL171W	Bristol VRT/SL3/6LXB	Eastern Coach Works	H43/31F	1981	RoadCar, 1995
JIL2029	Ford R1014	Plaxton Supreme V	C33F	1982	Summerfield, Southampton, 1985
RJI8922	DAF MB200DKFL600	Plaxton Paramount 3500	C53F	1985	Waters, Addlestone, 1989
SJI8099	Volvo B10M-61	Plaxton Paramount 3200 II	C53F	1986	Shearings, 1995
RJI8921	Volvo B10M-61	Plaxton Paramount 3200 II	C53F	1986	Shearings, 1992
RJI8923	Volvo B10M-61	Van Hool Alizée	C53F	1986	Shearings, 1992
RJI8919	DAF MB200DKVL615	Jonckheere Jubilee	C53F	1987	Clarke & Goodman, Pailton, 1989
RJI8920	Volvo B10M-61	Van Hool Alizée	C53F	1988	Ford's Coaches, Gunnislake, 1990
YRX481	DAF SB3000DKV601	Jonckheere Jubilee P599	C51FT	1989	
TJI8788	Kässbohrer Setra S215HD	Kässbohrer	C49FT	1992	Boon's Boreham, 1995
M302OTF	Dennis Javelin 8.5SDA2137	Berkhof E'llence 1000 Midi	C35F	1994	
M87SRD	MAN 11.190	Berkhof E'llence 1000 Midi	C35F	1995	
N222TAY	Dennis Javelin 12SDA2155	Berkhof Excellence 1000	C51FT	1995	
N333TAY	Toyota Coaster HZB50R	Caetano Optimo III	C21F	1995	
N444TAY	Toyota Coaster HZB50R	Caetano Optimo III	C21F	1995	
R111TAY	Dennis Javelin	Neoplan Transliner	C49FT	1997	

Previous Registrations:

JIL2029	VPR385X		RJI8923	C523DND
RJI8919	D99DNV		SJI8099	C353DND
RJI8920	E442RCV		TJI8788	RSU231
RJI8921	C354DND		YRX481	G838GNV
RJI8922	B229RRU			

Livery: White, orange, ivory and green

Travel Taylor operate school contract services using the fleet of Bristol VRs, with most comming from RoadCar in Lincoln and City of Oxford. Representing the coach fleet is M87SRD, a MAN 11.190 with Berkhof coachwork. It is seen here when new.

Several Tourex vehicles are used exclusively for school contract services and are liveried in yellow for this purpose. The School Bus Company is also shown on the buses. Pictured here are 20, MBW612N, a Leyland Leopard with Plaxton bodywork and Leyland Tiger 25, A788YOX. This latter vehicle carries Marshall Campaigner bodywork and is one of five former military coaches currently operating with the company. *David Longbottom*

TOUREX

Tourex Ltd, Lamarsh Road, Botley, Oxford, OX2 0LE

	MBW645N	Bedford YRT	Duple Dominant	C51F	1975	Percival's, Oxford, 1987
	786AFC	Leyland Leopard PSU3F/5R	Plaxton Supreme IV Exp	C53F	1981	Percival's, Oxford, 1987
12	MPT298P	Leyland Atlantean AN68/1R	Eastern Coach Works	H45/27D	1975	Oxford Bus Company, 1990
17	MPT294P	Leyland Atlantean AN68/1R	Eastern Coach Works	H45/27D	1975	Oxford Bus Company, 1990
19	HVD740N	AEC Reliance 6U3ZR	Plaxton Supreme III	C50F	1975	Leavy, Botley, 1993
20	MBW612N	Leyland Leopard PSU5/4R	Plaxton Supreme III	C50F	1975	Heyfordian, Upper Heyford, 1994
22	558BWL	Leyland Tiger TRCTL11/3R	Marshall Campaigner	B54F	1983	MoD, 1995
23	YJN166	Leyland Tiger TRCTL11/3R	Marshall Campaigner	B54F	1983	MoD, 1995
24	A734YOX	Leyland Tiger TRCTL11/3R	Marshall Campaigner	B54F	1983	MoD, 1996
25	A788YOX	Leyland Tiger TRCTL11/3R	Marshall Campaigner	B54F	1983	MoD, 1996
26	966MKE	Volvo B10M-61	Plaxton Supreme V	C53F	1982	Tappins, Didcot, 1996
27	D527DPM	Leyland Tiger TRCTL11/3RZ	Plaxton Derwent 2	B54F	1987	MoD, 1997
80	VWL96	Leyland Leopard PSU3F/5R	Plaxton Supreme IV Exp	C53F	1981	Percival's, Oxford, 1987

Heritage vehicles:-

	LYB941	Bedford OB	Duple Vista	C29F	1948	Longstaff, Carlton, 1989
	KLB713	AEC Regent III 0961	Park Royal	H30/26R	1950	non-PSV, 1991
	FJB739C	Bristol Lodekka FLF6G	Eastern Coach Works	H38/32F	1965	Percivals, Oxford, 1991
	NDL375G	Bedford VAM	Duple Viceroy	C45F	1969	Paul's Tours, Sandown, 1990
	VER262L	AEC Reliance 2U3ZR	Alexander AY	C53F	1972	Percivals, Oxford, 1991

Previous Registrations:

558BWL	20KB65, A484YOX	LYB941	From new
786AFC	LWL743W	MBW612N	KBW118N, 2110UK
966MKE	NBL906X	MBW645N	JVS927N, VFC59
A734YOX	20KB67	VER262L	VER262L, 558BWL
A788YOX	20KB52	VWL96	LWL744W
D527DPM	82KF40	YJN166	20KB44, A537YOX
KLB713	from new		

Livery: Yellow (school buses)

The Traditional Motor Bus Company

The Traditional Motor Bus Company, 16 Forest Close, Newport, Isle of Wight

2	TDL564K	Bristol RELL6G	Eastern Coach Works	OB53F	1971	Southern Vectis, 1998
3	VDL613S	Bristol VRT/SL3/6LXB	Eastern Coach Works	CO43/31F	1978	Southern Vectis, 1998
4	HVD740N	Bristol VRT/SL3/6LXB	Eastern Coach Works	CO43/31F	1978	Southern Vectis, 1998

Depot:- c/o Seaview Services, Faulkner Lane, Sandown.

WESTBROOK TRAVEL

Newbus Ltd, 25B Blackwater Road, Newport, Isle of Wight, PO30 3BB

Depot:- Seaview (Park Lane, Nettlestone)

SDL638J	Bristol VRT/SL2/6G	Eastern Coach Works	H39/31F	1971	Southern Vectis, 1995
BHN658N	Bristol VRT/SL2/6G	Eastern Coach Works	O43/31F	1974	Keighley & District, 1990
GTA51N	Bristol VRT/SL2/6G	Eastern Coach Works	PO43/32F	1975	Western National, 1993
UFX858S	Bristol VRT/SL3/6LXB	Eastern Coach Works	CO43/31F	1977	Southern Vectis, 1998
KAD359V	Leyland Leopard PSU5C/4R	Plaxton Supreme IV	C57F	1980	Rover Coaches, Bromsgrove, 1992

Livery: Yellow, cream and maroon.

WHITE BUS SERVICES

C E Jeatt & Sons Ltd, North Street Garage, Winkfield, Windsor, SL4 4TF

w	STL725J	Bedford YRQ	Willowbrook 001	DP43F	1971	Simmons, Great Gonerby, 1981
w	SNK255N	Bedford YRQ	Willowbrook Expressway	C45F	1974	
	KDT281P	Bedford YRQ	Plaxton Supreme III	C45F	1975	Mauler, Winkfield, 1990
	RLW778R	Bedford YMT	Duple Dominant	C53F	1977	Mauler, Winkfield, 1990
	EAJ327V	Bedford YMT	Plaxton Supreme IV	C53F	1979	Flear, Middlesbrough, 1985
	HRO958V	Bedford YLQ	Duple Dominant	B45F	1979	
	JMJ633V	Bedford YMT	Plaxton Supreme IV Exp	C53F	1979	Moore, Windsor, 1987
	JNM747Y	Bedford YNT	Plaxton Paramount 3200	C53F	1983	Grey of Ely, 1997
	B633DDW	Bedford YNT	Plaxton Paramount 3200 II	C53F	1985	Fernhill Travel, Bracknell, 1995
	B542OJF	Bedford YNT	Duple Laser	C53F	1985	Victoria, Tean, 1997
	B30MSF	Bedford YNT	Duple Laser 2	C49F	1985	Glyn Evans, Manmoel, 1998
	C668WRT	Bedford YNT	Duple Dominant	B63F	1986	Chambers, Bures, 1995
	D473WPM	Iveco Daily 49.10	Robin Hood City Nippy	B21F	1986	Stagecoach South, 1997

Livery: White

Previous Registrations:-

JNM747Y   JNM747Y, ESU307

Westbrook Travel operate four Bristol VRs with various styles of roof from open-top to closed. Pictured on the Esplanade in Ryde is partially-open-top GTA51N.
Don Vincent.

At the foot of Windsor Castle, White Bus Services' Duple Dominant bus HRO958V is seen waiting time before operating the Ascot service. Typical of the fleet, it is based on a Bedford chassis.
Robert Edworthy

Only the 3200 version of Plaxton's Paramount has been mounted onto a Bedford chassis with two currently operating in the fleet of White Bus Services. Pictured in Millbank on school excursion work is JNM747Y.
Colin Lloyd

Wight Bus is the trading name of the transport department of the Isle of Wight Council who operate a fleet of modern vehicles mostly on school contracts. Shown here are H611CDL, a Leyland Swift with Reeve Burgess bodywork and P142TDL, one of six Dennis Darts delivered in 1996. These each have the UVG Urban Star body. *Don Vincent*

WIGHT BUS

Isle of Wight Council, 21 Whitcombe Road, Carisbrooke, Isle of Wight, PO30 1YS

5253	M977DNJ	LDV 400	SEM	M16	1995	
5802	A101FPL	Leyland Olympian ONTL11/2R	Eastern Coach Works	DPH45/27F	1984	Northumbria, 1993
5815	H611CDL	Leyland Swift ST2R44C97T5	Reeve Burgess Harrier	B41F	1990	
5816	P81VDL	Dennis Javelin	UVG Unistar	B72F	1997	
5817	P82VDL	Dennis Javelin	UVG Unistar	B72F	1997	
5818	P83VDL	Dennis Javelin	UVG Unistar	B72F	1997	
5819	J142JDL	Dennis Javelin 11SDA1921	Wadham Stringer	B67F	1991	
5820	H840DDL	Dennis Javelin 11SDA1923	Wright	B65F	1991	
5821	R301BDL	Mercedes-Benz Vario O814	UVG CityStar	B30FL	1997	
5822	E117JDL	Mercedes-Benz 609D	Steedrive	B26FL	1988	
5823	J797HDL	Mercedes-Benz 609D	Leicester Carriage Builders	B21FL	1991	
5824	J796HDL	Mercedes-Benz 609D	Leicester Carriage Builders	B19F	1991	
5825	P231TDL	Mercedes-Benz 811D	UVG CityStar	B33F	1996	
5827	R302BDL	Mercedes-Benz Vario O814	UVG CityStar	B30FL	1997	
5828	R303BDL	Mercedes-Benz Vario O814	UVG CityStar	B30FL	1997	
5834	R304BDL	Mercedes-Benz Vario O814	UVG CityStar	B30FL	1997	
5835	B230LDL	Mercedes-Benz L608D	Mellor	B26FL	1985	
5837	E793GDL	Mercedes-Benz 609D	Withey	B26FL	1987	
5838	E795GDL	Mercedes-Benz 609D	Withey	B26FL	1987	
5841	P124TDL	Dennis Javelin 12SDA2155	Caetano Algarve II	C57F	1996	
5842	P125TDL	Dennis Javelin 12SDA2155	Caetano Algarve II	C57F	1996	
5843	P137TDL	Dennis Dart	UVG Urban Star	B43F	1996	
5844	P138TDL	Dennis Dart	UVG Urban Star	B43F	1996	
5845	P139TDL	Dennis Dart	UVG Urban Star	B43F	1996	
5846	P140TDL	Dennis Dart	UVG Urban Star	B43F	1996	
5847	P141TDL	Dennis Dart	UVG Urban Star	B43F	1996	
5848	P142TDL	Dennis Dart	UVG Urban Star	B43F	1996	
6202	M975DNJ	LDV 400	SEM	M10L	1995	
6203	M976DNJ	LDV 400	SEM	M16	1995	
6219	F544ODL	Freight Rover Sherpa	Steedrive	B17FL	1988	

Livery: White, yellow and black

Depot:- Carisbrooke (Whitcombe Road); Sandown (Faulkner Lane).

In 1996 Caetano provided two coach bodies for Wight Bus. Based on Dennis Javelin chassis, they seat 57 passengers. Pictured in Shanklin in June 1998 is 5842, P125TDL.
Les Peters

WORTH'S

Worths Motor Services Ltd, The Garage, Enstone, Oxfordshire, OX7 4LQ

OJD401R	Leyland Fleetline FE30AGR	Park Royal	H44/24D	1977	Tappins, Didcot, 1993
XKV488S	Ford R1114	Plaxton Supreme III Express	C53F	1978	Pathfinder, Freckleton, 1985
FFC322V	Volvo B58-61	Plaxton Supreme IV	C57F	1980	
FUD322V	Volvo B58-61	Plaxton Supreme IV	C57F	1980	
JWL322W	Volvo B58-61	Plaxton Supreme IV	C57F	1980	
SKG406Y	Volvo B10M-61	Plaxton Paramount 3200	C57F	1983	K&P John, Llanharry, 1990
A112MUD	Leyland Tiger TRCTL11/3RH	Plaxton Paramount 3200 E	C51F	1984	The Oxford Bus Co, 1996
A114PBW	Leyland Tiger TRCTL11/3RH	Plaxton Paramount 3200 E	C51F	1984	The Oxford Bus Co, 1996
A118PBW	Leyland Tiger TRCTL11/3RH	Plaxton Paramount 3200 E	C50F	1984	The Oxford Bus Co, 1996
B123UUD	Leyland Tiger TRCTL11/3RH	Plaxton P'mount 3200 IIE	C51F	1984	The Oxford Bus Co, 1996
B124UUD	Leyland Tiger TRCTL11/3RH	Plaxton P'mount 3200 IIE	C51F	1984	The Oxford Bus Co, 1996
551DJB	Volvo B10M-61	Plaxton Paramount 3500 II	C53F	1986	Wallace Arnold, 1991
E971VUD	Iveco Daily 49.10	Robin Hood City Nippy	C25F	1987	NatWest Bank, Heythrop, 1995
774YPG	Volvo B10M-61	Plaxton Paramount 3200 III	C49F	1988	
XSK144	Volvo B10M-61	Plaxton Paramount 3200 III	C57F	1988	
KAZ2755	Volvo B10M-61	Plaxton Paramount 3200 III	C57F	1989	
IUI6722	Volvo B10M-60	Plaxton Paramount 3200 III	C55F	1989	Independent, Horsforth, 1994
G144MNH	Volvo B10M-60	Jonckheere Deauville P599	C51FT	1990	Harris, Catshill, 1995
G844VAY	Volvo B10M-60	Duple 320	C57F	1989	Crawford, Neilston, 1992
H443JLJ	Volvo B10M-60	Plaxton Paramount 3200 III	C57F	1990	Bere Regis & District, 1993
P7WMS	Volvo B10M-62	Berkhof Axial	C51FT	1997	
R8WMS	Volvo B10M-62	Plaxton Excalibur	C51FT	1998	
S6WMS	Volvo B10M-62	Plaxton Excalibur	C51FT	1998	

Heritage vehicles:-

LUD606	Bedford SBG	Duple Bella Vega	C41F	1957	

Previous Registrations:

551DJB	C121CWR	KAZ2755	F322MFC
774YPG	F318GWL	XSK144	F396HFC

Depots:- The Garage, Enstone and Burford Road, Chipping Norton.

Livery:- Silver and blue

Prominently displaying a large Volvo B10M badge is Worth's **KAZ2755** which, like many in the fleet, carries a Plaxton Paramount 3200 body. Like many operators in the rural areas, school contract services form a major proportion of the work, which should increase with the proposals to target school car journeys in the Government's recent White Paper on transport.
Colin Lloyd

Vehicle Index

Reg	Operator	Reg	Operator	Reg	Operator	Reg	Operator
64AAE	Easson's	859DYE	Reading Mainine	8589EL	Luckett	A869SUL	City Line, Oxford
66BXC	Easson's	868AVO	Heyfordian	8686DN	Luckett	AAE645V	First Provincial
67DNR	Easson's	894FUY	Priory of Gosport	8779KV	Heyfordian	AAE652V	First Provincial
770EWL	Tappins	943YKN	Heyfordian	8874PH	Hodge's	AAE653V	First Citybus
774YPG	Worth's	966MKE	Tourex	8896PH	Hodge's	AAE663V	First Citybus
98CLJ	Grayline	987FOU	Princess Summerbee	9197WF	Heyfordian	AAU136A	Charlton Services
282GOT	Princess Summerbee	991FOT	Princess Summerbee	9258VC	Stagecoach Oxford	AAX311A	Island Coach
292CLT	First Beeline	997GAT	Altonian	9467MU	Heyfordian	ADC176A	Bennetts Silverline
357CLT	Reading Mainine	1264LG	Heyfordian	9489PH	Hodge's	AFG428S	Brijan Tours
400DCD	Stagecoach South	1430PP	Heyfordian	9682FH	Heyfordian	AFJ738T	Stagecoach Oxford
401DCD	Stagecoach South	1435VZ	Heyfordian	9769UK	Heyfordian	AFJ748T	First Provincial
402DCD	Stagecoach South	1598PH	Hodge's	9785SM	Cheney Coaches	AFJ752T	First Provincial
403DCD	Stagecoach South	1636VB	Heyfordian	9945NE	Heyfordian	AFJ763T	First Provincial
404DCD	Stagecoach South	2110UK	Heyfordian	9958PH	Hodge's	AHU514V	First Provincial
405DCD	Stagecoach South	2185NU	Heyfordian	A3ALP	Buddens	ALD948B	Reading Mainine
406AOT	Princess Summerbee	225ASV	Marchwood	A6LTG	Luckett	ALD966B	Reading Mainine
406DCD	Stagecoach South	2462FD	Heyfordian	A7HLC	Luckett	ALD989B	Reading Mainine
407DCD	Stagecoach South	246KOT	Buddens	A11UFB	John Pike	ALD990B	Reading Mainine
408DCD	Stagecoach South	2482NX	Heyfordian	A12HLC	Luckett	ALJ568A	Solent Holidays
409DCD	Stagecoach South	2568PH	Hodge's	A13HLC	Luckett	ALM11B	Reading Mainine
410DCD	Stagecoach South	2622NU	Heyfordian	A14LLT	Luckett	ALM34B	Reading Mainine
411DCD	Stagecoach South	2705TD	Heyfordian	A15LLT	Luckett	ALM37B	Reading Mainine
412DCD	Stagecoach South	2779UE	Heyfordian	A16HLC	Luckett	ALM71B	Reading Mainine
413DCD	Stagecoach South	2969HJ	Chiltern Queens	A17HLC	Luckett	ALM89B	Reading Mainine
414DCD	Stagecoach South	297OJT	Buddens	A18HLC	Luckett	AST151W	First Provincial
415DCD	Stagecoach South	3063VC	Stagecoach Oxford	A18LTG	Luckett	AST153W	First Provincial
416DCD	Stagecoach South	3078RA	Heyfordian	A19HLC	Luckett	AST154W	First Provincial
417DCD	Stagecoach South	3103PH	Charlton Services	A19LTG	Luckett	AST156W	First Provincial
418DCD	Stagecoach South	3139KV	Heyfordian	A20HLC	Luckett	AST159W	First Provincial
419DCD	Stagecoach South	3150MC	Heyfordian	A20LTG	Luckett	AST415A	Reading Mainine
420DCD	Stagecoach South	3762KX	Heyfordian	A101FPL	Wight Bus	AST416A	Reading Mainine
421DCD	Stagecoach South	3900PH	Hodge's	A108TRP	Frimley	AYJ91T	Stagecoach South
422DCD	Stagecoach South	4068MH	Heyfordian	A10HLC	Luckett	AYJ92T	Stagecoach South
423DCD	Stagecoach South	4078NU	Heyfordian	A112MUD	Worth's	AYJ95T	Stagecoach South
424DCD	Stagecoach South	4128AP	Heyfordian	A113MUD	Charlton Services	AYJ97T	Stagecoach South
435SFC	Coliseum	4402PH	Hodge's	A114PBW	Worth's	AYJ100T	Stagecoach South
449BHU	Grayline	4631PH	Hodge's	A118PBW	Worth's	AYJ102T	Stagecoach South
461XPB	Tappins	4817F	Gange's Coaches	A136GTA	Grand Tours	AYJ107T	Stagecoach South
472YMF	Stagecoach South	4827WD	Heyfordian	A158OOT	John Pike	B4OAK	Oakley Coaches
473CDL	Southern Vectis	5057VC	Heyfordian	A201MEL	Solent Blueline	B7BED	Oakley Coaches
479COT	Princess Summerbee	5089LG	Heyfordian	A202MEL	Solent Blueline	B30DSF	Wight Bus
481HYE	Heyfordian	5134PH	Hodge's	A203MEL	Solent Blueline	B121WUV	Stagecoach South
489AOU	Princess Summerbee	5226PH	Hodge's	A204MEL	Solent Blueline	B123UUD	Worth's
498ANX	Jacobs	5300RU	John Pike	A205MEL	Solent Blueline	B124UUD	Worth's
500EFC	Tappins	5701DP	Heyfordian	A207JTT	Gange's Coaches	B124WUV	Stagecoach South
549KYA	Princess Summerbee	5881PH	Hodge's	A277ROW	First Citybus	B125WUV	Stagecoach South
551DJB	Worth's	6230NU	Heyfordian	A301KJT	First Provincial	B161FWJ	Tappins
558BWL	Tourex	6258VZ	Buddens	A302KJT	First Provincial	B163FWJ	Tappins
583CLT	Reading Mainine	6595KV	Heyfordian	A314NMJ	Princess Summerbee	B230LDL	Wight Bus
591STT	Chiltern Queens	6940MD	Heyfordian	A462ODY	Mervyn's Coaches	B373NAB	Island Coach
627DYE	Reading Mainine	6960TU	Heyfordian	A463JJF	Carterton	B413CMC	Aldermaston Coaches
636VHX	Coliseum	6967PH	Hodge's	A484JRU	Jacobs	B414CMC	Aldermaston Coaches
640DYE	Reading Mainine	7034KW	Heyfordian	A494JEC	Carterton	B449WTC	First Provincial
650DYE	Reading Mainine	7107PH	Hodge's	A501HUT	Island Coach	B498JDL	Gange's Coaches
653GBU	Tappins	7209RU	Heyfordian	A604TGO	Jacobs	B542OJF	White Bus
666VMX	Luckett	7223MY	Heyfordian	A695FDL	Solent Blueline	B552AKE	Home James
670DHO	Marchwood	7298RU	Heyfordian	A697DDL	Solent Blueline	B586EGT	Cheney Coaches
735DYE	Reading Mainine	7396LJ	Heyfordian	A698DDL	Southern Vectis	B630DDW	Oakley Coaches
741UKL	Mervyn's Coaches	7845LJ	Heyfordian	A699DDL	Solent Blueline	B631XOW	First Provincial
748ECR	Heyfordian	7958NU	Heyfordian	A700DDL	Solent Blueline	B633DDW	White Bus
752FUV	Priory of Gosport	8177KP	Jacobs	A734YOX	Tourex	B635DDW	Oakley Coaches
786AFC	Tourex	8212FN	Heyfordian	A788YOX	Tourex	B672TPO	Angela
809DYE	First Beeline	8252MX	Heyfordian	A823SUL	Stagecoach South	B911SPR	Chiltern Queens
832DDV	Jacobs	8548VF	Heyfordian	A836PPP	Aldermaston Coaches	B919NPC	Oakley Coaches

Reg	Operator	Reg	Operator	Reg	Operator	Reg	Operator
B971FBL	Aldermaston Coaches	CEL105T	Marchwood	D562HPO	First Provincial	E260PEL	Tappins
B995CUS	Jacobs	CJH117V	Stagecoach South	D578MVR	Horseman	E271HDL	M Travel
BBW20V	Chiltern Queens	CJH119V	Stagecoach South	D579MVR	Horseman	E274HDL	M Travel
BBW21V	City Line, Oxford	CJH120V	Stagecoach South	D582MVR	Horseman	E275HDL	M Travel
BBW22V	Chiltern Queens	CJH124V	Stagecoach South	D613WEY	Courtney	E276HDL	M Travel
BBW23V	City Line, Oxford	CJH145V	Stagecoach South	D647ETR	Marchwood	E289HRV	First Citybus
BBW213Y	City Line, Oxford	CJH164V	Reading Buses	D648ETR	Marchwood	E290HRV	First Citybus
BBW214Y	City Line, Oxford	CJH165V	Reading Buses	D708VRX	John Pike	E309BWL	Stagecoach Oxford
BBW215Y	City Line, Oxford	CJH166V	Reading Buses	D751DLO	First Beeline	E357AMR	Priory of Gosport
BBW216Y	City Line, Oxford	CJH168V	Reading Buses	D752DLO	First Beeline	E454SON	Reading Buses
BBW217Y	City Line, Oxford	CJH169V	Reading Buses	D753DLO	First Beeline	E456SON	Reading Buses
BBW218Y	City Line, Oxford	CJH170V	Reading Buses	D754DLO	First Beeline	E457SON	Reading Buses
BCW827V	Stagecoach South	CJH171V	Reading Buses	D756DLO	First Beeline	E458SON	Reading Buses
BED2T	Oakley Coaches	CJH172V	Reading Buses	D781VMO	Horseman	E459SON	Reading Buses
BFS14L	Tappins	CJJ677W	Stagecoach South	D782VMO	Horseman	E460SON	Reading Buses
BFS34L	Tappins	CJJ679W	Stagecoach South	D783VMO	Horseman	E462SON	Reading Buses
BFS48L	Tappins	CPE162Y	Altonian	D784VMO	Horseman	E463SON	Reading Buses
BFS49L	Tappins	CPO98W	Stagecoach South	D785VMO	Horseman	E464SON	Reading Buses
BFS50L	Tappins	CPO100W	Stagecoach South	D789NDV	Stagecoach Oxford	E465SON	Reading Buses
BHN658N	Westbrook	CRU301L	John Pike	D822UTF	City Line, Oxford	E466SON	Reading Buses
BHO442V	Marchwood	CSU243	Charlton Services	D823UTF	City Line, Oxford	E467SON	Reading Buses
BJG671V	Stagecoach South	CSU432	Charlton Services	D824UTF	City Line, Oxford	E468SON	Reading Buses
BJG672V	Stagecoach South	CTM406T	First Citybus	D851CNV	Altonian	E469SON	Reading Buses
BJG673V	Stagecoach South	CTM412T	Hellyers	D893MWR	Altonian	E471SON	Tappins
BJG674V	Stagecoach South	CUD219Y	City Line, Oxford	D898NUA	Reading Buses	E492CPE	Priory of Gosport
BJG675V	Stagecoach South	CUD220Y	City Line, Oxford	D898YCF	Courtney	E503YSU	Burghfield Mini
BKE859T	Stagecoach South	CUD221Y	City Line, Oxford	D939KNW	Reading Buses	E512PWR	Grayline
BOU3V	First Provincial	CUD222Y	City Line, Oxford	DAZ4518	Angela	E533PRU	Chiltern Queens
BOU4V	First Provincial	CUD223Y	City Line, Oxford	DAZ5045	Angela	E557GFR	Reading Buses
BPO109W	Home James	CUD224Y	City Line, Oxford	DAZ5046	Angela	E558GFR	Reading Buses
BUS5X	Reading Buses	CUL79V	Stagecoach South	DBK262W	First Citybus	E601HTF	Reading Buses
C31SNH	Island Coach	CUL168V	Stagecoach South	DBK263W	First Citybus	E602HTF	Reading Buses
C114PUJ	Chiltern Queens	CUL169V	Stagecoach South	DBK264W	First Citybus	E603HTF	Reading Buses
C116GVU	Aldermaston	CUL180V	Stagecoach South	DBK265W	First Citybus	E604HTF	Reading Buses
C119BRV	Princess Summerbee	CUL190V	Stagecoach South	DBK266W	First Citybus	E605HTF	Reading Buses
C220XRU	Solent Blueline	CUL198V	Stagecoach South	DBV23W	Solent Blueline	E606HTF	Reading Buses
C221XRU	Solent Blueline	CUL215V	Stagecoach South	DDZ1639	Priory of Gosport	E664AUD	Bennetts Silverline
C226XRU	Solent Blueline	CUL225V	Stagecoach South	DPX683W	Southern Vectis	E682UNE	Horseman
C265SDL	Southern Vectis	CUV201C	Reading Mainline	DPX684W	Southern Vectis	E683UNE	Horseman
C268SDL	Southern Vectis	D21NWO	Oakley Coaches	DPX685W	Southern Vectis	E684UNE	Horseman
C316TDL	Seaview Services	D22NWO	Oakley Coaches	DVJ398W	Cheney Coaches	E685UNE	Horseman
C323UFP	Tappins	D34ENH	Chiltern Queens	DYA197A	Burghfield Mini	E687UNE	Horseman
C324UFP	Tappins	D52TLV	Priory of Gosport	DYA199A	Burghfield Mini	E694UNE	Horseman
C325UFP	Tappins	D73HRU	Tappins	DYA238A	Burghfield Mini	E695UNE	Horseman
C355SVV	Oakley Coaches	D74HRU	Tappins	DYA26A	Burghfield Mini	E696UNE	Horseman
C381NHJ	Priory of Gosport	D75HRU	Tappins	DYA272A	Burghfield Mini	E697UNE	Horseman
C433BHY	First Citybus	D82UTF	Reading Buses	DYA27A	Burghfield Mini	E698UNE	Horseman
C443BHY	First Citybus	D83UTF	Reading Buses	DYA28A	Burghfield Mini	E716CPC	Altonian
C476TAY	M Travel	D84UTF	Reading Buses	DYA49A	Burghfield Mini	E739JAY	Priory of Gosport
C534BHY	M Travel	D103PTT	Stagecoach Oxford	DYA52A	Burghfield Mini	E746SKR	Stagecoach South
C588VAA	Home James	D119VFV	Priory of Gosport	DYA54A	Burghfield Mini	E747SKR	Stagecoach South
C592VUT	Princess Summerbee	D122PTT	Stagecoach Oxford	DYA79A	Burghfield Mini	E748SKR	Stagecoach South
C606WTP	Priory of Gosport	D126YDL	Gange's Coaches	DYA92A	Burghfield Mini	E749SKR	Stagecoach South
C644SJM	Chiltern Queens	D132PTT	Stagecoach Oxford	DYA93A	Burghfield Mini	E750SKR	Stagecoach South
C650XDF	Bennetts Silverline	D137PTT	Stagecoach Oxford	DYA97A	Burghfield Mini	E751SKR	Stagecoach South
C652XDF	McLeans	D211VEV	Stagecoach South	E23ETN	Frimley	E752SKR	Stagecoach South
C657XDF	Bennetts Silverline	D212MKK	Jacobs	E68MCR	Easson's	E753SKR	Stagecoach South
C658XDF	Bennetts Silverline	D213MKK	Jacobs	E68SUH	Grayline	E754UKR	Stagecoach South
C668JKG	Bennetts Silverline	D237YRX	Horseman	E106JES	Burghfield Mini	E755UKR	Stagecoach South
C668WRT	White Bus	D238YRX	Horseman	E117JDL	Wight Bus	E755VJO	City Line, Oxford
C805FMC	Oakley Coaches	D248KKL	Home James	E129AAL	Burghfield Mini	E793GDL	Wight Bus
C942DHT	Altonian	D254OOJ	Priory of Gosport	E205OEL	Jacobs	E795GDL	Wight Bus
C984UDL	Gange's Coaches	D259JPR	County Travel	E215PWY	Grayline	E829ATT	Stagecoach Oxford
CAY211Y	Priory of Gosport	D262HFX	Chiltern Queens	E225CFC	City Line, Oxford	E837EUT	Altonian
CAY212Y	Priory of Gosport	D273WPM	White Bus	E226CFC	City Line, Oxford	E904LVE	Grayline
CBV2S	Stagecoach South	D504NWG	Chiltern Queens	E227CFC	City Line, Oxford	E911DRD	Reading Buses
CCG830V	Aldermaston Coaches	D506NWG	Chiltern Queens	E228CFC	City Line, Oxford	E912DRD	Reading Buses
CD7045	Stagecoach South	D514NDA	Priory of Gosport	E229CFC	City Line, Oxford	E913DRD	Reading Buses
CDL899	Southern Vectis	D527DPM	Tourex	E236VUD	Reading Buses	E914DRD	Reading Buses
CDT587T	Cheney Coaches	D560YCW	Reading Buses	E247KCF	Reading Buses	E915DRD	Reading Buses

Reg	Operator	Reg	Operator	Reg	Operator	Reg	Operator
E916DRD	Reading Buses	F309MYJ	Stagecoach South	F767EKM	Stagecoach South	G55XLO	First Beeline
E917DRD	Reading Buses	F311EJO	Stagecoach Oxford	F767FDV	Stagecoach Oxford	G56XLO	First Beeline
E971VUD	Worth's	F312EJO	Stagecoach Oxford	F768FDV	Stagecoach Oxford	G59WCF	Burghfield Mini
E986NMK	Priory of Gosport	F314EJO	Stagecoach Oxford	F769FDV	Stagecoach Oxford	G71APO	Stagecoach South
E996UYG	Reading Buses	F318EJO	Stagecoach Oxford	F770FDV	Stagecoach Oxford	G73APO	Stagecoach South
E999UYG	Reading Buses	F323EJO	Stagecoach Oxford	F771EKM	Stagecoach South	G75BRU	Jacobs
EAJ327V	White Bus	F324EJO	Stagecoach Oxford	F771OJH	Reading Buses	G100VMM	Reading Buses
EAP973V	Stagecoach South	F344TSC	Chiltern Queens	F772EKM	Stagecoach South	G104WRV	First Citybus
EAP986V	Stagecoach South	F350OOR	Jacobs	F773EKM	Stagecoach South	G105WRV	First Citybus
EAP988V	Stagecoach South	F360SDP	Reading Buses	F774EKM	Stagecoach South	G106WRV	First Citybus
EBM440T	Charlton Services	F361SDP	Reading Buses	F774OJH	Reading Buses	G108PGT	City Line, Oxford
EBW106Y	Chiltern Queens	F362SDP	Reading Buses	F775EKM	Stagecoach South	G108WRV	First Citybus
EBW107Y	Chiltern Queens	F363SDP	Reading Buses	F776FDV	Stagecoach Oxford	G109PGT	City Line, Oxford
EDF269T	Charlton Services	F364SDP	Reading Buses	F781KKP	Stagecoach South	G109XOW	First Citybus
EEL893V	First Provincial	F365YFX	John Pike	F782KKP	Stagecoach South	G110PGT	City Line, Oxford
ENJ909V	Stagecoach South	F382KVM	Burghfield Mini	F816TMD	Oakley Coaches	G110XOW	First Citybus
ENJ910V	Stagecoach South	F400DUG	Tappins	F817URN	Solent Blueline	G111XOW	First Citybus
ENJ911V	Stagecoach South	F402KOD	Stagecoach Oxford	F845YJX	Horseman	G112APC	Home James
ENJ912V	Stagecoach South	F403KOD	Stagecoach Oxford	F850NJO	McLeans	G112PGT	City Line, Oxford
ENJ914V	Stagecoach South	F409KOD	Stagecoach Oxford	F851YJX	County Travel	G112XOW	First Citybus
EOI4376	Grayline	F419YFX	Jacobs	F85MJH	Reading Buses	G113XOW	First Citybus
ERE235Y	Priory of Gosport	F451XFX	Jacobs	F862LCU	Solent Blueline	G114PGT	City Line, Oxford
ERV115W	Stagecoach South	F481ENH	Jacobs	F863LCU	Solent Blueline	G115PGT	City Line, Oxford
ERV116W	Stagecoach South	F505CBO	City Line, Oxford	F86MJH	Reading Buses	G116PGT	City Line, Oxford
ERV117W	Stagecoach South	F516GGJ	Charlton Services	F86TDL	Southern Vectis	G117PGT	City Line, Oxford
ERV118W	Stagecoach South	F531NRD	Reading Buses	F888XOE	Courtney	G118PGT	City Line, Oxford
ESU940	Heyfordian	F532NRD	Reading Buses	F904YNV	Daish's Hotel	G119PGT	City Line, Oxford
EYE229V	Stagecoach South	F533NRD	Reading Buses	F905YNV	Daish's Hotel	G120PGT	City Line, Oxford
EYE233V	Stagecoach South	F534NRD	Reading Buses	F950HTT	Jacobs	G124PGT	City Line, Oxford
EYE237V	Stagecoach South	F535NRD	Reading Buses	F986TTF	Chiltern Queens	G144MNH	Worth's
EYE240V	Stagecoach South	F544ODL	Wight Bus	F995XOV	M Travel	G144ULG	Seaview Services
EYE244V	Stagecoach South	F548WGL	Altonian	FBZ7356	Heyfordian	G168RBD	Daish's Hotel
EYE250V	Stagecoach South	F556NJM	City Line, Oxford	FBZ7357	Heyfordian	G210SSL	Stagecoach South
F22VFX	Solent Holidays	F557NJM	City Line, Oxford	FDC411V	Oakley Coaches	G211SSL	Stagecoach South
F55TPR	John Pike	F558NJM	City Line, Oxford	FDC412V	Oakley Coaches	G212SSL	Stagecoach South
F69RBK	Easson's	F559NJM	City Line, Oxford	FDL677V	Solent Blueline	G213SSL	Stagecoach South
F87MJH	Reading Buses	F560NJM	City Line, Oxford	FDL678V	Solent Blueline	G214SSL	Stagecoach South
F101GRM	First Beeline	F601MSL	Stagecoach South	FDL679V	Southern Vectis	G217TKK	Burghfield Mini
F102RTR	First Citybus	F602MSL	Stagecoach South	FDL680V	Solent Blueline	G226TKK	Burghfield Mini
F165XLJ	Tappins	F603MSL	Stagecoach South	FDL681V	Southern Vectis	G230VWL	City Line, Oxford
F166XLJ	Tappins	F604MSL	Stagecoach South	FDL682V	Southern Vectis	G231VWL	City Line, Oxford
F172LBL	First Beeline	F605MSL	Stagecoach South	FDV829V	Stagecoach South	G232VWL	City Line, Oxford
F173LBL	First Beeline	F606MSL	Stagecoach South	FDV830V	Stagecoach South	G233VWL	City Line, Oxford
F174LBL	First Beeline	F610VLJ	Jacobs	FDV831V	Stagecoach South	G234DFX	Burghfield Mini
F175LBL	First Beeline	F633OHD	Horseman	FDV839V	Stagecoach South	G234VWL	City Line, Oxford
F176LBL	First Beeline	F634OHD	Horseman	FFC322V	Worth's	G235VWL	City Line, Oxford
F177XAV	Princess Summerbee	F635OHD	Horseman	FGN891X	Jacobs	G243CLD	Cheney Coaches
F215AVH	Princess Summerbee	F636OHD	Horseman	FIL4904	Bennetts Silverline	G274BEL	Hellyers
F221DDY	Courtney	F638OHD	Horseman	FIL7662	Heyfordian	G277BEL	Courtney
F232DWF	Fleet Coaches	F651RBP	Stagecoach South	FIL7664	Heyfordian	G283BEL	Hellyers
F246RJX	Marchwood	F706RDL	Solent Blueline	FIL8317	Heyfordian	G284BEL	Hellyers
F247RJX	Marchwood	F707RDL	Solent Blueline	FIL8441	Heyfordian	G301XCR	First Citybus
F248RJX	Marchwood	F708SDL	Solent Blueline	FJB739C	Tourex	G302XCR	First Citybus
F254MGB	Courtney	F709SDL	Solent Blueline	FKX291T	Horseman	G303XCR	First Citybus
F274JWL	McLeans	F710SDL	Southern Vectis	FNS162T	Reading Buses	G304XCR	First Citybus
F275UOR	Brijan Tours	F711SDL	Southern Vectis	FPR705E	Gange's Coaches	G305XCR	First Citybus
F283SDL	Southern Vectis	F712SDL	Southern Vectis	FTR267X	First Citybus	G343WHY	Cheney Coaches
F284SDL	Southern Vectis	F730OOT	County Travel	FTR268X	First Citybus	G364FOP	Marchwood
F285SDL	Southern Vectis	F731OOT	Marchwood	FTR269X	First Citybus	G378EJT	Jacobs
F286SDL	Southern Vectis	F746FDV	Stagecoach Oxford	FTR270X	First Citybus	G417VAY	Tappins
F287SDL	Southern Vectis	F755OJH	Reading Buses	FTR271X	First Citybus	G418VAY	Tappins
F299GDB	Burghfield Mini	F761EKM	Stagecoach South	FUD322V	Worth's	G419VAY	Tappins
F301MYJ	Stagecoach South	F762EKM	Stagecoach South	FWL778Y	City Line, Oxford	G423WFP	Priory of Gosport
F302MYJ	Stagecoach South	F763EKM	Stagecoach South	FWL779Y	City Line, Oxford	G425BJT	Jacobs
F303MYJ	Stagecoach South	F764EKM	Stagecoach South	FWL780Y	City Line, Oxford	G435ETW	Burghfield Mini
F304MYJ	Stagecoach South	F764FDV	Stagecoach Oxford	FWL781Y	City Line, Oxford	G457MGG	Daish's Hotel
F305MYJ	Stagecoach South	F765EKM	Stagecoach South	G22UWL	Cheney Coaches	G471OKP	Burghfield Mini
F306MYJ	Stagecoach South	F765FDV	Stagecoach Oxford	G43HDW	Daish's Hotel	G483BJT	Jacobs
F307MYJ	Stagecoach South	F766EKM	Stagecoach South	G51WPF	Fleet Coaches	G495BJT	Jacobs
F308MYJ	Stagecoach South	F766FDV	Stagecoach Oxford	G52CAB	Home James	G501XBL	Reading Buses

Scan Coaches purchased a batch of Scania K92CRB buses for a London tendered bus operation. When the tender was lost at a subsequent re-tendering round, the vehicles were sold and have found homes in a number of fleets. Fitted with Jonckheere TransCity dual-door bodywork, C355SVV came into the Oakley Coaches fleet having previously been used at Aviemore. *Graham Ashworth*

Reg	Operator	Reg	Operator	Reg	Operator	Reg	Operator
G502XBL	Reading Buses	G705TCD	Stagecoach South	G777WFC	City Line, Oxford	G952TDV	Stagecoach Oxford
G503XBL	Reading Buses	G705XLY	Burghfield Mini	G778WFC	City Line, Oxford	G954TDV	Stagecoach Oxford
G504LWU	Tappins	G706TCD	Stagecoach South	G779WFC	City Line, Oxford	G960ATP	Altonian
G504XBL	Reading Buses	G707TCD	Stagecoach South	G780WFC	City Line, Oxford	G961CJB	Burghfield Mini
G505LWU	Tappins	G708TCD	Stagecoach South	G781WFC	City Line, Oxford	G974ARV	Stagecoach South
G505XBL	Reading Buses	G709TCD	Stagecoach South	G782WFC	City Line, Oxford	G975ARV	Stagecoach South
G506LWU	Tappins	G710TCD	Stagecoach South	G783WFC	City Line, Oxford	G977ARV	Stagecoach South
G506XBL	Reading Buses	G711PGT	City Line, Oxford	G800RNC	Courtney	G978ARV	Stagecoach South
G507LWU	Tappins	G713WDL	Southern Vectis	G802RNC	Courtney	GAZ8573	Charlton Services
G507XBL	Reading Buses	G714WDL	Southern Vectis	G803BLF	Burghfield Mini	GDZ8449	Oakley Coaches
G508LWU	Tappins	G715WDL	Southern Vectis	G804BLF	Burghfield Mini	GFJ658N	Frimley
G508XBL	Reading Buses	G716WDL	Southern Vectis	G805BLF	Burghfield Mini	GFN546N	Stagecoach South
G509LWU	Tappins	G717WDL	Southern Vectis	G807RTS	Stagecoach South	GFO366	Priory of Gosport
G509XBL	Reading Buses	G718WDL	Southern Vectis	G808RTS	Stagecoach South	GGM81W	Stagecoach South
G510LWU	Tappins	G719WDL	Southern Vectis	G809RTS	Stagecoach South	GIL8488	Frimley
G510XBL	Reading Buses	G720WDL	Southern Vectis	G821UMU	Altonian	GIL8674	Grand Tours
G511LWU	Tappins	G721WDL	Solent Blueline	G831UDV	Stagecoach Oxford	GIL8939	Grand Tours
G512LWU	Tappins	G722WDL	Solent Blueline	G832UDV	Stagecoach Oxford	GJI7173	Charlton Services
G513LWU	Tappins	G723XDL	Southern Vectis	G833UDV	Stagecoach Oxford	GKL827N	Priory of Gosport
G518RKM	Burghfield Mini	G724XDL	Southern Vectis	G834UDV	Stagecoach Oxford	GPC731N	Reading Buses
G551SKP	Home James	G725XDL	Southern Vectis	G835UDV	Stagecoach Oxford	GPJ895N	Reading Buses
G561HAX	Burghfield Mini	G726XDL	Southern Vectis	G836UDV	Stagecoach Oxford	GPJ896N	Reading Buses
G565YTR	Southern Vectis	G727XDL	Southern Vectis	G837UDV	Stagecoach Oxford	GTA51N	Westbrook
G574HAX	Burghfield Mini	G730CFX	Jacobs	G838PJA	Burghfield Mini	GUW445W	City Line, Oxford
G608SGU	Reading Buses	G740CFX	Jacobs	G838UDV	Stagecoach Oxford	GUW451W	City Line, Oxford
G660DLJ	Jacobs	G769WFC	City Line, Oxford	G839UDV	Stagecoach Oxford	GUW453W	City Line, Oxford
G674YLP	Burghfield Mini	G770WFC	City Line, Oxford	G840UDV	Stagecoach Oxford	GUW458W	City Line, Oxford
G681DLJ	Burghfield Mini	G771WFC	City Line, Oxford	G841UDV	Stagecoach Oxford	GUW470W	First Beeline
G682DLJ	Burghfield Mini	G772WFC	City Line, Oxford	G842UDV	Stagecoach Oxford	GUW482W	City Line, Oxford
G701TCD	Stagecoach South	G773WFC	City Line, Oxford	G843UDV	Stagecoach Oxford	GUW495W	City Line, Oxford
G702TCD	Stagecoach South	G774EPF	Solent Holidays	G844VAY	Worth's	GUW497W	First Beeline
G703TCD	Stagecoach South	G774WFC	City Line, Oxford	G895XPX	First Citybus	GYE280W	City Line, Oxford
G703XLY	Burghfield Mini	G775WFC	City Line, Oxford	G950TDV	Stagecoach Oxford	GYJ919V	Stagecoach South
G704TCD	Stagecoach South	G776WFC	City Line, Oxford	G951TDV	Stagecoach Oxford	GYJ920V	Stagecoach South

The latest arrivals with First Provincial are a further batch of Dennis Darts with Plaxton Pointer bodywork, to the mark 2 specification. Representing the delivery is 615, R615YCR. *Kevin Vincent*

GYJ921V	Stagecoach South	H562FLE	Cheney Coaches	H806BKK	Stagecoach South	HDZ5401	First Beeline
GYJ922V	Stagecoach South	H611CDL	Wight Bus	H807BKK	Stagecoach South	HDZ5402	First Beeline
H13BED	Oakley Coaches	H613NJB	Reading Buses	H808BKK	Stagecoach South	HDZ5403	First Beeline
H51SYG	Grand Tours	H634HBW	Pearces	H809BKK	Stagecoach South	HDZ5404	First Beeline
H109HDV	Stagecoach Oxford	H639UWR	Stagecoach Oxford	H810BKK	Stagecoach South	HDZ5405	First Beeline
H171GTA	First Provincial	H640UWE	Courtney	H815CBP	Stagecoach South	HDZ5406	First Beeline
H173GTA	First Provincial	H640UWR	Stagecoach Oxford	H816CBP	Stagecoach South	HDZ5407	First Beeline
H175GTA	First Provincial	H641UWR	Stagecoach Oxford	H817CBP	Stagecoach South	HDZ5408	First Beeline
H176GTA	First Provincial	H650UWR	Stagecoach Oxford	H818CBP	Stagecoach South	HDZ5409	First Beeline
H179GTA	First Provincial	H673KPR	Jacobs	H819CBP	Stagecoach South	HDZ5410	First Beeline
H186EJF	County Travel	H675LOX	Aldermaston Coaches	H840DDL	Wight Bus	HDZ5411	First Beeline
H189RWF	City Line, Oxford	H679BTP	Stagecoach South	H847UUA	Reading Buses	HDZ5413	First Beeline
H191RWF	City Line, Oxford	H680BTP	Stagecoach South	H848AHS	Heyfordian	HDZ5414	First Beeline
H211TCP	Brijan Tours	H687EDL	Gange's Coaches	H896JPG	Fleet Coaches	HDZ5415	First Beeline
H224TCP	Horseman	H712KPR	Marchwood	H901EDL	Seaview Services	HDZ5416	First Beeline
H225TCP	Horseman	••H728DDL	Solent Blueline	H905LVX	Jacobs	HDZ5417	First Beeline
H226TCP	Horseman	H729DDL	Solent Blueline	H975EOR	Marchwood	HDZ5418	First Beeline
H227TCP	Horseman	H731DDL	Solent Blueline	H991FTT	First Provincial	HDZ5419	First Beeline
H228TCP	Horseman	H732DDL	Solent Blueline	H997FTT	First Provincial	HDZ5420	First Beeline
H229TCP	Horseman	H733DDL	Solent Blueline	HAV1Y	Island Coach	HDZ5421	First Beeline
H261GRY	Tappins	H734DDL	Solent Blueline	HCF173W	Reading Buses	HDZ5422	First Beeline
H262GRY	Tappins	H758DTM	Altonian	HCF174W	Reading Buses	HDZ5423	First Beeline
H289DDL	Southern Vectis	H783GTA	First Provincial	HCF175W	Reading Buses	HDZ5424	First Beeline
H306DRV	First Citybus	H787GTA	First Provincial	HCF176W	Reading Buses	HDZ5425	First Beeline
H308DRV	First Citybus	H787JFC	Cheney Coaches	HCF177W	Reading Buses	HDZ5426	First Beeline
H329POG	Courtney	H788GTA	First Provincial	HCF178W	Reading Buses	HDZ5427	First Beeline
H427XGK	City Line, Oxford	H788RWJ	Chiltern Queens	HCF179W	Reading Buses	HDZ5429	First Beeline
H443JLJ	Worth's	H790GTA	Stagecoach Oxford	HCF180W	Reading Buses	HDZ5430	First Beeline
H458FLD	Aldermaston Coaches	H801BKK	Stagecoach South	HCF181W	Reading Buses	HDZ5431	First Beeline
H459FLD	Aldermaston Coaches	H802BKK	Stagecoach South	HCF182W	Reading Buses	HDZ5432	First Beeline
H463GTM	First Provincial	H803BKK	Stagecoach South	HCF183W	Reading Buses	HDZ5433	First Beeline
H48VNH	Home James	H804BKK	Stagecoach South	HDL232V	Princess Summerbee	HDZ5434	First Beeline
H523CTR	First Provincial	H805BKK	Stagecoach South	HDL255E	Gange's Coaches	HDZ5435	First Beeline

Reg	Operator	Reg	Operator	Reg	Operator	Reg	Operator
HDZ5436	First Beeline	J238KDL	Southern Vectis	J612SJB	Reading Buses	K161PPO	First Provincial
HDZ5437	First Beeline	J401LKO	Stagecoach South	J623GCR	Stagecoach South	K162PPO	First Provincial
HDZ5438	First Beeline	J402LKO	Stagecoach South	J624GCR	Stagecoach South	K163PPO	First Provincial
HDZ5439	First Beeline	J403LKO	Stagecoach South	J701YRM	Stagecoach South	K164PPO	First Provincial
HDZ5442	First Beeline	J408AWF	Home James	J702YRM	Stagecoach South	K165PPO	First Provincial
HDZ5443	First Beeline	J411AWF	Fleet Coaches	J703YRM	Stagecoach South	K170FYG	Reading Buses
HDZ5444	First Beeline	J412AWF	Fleet Coaches	J704CWT	Home James	K200OMP	Pearces
HDZ5445	First Beeline	J420HDS	Stagecoach Oxford	J720GAP	Stagecoach South	K208SFP	McLeans
HDZ5447	First Beeline	J424HDS	Stagecoach Oxford	J721GAP	Stagecoach South	K215CBD	Buddens
HDZ5448	First Beeline	J456FSR	Stagecoach Oxford	J722GAP	Stagecoach South	K216CBD	Buddens
HDZ5449	First Beeline	J461JRV	Priory of Gosport	J786KHD	Reading Buses	K235NHC	Stagecoach South
HDZ5450	First Beeline	J501GCD	Stagecoach South	J788KHD	Reading Buses	K236NHC	Stagecoach South
HDZ5451	First Beeline	J502GCD	Stagecoach South	J796HDL	Wight Bus	K237NHC	Stagecoach South
HDZ5452	First Beeline	J503GCD	Stagecoach South	J797HDL	Wight Bus	K238NHC	Stagecoach South
HDZ5453	First Beeline	J504GCD	Stagecoach South	J799KHD	Reading Buses	K238PRV	Buddens
HFG923V	Stagecoach South	J505GCD	Stagecoach South	J811NKK	Stagecoach South	K239NHC	Stagecoach South
HIL2295	Heyfordian	J506GCD	Stagecoach South	J812NKK	Stagecoach South	K240NHC	Stagecoach South
HIL3670	John Pike	J507GCD	Stagecoach South	J813NKK	Stagecoach South	K279XJB	First Beeline
HIL6649	McLeans	J508GCD	Stagecoach South	J814NKK	Stagecoach South	K281XJB	First Beeline
HIL6802	John Pike	J509GCD	Stagecoach South	J856NKK	Stagecoach South	K282XJB	First Beeline
HIL7978	Coliseum	J510GCD	Stagecoach South	J907GTC	Courtney	K283XJB	First Beeline
HJI8686	Home James	J511GCD	Stagecoach South	J909NKP	Stagecoach South	K301GDT	Tappins
HKE680L	Newnham Coaches	J512GCD	Stagecoach South	J965JNL	Reading Buses	K302GDT	Tappins
HKE690L	Stagecoach South	J513GCD	Stagecoach South	J966JNL	Reading Buses	K337ABH	Brijan Tours
HOD75	Mervyn's Coaches	J514GCD	Stagecoach South	JAX25W	Aldermaston	K373HHK	Cheney Coaches
HPK503N	Stagecoach South	J515GCD	Stagecoach South	JBP129P	First Provincial	K505RJX	Reading Buses
HPK505N	Stagecoach South	J516GCD	Stagecoach South	JBP132P	First Provincial	K540EHE	Buddens
HRO958V	White Bus	J517GCD	Stagecoach South	JBP133P	First Provincial	K544EHE	Buddens
HRY698V	Hodge's	J517LRY	Grand Tours	JBZ4909	Aldermaston Coaches	K545EHE	Buddens
HSK843	Island Coach	J518GCD	Stagecoach South	JCK849W	Stagecoach South	K553NHC	Stagecoach South
HSV336	Princess Summerbee	J519GCD	Stagecoach South	JDL724W	Gange's Coaches	K554NHC	Stagecoach South
HSV720	Heyfordian	J520GCD	Stagecoach South	JDX574V	Cheney Coaches	K556NHC	Stagecoach South
HUD493W	Travel Taylor	J521GCD	Stagecoach South	JFO256	Reading Mainline	K557NHC	Stagecoach South
HUD497W	Travel Taylor	J522GCD	Stagecoach South	JHF682	Altonian	K558NHC	Stagecoach South
HUF451X	Stagecoach South	J523GCD	Stagecoach South	JIL2029	Travel Taylor	K559NHC	Stagecoach South
HUF579X	Stagecoach South	J524GCD	Stagecoach South	JIL3713	Amport & District	K561NHC	Stagecoach South
HUF592X	Stagecoach South	J525GCD	Stagecoach South	JIL3969	Amport & District	K562NHC	Stagecoach South
HUF593X	Stagecoach South	J526GCD	Stagecoach South	JJG898P	Stagecoach South	K563NHC	Stagecoach South
HUF603X	Stagecoach South	J527GCD	Stagecoach South	JMJ633V	White Bus	K564NHC	Stagecoach South
HUF604X	Stagecoach South	J528GCD	Stagecoach South	JNJ194V	Stagecoach South	K565NHC	Stagecoach South
HUF625X	Stagecoach South	J528WTW	Altonian	JNJ718V	Stagecoach South	K566NHC	Stagecoach South
HUF626X	Stagecoach South	J529GCD	Stagecoach South	JNM747Y	White Bus	K567NHC	Stagecoach South
HUF639X	Stagecoach South	J530GCD	Stagecoach South	JUD597W	Pearces	K568NHC	Stagecoach South
HVD740N	Tourex	J531GCD	Stagecoach South	JUO983	Marchwood	K569NHC	Stagecoach South
HWJ921W	Travel Taylor	J532GCD	Stagecoach South	JWL322W	Worth's	K570NHC	Stagecoach South
HWJ926W	Travel Taylor	J533GCD	Stagecoach South	JWV127W	City Line, Oxford	K571NHC	Stagecoach South
HWJ927W	Travel Taylor	J534GCD	Stagecoach South	JWV128W	City Line, Oxford	K572NHC	Stagecoach South
IAZ4816	Hellyers	J535GCD	Stagecoach South	JWV253W	Stagecoach South	K573NHC	Stagecoach South
IIL1355	Cheney Coaches	J536GCD	Stagecoach South	JWV255W	Stagecoach South	K574NHC	Stagecoach South
IIL1832	Tappins	J537GCD	Stagecoach South	JWV269W	Stagecoach South	K575NHC	Stagecoach South
IIL3503	Stagecoach South	J538GCD	Stagecoach South	JYJ269N	Stagecoach South	K576NHC	Stagecoach South
IIL3505	Stagecoach South	J539GCD	Stagecoach South	K1HCL	Horseman	K577NHC	Stagecoach South
IIL8746	Priory of Gosport	J540GCD	Stagecoach South	K2HCL	Horseman	K578NHC	Stagecoach South
IUI5035	John Pike	J541GCD	Stagecoach South	K100OMP	Pearces	K579NHC	Stagecoach South
IUI5036	John Pike	J542GCD	Stagecoach South	K118BUD	City Line, Oxford	K580NHC	Stagecoach South
IUI5037	John Pike	J543GCD	Stagecoach South	K119BUD	City Line, Oxford	K584ODY	Stagecoach South
IUI5045	John Pike	J544GCD	Stagecoach South	K120BUD	City Line, Oxford	K585ODY	Stagecoach South
IUI6722	Worth's	J545GCD	Stagecoach South	K121BUD	City Line, Oxford	K586ODY	Stagecoach South
J35UHP	Buddens	J546GCD	Stagecoach South	K122BUD	City Line, Oxford	K587ODY	Stagecoach South
J45GCX	Marchwood	J547GCD	Stagecoach South	K123BUD	City Line, Oxford	K588ODY	Stagecoach South
J100OFC	Pearces	J548GCD	Stagecoach South	K124BUD	City Line, Oxford	K619XOD	First Provincial
J137LLK	County Travel	J549GCD	Stagecoach South	K125BUD	City Line, Oxford	K621XOD	First Provincial
J142JDL	Wight Bus	J550GCD	Stagecoach South	K126BUD	City Line, Oxford	K622XOD	First Provincial
J174PKJ	John Pike	J551GCD	Stagecoach South	K126XRU	Jacobs	K623XOD	First Provincial
J232KDL	Solent Blueline	J552GCD	Stagecoach South	K127BUD	City Line, Oxford	K633XOD	First Provincial
J233KDL	Solent Blueline	J607SJB	Reading Buses	K127XRU	Jacobs	K651DBL	First Beeline
J234KDL	Solent Blueline	J608SJB	Reading Buses	K128BUD	City Line, Oxford	K652DBL	First Beeline
J235KDL	Solent Blueline	J609SJB	Reading Buses	K129BUD	City Line, Oxford	K653DBL	First Beeline
J236KDL	Southern Vectis	J610SJB	Reading Buses	K130BUD	City Line, Oxford	K655NHC	Stagecoach South
J237KDL	Southern Vectis	J611SJB	Reading Buses	K160PPO	First Provincial	K660NHC	Stagecoach South

Reg	Operator	Reg	Operator	Reg	Operator	Reg	Operator
K665NGB	Home James	K871ODY	Stagecoach South	L4BSL	Bennetts Silverline	L314BOD	First Provincial
K701UTT	First Provincial	K872ODY	Stagecoach South	L11VWL	Pearces	L315BOD	First Provincial
K702BBL	Reading Buses	K873ODY	Stagecoach South	L89EWO	Courtney	L316BOD	First Provincial
K703BBL	Reading Buses	K874ODY	Stagecoach South	L120OWF	Priory of Gosport	L317BOD	First Provincial
K703UTT	First Provincial	K875ODY	Stagecoach South	L150HUD	City Line, Oxford	L319BOD	First Provincial
K704UTT	First Provincial	K876ODY	Stagecoach South	L151HUD	City Line, Oxford	L320BOD	First Provincial
K705UTT	First Provincial	K877ODY	Stagecoach South	L152HUD	City Line, Oxford	L322BOD	First Provincial
K706UTT	First Provincial	K878ODY	Stagecoach South	L153HUD	City Line, Oxford	L323BOD	First Provincial
K707UTT	First Provincial	K879ODY	Stagecoach South	L154HUD	City Line, Oxford	L324BOD	First Provincial
K708UTT	First Provincial	K880ODY	Stagecoach South	L155HUD	City Line, Oxford	L350MKU	Horseman
K709UTT	First Provincial	K910TKP	Stagecoach South	L155LBW	Stagecoach Oxford	L351MKU	Horseman
K710UTT	First Provincial	K911VDV	First Provincial	L156LBW	Stagecoach Oxford	L381RYC	Marchwood
K712UTT	First Provincial	K912VDV	First Provincial	L157LBW	Stagecoach Oxford	L382RYC	Marchwood
K714ASC	Stagecoach South	K914VDV	First Provincial	L158LBW	Stagecoach Oxford	L499BEL	Jacobs
K715ASC	Stagecoach South	K915VDV	First Provincial	L159LBW	Stagecoach Oxford	L509EHD	Marchwood
K715UTT	First Provincial	K916VDV	First Provincial	L166TRV	First Provincial	L510EHD	Marchwood
K716ASC	Stagecoach South	K917VDV	First Provincial	L167TRV	First Provincial	L526YDL	Solent Blueline
K716UTT	First Provincial	K918VDV	First Provincial	L168TRV	First Provincial	L527YDL	Solent Blueline
K717ASC	Stagecoach South	K919VDV	First Provincial	L169TRV	First Provincial	L528YDL	Solent Blueline
K723UTT	First Provincial	K920VDV	First Provincial	L170TRV	First Provincial	L529EHD	Reading Buses
K728UTT	First Provincial	K921VDV	First Provincial	L171TRV	First Provincial	L540XJU	Tappins
K729UTT	First Provincial	K922VDV	First Provincial	L172TRV	First Provincial	L601VCD	Stagecoach South
K735ODL	Southern Vectis	K923VDV	First Provincial	L173TRV	First Provincial	L602VCD	Stagecoach South
K736ODL	Southern Vectis	K928VDV	First Provincial	L174TRV	First Provincial	L603VCD	Stagecoach South
K737ODL	Southern Vectis	K929VDV	First Provincial	L175TRV	First Provincial	L609TDY	Stagecoach South
K738ODL	Southern Vectis	K930VDV	First Provincial	L176TRV	First Provincial	L615LJM	Reading Buses
K739ODL	Southern Vectis	K931VDV	First Provincial	L177TRV	First Provincial	L616LJM	Reading Buses
K740ODL	Southern Vectis	KAD359V	Westbrook	L178TRV	First Provincial	L616TDY	Stagecoach South
K741ODL	Southern Vectis	KAZ2755	Worth's	L188SDY	Stagecoach South	L617LJM	Reading Buses
K742ODL	Southern Vectis	KBZ7145	Tappins	L195YDU	Grayline	L617TDY	Stagecoach South
K743ODL	Southern Vectis	KDL202W	Southern Vectis	L201BPL	Horseman	L618LJM	Reading Buses
K789DAO	Stagecoach South	KDL203W	Southern Vectis	L202BPL	Horseman	L618TDY	Stagecoach South
K790DAO	Stagecoach South	KDT281P	White Bus	L203BPL	Horseman	L619LJM	Reading Buses
K791DAO	Stagecoach South	KDZ8761	Seaview Services	L205BPL	Horseman	L620LJM	Reading Buses
K801CAN	First Beeline	KIB7027	Grayline	L205GMO	First Beeline	L624TDY	Stagecoach South
K801DCF	Reading Buses	KIB8111	Coliseum	L206BPL	Horseman	L625TDY	Stagecoach South
K801WFJ	First Provincial	KIW5922	Princess Summerbee	L206GMO	First Beeline	L626TDY	Stagecoach South
K802CAN	First Beeline	KJD521P	Frimley	L207BPL	Horseman	L627TDY	Stagecoach South
K802DCF	Reading Buses	KJO504W	Travel Taylor	L207GMO	First Beeline	L628TDY	Stagecoach South
K802WFJ	First Provincial	KJO510W	Travel Taylor	L208BPL	Horseman	L629TDY	Stagecoach South
K803DCF	Reading Buses	KJU771V	Cheney Coaches	L208GMO	First Beeline	L630TDY	Stagecoach South
K804DCF	Reading Buses	KLB713	Tourex	L210BPL	Horseman	L631TDY	Stagecoach South
K805DCF	Reading Buses	KOW272Y	First Citybus	L211BPL	Horseman	L632TDY	Stagecoach South
K807EET	Priory of Gosport	KOW273Y	First Citybus	L212BPL	Horseman	L633TDY	Stagecoach South
K811EET	Fleet Coaches	KOW274Y	First Citybus	L212GJO	Stagecoach Oxford	L634TDY	Stagecoach South
K819WFJ	First Provincial	KOW275Y	First Citybus	L213BPL	Horseman	L635TDY	Stagecoach South
K821TKP	Stagecoach South	KOW276Y	First Citybus	L214BPL	Horseman	L671OHL	Fleet Coaches
K822TKP	Stagecoach South	KPA355P	Reading Buses	L215BPL	Horseman	L671RUA	Reading Buses
K823TKP	Stagecoach South	KPA369P	Stagecoach South	L227THP	Solent Blueline	L672OHL	Fleet Coaches
K824TKP	Stagecoach South	KPA374P	Stagecoach South	L241SDY	Stagecoach South	L673OHL	Fleet Coaches
K825TKP	Stagecoach South	KPA379P	Stagecoach South	L242SDY	Stagecoach South	L680MET	Priory of Gosport
K853ODY	Stagecoach South	KRE281P	Reading Buses	L243SDY	Stagecoach South	L705FRD	Reading Buses
K853YTG	John Pike	KRE283P	Reading Buses	L244SDY	Stagecoach South	L706FRD	Reading Buses
K854ODY	Stagecoach South	KRU838W	Stagecoach South	L245SDY	Stagecoach South	L707LJM	Reading Buses
K855ODY	Stagecoach South	KYN288X	Stagecoach South	L246SDY	Stagecoach South	L723JUD	Stagecoach Oxford
K856ODY	Stagecoach South	KYN305X	Stagecoach South	L247FDV	Stagecoach Oxford	L724JUD	Stagecoach Oxford
K857ODY	Stagecoach South	KYN308X	City Line, Oxford	L247SDY	Stagecoach South	L730BPR	Jacobs
K858ODY	Stagecoach South	KYN487X	Stagecoach South	L248FDV	Stagecoach Oxford	L737EPC	Buddens
K859ODY	Stagecoach South	KYV345X	Stagecoach South	L248SDY	Stagecoach South	L740YGE	Heyfordian
K860ODY	Stagecoach South	KYV348X	Stagecoach South	L249SDY	Stagecoach South	L743YGE	Heyfordian
K861ODY	Stagecoach South	KYV361X	Stagecoach South	L250SDY	Stagecoach South	L745YGE	Heyfordian
K862ODY	Stagecoach South	KYV391X	City Line, Oxford	L295CJT	Jacobs	L751FRD	Reading Buses
K863ODY	Stagecoach South	KYV397X	Stagecoach South	L309RTP	First Citybus	L752FRD	Reading Buses
K864ODY	Stagecoach South	KYV420X	Stagecoach South	L310RTP	First Citybus	L801HJO	Stagecoach Oxford
K865ODY	Stagecoach South	KYV424X	Stagecoach South	L311BOD	First Provincial	L802HJO	Stagecoach Oxford
K866ODY	Stagecoach South	KYV451X	Stagecoach South	L311RTP	First Citybus	L803HJO	Stagecoach Oxford
K867ODY	Stagecoach South	KYV474X	Stagecoach South	L312BOD	First Provincial	L804HJO	Stagecoach Oxford
K868ODY	Stagecoach South	KYV511X	Stagecoach South	L312RTP	First Citybus	L806FRD	Reading Buses
K869ODY	Stagecoach South	KYV519X	City Line, Oxford	L313BOD	First Provincial	L807FRD	Reading Buses
K870ODY	Stagecoach South	KYV523X	Stagecoach South	L313RTP	First Citybus	L808FRD	Reading Buses

Heyfordian L740YGE leads sister vehicle L743YGE round Hyde Park corner in March 1998. The Joncktheere bodywork on the pair is the Deauville 45 model that was built at Roeselare in Belgium. Jonckheere have since become part of the Berkhof-Jonkheere group with several body-building businesses in Europe. *Colin Lloyd*

L826BKK	Stagecoach South	LIL2174	Oakley Coaches	M87SRD	Travel Taylor	M192XTR	First Provincial
L827BKK	Stagecoach South	LIL9923	Brijan Tours	M93WBW	Stagecoach Oxford	M193XTR	First Provincial
L828BKK	Stagecoach South	LJI8154	Brijan Tours	M94WBW	Stagecoach Oxford	M194XTR	First Provincial
L829BKK	Stagecoach South	LMO185X	Reading Buses	M95WBW	Stagecoach Oxford	M195XTR	First Provincial
L830BKK	Stagecoach South	LMO186X	Reading Buses	M96WBW	Stagecoach Oxford	M196XTR	First Provincial
L881SDY	Stagecoach South	LMO187X	Reading Buses	M96WBW	Stagecoach Oxford	M197XTR	First Provincial
L882SDY	Stagecoach South	LMO188X	Reading Buses	M97WBW	Stagecoach Oxford	M198PCF	Aldermaston Coaches
L883SDY	Stagecoach South	LMO189X	Reading Buses	M98WBW	Stagecoach Oxford	M198XTR	First Provincial
L883STR	Home James	LMO190X	Reading Buses	M101WBW	Stagecoach Oxford	M199UYB	Priory of Gosport
L884SDY	Stagecoach South	LMO191X	Reading Buses	M103XBW	Stagecoach Oxford	M199XTR	First Provincial
L885SDY	Stagecoach South	LMO192X	Reading Buses	M104BPX	Marchwood	M201XTR	First Provincial
L886SDY	Stagecoach South	LMO193X	Reading Buses	M104XBW	Stagecoach Oxford	M202XTR	First Provincial
L887SDY	Stagecoach South	LPF603P	Reading Buses	M105CCD	Stagecoach South	M203XTR	First Provincial
L941URL	John Pike	LPF605P	Stagecoach South	M105XBW	Stagecoach Oxford	M204BPO	First Provincial
LBO6X	Bennetts Silverline	LSV670	Stagecoach Oxford	M106CCD	Stagecoach South	M205BPO	First Provincial
LDS280A	Reading Mainine	LTP634R	First Provincial	M106XBW	Stagecoach Oxford	M206BPO	First Provincial
LDZ2502	Heyfordian	LVS441V	Hellyers	M107XBW	Stagecoach Oxford	M207BPO	First Provincial
LDZ2503	Heyfordian	LVS442V	Hellyers	M108CCD	Stagecoach South	M212UYD	Priory of Gosport
LDZ3474	Seaview Services	LWU471V	First Provincial	M145KJF	Angela	M214TNO	Solent Holidays
LFJ870W	Stagecoach South	LYB941	Tourex	M149KJF	Buddens	M214UYD	Priory of Gosport
LFJ874W	Stagecoach South	M3BUD	Buddens	M179XTR	First Provincial	M220DWV	Stagecoach South
LFJ875W	Stagecoach South	M4PJT	Amport & District	M180XTR	First Provincial	M23UUA	Reading Buses
LFJ880W	Stagecoach South	M8BSL	Bennetts Silverline	M181XTR	First Provincial	M241XPO	Solent Blueline
LHG449T	Solent Blueline	M15BUD	Buddens	M182XTR	First Provincial	M242XPO	Solent Blueline
LHG450T	Solent Blueline	M59VJO	Stagecoach Oxford	M183XTR	First Provincial	M243XPO	Solent Blueline
LHG451T	Solent Blueline	M61VJO	Stagecoach Oxford	M184XTR	First Provincial	M244XPO	Solent Blueline
LHG452T	Solent Blueline	M62VJO	Stagecoach Oxford	M185XTR	First Provincial	M245BPO	Solent Blueline
LHG454T	Solent Blueline	M71BPX	Home James	M186XTR	First Provincial	M246BPO	Solent Blueline
LHG455T	Solent Blueline	M74VJO	Stagecoach Oxford	M187XTR	First Provincial	M247BPO	Solent Blueline
LHG456T	Solent Blueline	M75VJO	Stagecoach Oxford	M188XTR	First Provincial	M247TAK	IoW Tours
LHG457T	Solent Blueline	M76VJO	Stagecoach Oxford	M189XTR	First Provincial	M248BPO	Solent Blueline
LHG459T	Solent Blueline	M78VJO	Stagecoach Oxford	M190XTR	First Provincial	M249BPO	Solent Blueline
LHO420T	Gange's Coaches	M84WBW	Stagecoach Oxford	M191XTR	First Provincial	M250BPO	Solent Blueline

New Year's day, 1998, saw the Winchester bus rally and one of the attendees, Solent Blue Line 736, M736BBP, is seen passing Silver Star Atlantean. This East Lancashire body style was used by several operators for their express-specification double-deck buses. *Glyn Matthews*

M251BPO	Solent Blueline	M413DBY	Amport & District	M623PDP	Reading Buses	M682LRU	Buddens
M252BPO	Solent Blueline	M477UYA	Priory of Gosport	M627FNS	City Line, Oxford	M683LRU	Buddens
M272SBT	Reading Buses	M497XWF	Buddens	M628FNS	City Line, Oxford	M684LRU	Buddens
M300MFC	Pearces	M499XWF	Buddens	M629FNS	City Line, Oxford	M685MRP	Amport & District
M302OTF	Travel Taylor	M501VJO	City Line, Oxford	M630FNS	City Line, Oxford	M735BBP	Solent Blueline
M302VET	Buddens	M502VJO	City Line, Oxford	M636BCD	Stagecoach South	M736BBP	Solent Blueline
M305VET	Buddens	M503VJO	City Line, Oxford	M637BCD	Stagecoach South	M738KCU	Carterton
M311YSC	Stagecoach South	M504VJO	City Line, Oxford	M638BCD	Stagecoach South	M745HDL	Southern Vectis
M312YSC	Stagecoach South	M505NCG	John Pike	M639BCD	Stagecoach South	M745HDL	Southern Vectis
M313YSC	Stagecoach South	M505VJO	City Line, Oxford	M642HDV	First Provincial	M746HDL	Southern Vectis
M314YOT	First Citybus	M506VJO	City Line, Oxford	M643HDV	First Provincial	M748HDL	Southern Vectis
M315YOT	First Citybus	M507VJO	City Line, Oxford	M644HDV	First Provincial	M749HDL	Southern Vectis
M316YOT	First Citybus	M508VJO	City Line, Oxford	M645HDV	First Provincial	M750HDL	Southern Vectis
M317YOT	First Citybus	M509VJO	City Line, Oxford	M646HDV	First Provincial	M751HDL	Southern Vectis
M318YOT	First Citybus	M510VJO	City Line, Oxford	M647HDV	First Provincial	M758GDL	Southern Vectis
M319YOT	First Citybus	M511PDP	Reading Buses	M650BCD	Stagecoach South	M759GDL	Southern Vectis
M320YOT	First Citybus	M511VJO	City Line, Oxford	M651BCD	Stagecoach South	M771BHU	John Pike
M321YOT	First Citybus	M512PDP	Reading Buses	M652BCD	Stagecoach South	M791TCF	First Beeline
M322YOT	First Citybus	M512VJO	City Line, Oxford	M653SBL	Horseman	M792TCF	First Beeline
M323YOT	First Citybus	M513PDP	Reading Buses	M654SBL	Horseman	M793TCF	First Beeline
M334KRY	Amport & District	M513VJO	City Line, Oxford	M655SBL	Horseman	M794TCF	First Beeline
M404BFG	Stagecoach South	M514VJO	City Line, Oxford	M656SBL	Horseman	M79VJO	Stagecoach Oxford
M404OKM	Stagecoach South	M515VJO	City Line, Oxford	M657SBL	Horseman	M809PDP	Reading Buses
M405BFG	Stagecoach South	M516VJO	City Line, Oxford	M658SBL	Horseman	M810PDP	Reading Buses
M405OKM	Stagecoach South	M517VJO	City Line, Oxford	M659SBL	Horseman	M810PGM	First Beeline
M406BFG	Stagecoach South	M518VJO	City Line, Oxford	M662ECD	Stagecoach South	M811PDP	Reading Buses
M406OKM	Stagecoach South	M519VJO	City Line, Oxford	M663ECD	Stagecoach South	M811PGM	First Beeline
M407BFG	Stagecoach South	M520VJO	City Line, Oxford	M664ECD	Stagecoach South	M812PGM	First Beeline
M407OKM	Stagecoach South	M576JBC	Hellyers	M665ECD	Stagecoach South	M813PGM	First Beeline
M408BFG	Stagecoach South	M614NRD	Reading Buses	M667ECD	Stagecoach South	M814PGM	First Beeline
M408OKM	Stagecoach South	M615APN	Stagecoach South	M668ECD	Stagecoach South	M815PGM	First Beeline
M409BFG	Stagecoach South	M621PDP	Reading Buses	M669ECD	Stagecoach South	M816PGM	First Beeline
M410BFG	Stagecoach South	M622PDP	Reading Buses	M670ECD	Stagecoach South	M817PGM	First Beeline

Reg	Operator	Reg	Operator	Reg	Operator	Reg	Operator
M818PGM	First Beeline	N42FWU	Marchwood	N243PDL	Southern Vectis	N376LPN	Stagecoach South
M819PGM	First Beeline	N42MJO	Stagecoach Oxford	N253ECR	Solent Blueline	N377LPN	Stagecoach South
M844LFP	Marchwood	N43MJO	Stagecoach Oxford	N254ECR	Solent Blueline	N378LPN	Stagecoach South
M845LFP	Marchwood	N45MJO	Stagecoach Oxford	N255ECR	Solent Blueline	N379LPN	Stagecoach South
M846LFP	Marchwood	N46MJO	Stagecoach Oxford	N256ECR	Solent Blueline	N37FWU	Marchwood
M849ABX	Home James	N47EJO	Stagecoach Oxford	N257ECR	Solent Blueline	N380LPN	Stagecoach South
M889ECD	Stagecoach South	N47MJO	Stagecoach Oxford	N258ECR	Solent Blueline	N381LPN	Stagecoach South
M889WAK	Hellyers	N48EJO	Stagecoach Oxford	N259FOR	Solent Blueline	N382LPN	Stagecoach South
M890ECD	Stagecoach South	N48MJO	Stagecoach Oxford	N260FOR	Solent Blueline	N383EAK	McLeans
M904OVR	Hellyers	N51KBW	Stagecoach Oxford	N261FOR	Southern Vectis	N383LPN	Stagecoach South
M911WJK	Stagecoach South	N52KBW	Stagecoach Oxford	N262FOR	Southern Vectis	N384EAK	McLeans
M912WJK	Stagecoach South	N53KBW	Stagecoach Oxford	N301FOR	Marchwood	N384LPN	Stagecoach South
M913WJK	Stagecoach South	N54KBW	Stagecoach Oxford	N302FOR	Marchwood	N385LPN	Stagecoach South
M914WJK	Stagecoach South	N56KBW	Stagecoach Oxford	N303FOR	Marchwood	N386LPN	Stagecoach South
M915WJK	Stagecoach South	N57KBW	Stagecoach Oxford	N304FOR	Marchwood	N387LPN	Stagecoach South
M916WJK	Stagecoach South	N58KBW	Stagecoach Oxford	N305FOR	County Travel	N388LPN	Stagecoach South
M917WJK	Stagecoach South	N59KBW	Stagecoach Oxford	N311AMC	Stagecoach South	N389LPN	Stagecoach South
M918WJK	Stagecoach South	N62KBW	Stagecoach Oxford	N312AMC	Stagecoach South	N390LPN	Stagecoach South
M923TYG	Amport & District	N63KBW	Stagecoach Oxford	N314AMC	Stagecoach South	N391LPN	Stagecoach South
M930TYG	Reading Buses	N64KBW	Stagecoach Oxford	N315AMC	Stagecoach South	N392LPN	Stagecoach South
M957VWY	Reading Buses	N107ECR	Jacobs	N316AMC	Stagecoach South	N393LPN	Stagecoach South
M967GDU	First Citybus	N129MBW	Pearces	N321AMC	Stagecoach South	N394LPN	Stagecoach South
M968RWL	Pearces	N136MPN	Stagecoach South	N322AMC	Stagecoach South	N395LPN	Stagecoach South
M975DNJ	Wight Bus	N156BFC	City Line, Oxford	N323AMC	Stagecoach South	N396LPN	Stagecoach South
M976DNJ	Wight Bus	N157BFC	City Line, Oxford	N324AMC	Stagecoach South	N397LPN	Stagecoach South
M977DNJ	Wight Bus	N158BFC	City Line, Oxford	N324ECR	First Citybus	N398LPN	Stagecoach South
MBW612N	Tourex	N159GOT	First Citybus	N325AMC	Stagecoach South	N399LEW	Cheney Coaches
MBW645N	Tourex	N160GOT	First Citybus	N325ECR	First Citybus	N399LPN	Stagecoach South
MBZ7136	Priory of Gosport	N161GOT	First Citybus	N326AMC	Stagecoach South	N413NRG	City Line, Oxford
MCR212R	First Citybus	N162GOT	First Citybus	N326ECR	First Citybus	N414NRG	City Line, Oxford
MDL952	Southern Vectis	N163GOT	First Citybus	N327ECR	First Citybus	N415NRG	City Line, Oxford
MDL953	Southern Vectis	N164GOT	First Citybus	N328ECR	First Citybus	N416NRG	City Line, Oxford
MDL955	Southern Vectis	N165GOT	First Citybus	N329ECR	First Citybus	N444TAY	Travel Taylor
MDS855V	First Provincial	N166GOT	First Citybus	N333TAY	Travel Taylor	N451PAP	Stagecoach South
MDS856V	First Provincial	N167GOT	First Citybus	N341MPN	Stagecoach South	N452PAP	Stagecoach South
MDS857V	First Provincial	N168GOT	First Citybus	N342MPN	Stagecoach South	N453PAP	Stagecoach South
MDS863V	First Provincial	N171LHU	Tappins	N343MPN	Stagecoach South	N454PAP	Stagecoach South
MDS867V	First Provincial	N172LHU	Tappins	N344MPN	Stagecoach South	N455PAP	Stagecoach South
MFF580	Reading Mainine	N173LHU	Tappins	N345MPN	Stagecoach South	N456PAP	Stagecoach South
MFN946F	Stagecoach South	N174LHU	Tappins	N346MPN	Stagecoach South	N457PAP	Stagecoach South
MIB649	Coliseum	N175LHU	Tappins	N347MPN	Stagecoach South	N458PAP	Stagecoach South
MIB650	Coliseum	N176LHU	Tappins	N348MPN	Stagecoach South	N459PAP	Stagecoach South
MIB651	Coliseum	N177LHU	Tappins	N349MPN	Stagecoach South	N460PAP	Stagecoach South
MIB652	Coliseum	N178LHU	Tappins	N350MPN	Stagecoach South	N461PAP	Stagecoach South
MIB653	Coliseum	N179LHU	Tappins	N351MPN	Stagecoach South	N462PAP	Stagecoach South
MIL1170	Amport & District	N180LHU	Tappins	N352MPN	Stagecoach South	N463PAP	Stagecoach South
MIL3726	Carterton	N191LPN	Stagecoach South	N353MPN	Stagecoach South	N464PAP	Stagecoach South
MIL4530	Courtney	N192LPN	Stagecoach South	N354MPN	Stagecoach South	N465ETR	First Citybus
MIW5799	Solent Holidays	N193LPN	Stagecoach South	N355MPN	Stagecoach South	N465PAP	Stagecoach South
MJI1676	Grayline	N194LPN	Stagecoach South	N356MPN	Stagecoach South	N466ETR	First Citybus
MJI1677	Grayline	N195LPN	Stagecoach South	N357MPN	Stagecoach South	N466PAP	Stagecoach South
MJI1678	Grayline	N196LPN	Stagecoach South	N358MPN	Stagecoach South	N467ETR	First Citybus
MJI1679	Grayline	N197LPN	Stagecoach South	N359MPN	Stagecoach South	N467PAP	Stagecoach South
MJI2379	Angela	N198LPN	Stagecoach South	N360LPN	Stagecoach South	N501MWW	Reading Buses
MJT880P	First Provincial	N199LPN	Stagecoach South	N361LPN	Stagecoach South	N514YTF	Reading Buses
MOD571P	First Provincial	N201LPN	Stagecoach South	N362LPN	Stagecoach South	N515YTF	Reading Buses
MOW636R	First Provincial	N202LPN	Stagecoach South	N363LPN	Stagecoach South	N516YTF	Reading Buses
MOW637R	First Provincial	N203LPN	Stagecoach South	N364LPN	Stagecoach South	N517YTF	Reading Buses
MPT294P	Tourex	N204LPN	Stagecoach South	N365LPN	Stagecoach South	N518YTF	Reading Buses
MPT298P	Tourex	N211WRD	First Beeline	N366LPN	Stagecoach South	N519YTF	Reading Buses
MRD1	Reading Buses	N212WRD	First Beeline	N367LPN	Stagecoach South	N520YTF	Reading Buses
MUD25W	Chiltern Queens	N213WRD	First Beeline	N368LPN	Stagecoach South	N521MJO	City Line, Oxford
N1VWL	Pearces	N214WRD	First Beeline	N369LPN	Stagecoach South	N521TRU	John Pike
N9BSL	Bennetts Silverline	N215WRD	First Beeline	N370LPN	Stagecoach South	N522MJO	City Line, Oxford
N10BSL	Bennetts Silverline	N216WRD	First Beeline	N371LPN	Stagecoach South	N523MJO	City Line, Oxford
N36FWU	Marchwood	N217WRD	First Beeline	N372LPN	Stagecoach South	N524MJO	City Line, Oxford
N38FWU	Marchwood	N222TAY	Travel Taylor	N372VRW	Home James	N589GBW	Grand Tours
N39FWU	Marchwood	N240PDL	Southern Vectis	N373LPN	Stagecoach South	N590TAY	Jacobs
N41FWU	Marchwood	N241PDL	Southern Vectis	N374LPN	Stagecoach South	N593DOR	Marchwood
N41MJO	Stagecoach Oxford	N242PDL	Southern Vectis	N375LPN	Stagecoach South	N601EBP	First Provincial

Reg	Operator	Reg	Operator	Reg	Operator	Reg	Operator
N601FJO	City Line, Oxford	N625XJM	First Beeline	N912NAP	Stagecoach South	N974NAP	Stagecoach South
N601KGF	Stagecoach South	N626XJM	First Beeline	N913DWJ	Buddens	N975NAP	Stagecoach South
N601XJM	First Beeline	N640LPN	Stagecoach South	N913NAP	Stagecoach South	N976NAP	Stagecoach South
N602EBP	First Provincial	N641LPN	Stagecoach South	N914NAP	Stagecoach South	N977NAP	Stagecoach South
NAL52FJO	City Line, Oxford	N642LPN	Stagecoach South	N915NAP	Stagecoach South	NAL53P	Carterton
N602KGF	Stagecoach South	N643LPN	Stagecoach South	N916DWJ	Buddens	NDD113W	Carterton
N602XJM	First Beeline	N644LPN	Stagecoach South	N916NAP	Stagecoach South	NDL375G	Tourex
N603EBP	First Provincial	N645LPN	Stagecoach South	N917DWJ	Buddens	NDL490G	Southern Vectis
N603FJO	City Line, Oxford	N649KWL	Pearces	N917NAP	Stagecoach South	NDL600W	Gange's Coaches
N603KGF	Stagecoach South	N660VJB	Horseman	N918NAP	Stagecoach South	NDR155M	Reading Buses
N603XJM	First Beeline	N661VJB	Horseman	N918NAP	Stagecoach South	NDZ3015	Stagecoach Oxford
N604EBP	First Provincial	N662VJB	Horseman	N919DWJ	Buddens	NDZ3016	Stagecoach Oxford
N604FJO	City Line, Oxford	N663VJB	Horseman	N919NAP	Stagecoach South	NDZ3146	Stagecoach Oxford
N604KGF	Stagecoach South	N664VJB	Horseman	N920DWJ	Buddens	NDZ3147	Stagecoach Oxford
N604XJM	First Beeline	N665VJB	Horseman	N920NAP	Stagecoach South	NDZ3148	Stagecoach Oxford
N605EBP	First Provincial	N669VJB	Horseman	N921DWJ	Buddens	NDZ3149	Stagecoach Oxford
N605FJO	City Line, Oxford	N670VJB	Horseman	N921NAP	Stagecoach South	NDZ3150	Stagecoach Oxford
N605KGF	Stagecoach South	N671VJB	Horseman	N922NAP	Stagecoach South	NFN88R	Stagecoach South
N605XJM	First Beeline	N672VJB	Horseman	N923NAP	Stagecoach South	NFX667	Stagecoach South
N606EBP	First Provincial	N673VJB	Horseman	N924NAP	Stagecoach South	NIB7625	County Travel
N606FJO	City Line, Oxford	N681AHL	Grayline	N925NAP	Stagecoach South	NIJ2636	Frimley
N606KGF	Stagecoach South	N687AHL	IoW Tours	N926NAP	Stagecoach South	NIL4580	Heyfordian
N606XJM	First Beeline	N688AHL	IoW Tours	N927NAP	Stagecoach South	NIL7247	Frimley
N607EBP	First Provincial	N698AHL	Solent Holidays	N928NAP	Stagecoach South	NIL7249	Frimley
N607FJO	City Line, Oxford	N709CYC	Priory of Gosport	N929NAP	Stagecoach South	NIL7251	Frimley
N607KGF	Stagecoach South	N710GRV	First Provincial	N930NAP	Stagecoach South	NIL7252	Frimley
N607XJM	First Beeline	N711GRV	First Provincial	N931NAP	Stagecoach South	NIL7253	Frimley
N608FJO	City Line, Oxford	N712GRV	First Provincial	N932NAP	Stagecoach South	NIL8237	Bennetts Silverline
N608XJM	First Beeline	N713GRV	First Provincial	N933NAP	Stagecoach South	NIW6503	Solent Holidays
N609FJO	City Line, Oxford	N714GRV	First Provincial	N934NAP	Stagecoach South	NIW6518	Cheney Coaches
N609KGF	Stagecoach Oxford	N715GRV	First Provincial	N935NAP	Stagecoach South	NOB323M	Newnham Coaches
N609XJM	First Beeline	N716GRV	First Provincial	N936NAP	Stagecoach South	NPJ483R	Reading Buses
N610FJO	City Line, Oxford	N717GRV	First Provincial	N937NAP	Stagecoach South	NRH803A	Reading Mainine
N610KGF	Stagecoach South	N718GRV	First Provincial	N938NAP	Stagecoach South	NRU308M	Grayline
N610XJM	First Beeline	N719GRV	First Provincial	N939NAP	Stagecoach South	NSU513	Home James
N611FJO	City Line, Oxford	N720GRV	First Provincial	N940NAP	Stagecoach South	NTC573R	First Provincial
N611LGC	Stagecoach Oxford	N721GRV	First Provincial	N941NAP	Stagecoach South	NTT575W	Priory of Gosport
N611XJM	First Beeline	N795WAN	First Beeline	N942NAP	Stagecoach South	NUW594Y	Stagecoach South
N612FJO	City Line, Oxford	N796WAN	First Beeline	N943NAP	Stagecoach South	NUW596Y	Stagecoach South
N612LGC	Stagecoach Oxford	N797WAN	First Beeline	N944NAP	Stagecoach South	NUW611Y	Stagecoach South
N612XJM	First Beeline	N798WAN	First Beeline	N945NAP	Stagecoach South	NUW645Y	Stagecoach South
N613FJO	City Line, Oxford	N808NHS	Heyfordian	N946NAP	Stagecoach South	NUW647Y	Stagecoach South
N613LGC	Stagecoach Oxford	N809NHS	Heyfordian	N947NAP	Stagecoach South	NUW661Y	City Line, Oxford
N613XJM	First Beeline	N810PDL	Southern Vectis	N948NAP	Stagecoach South	NUW663Y	Stagecoach South
N614FJO	City Line, Oxford	N811PDL	Southern Vectis	N949NAP	Stagecoach South	NUW670Y	Stagecoach South
N614LGC	Stagecoach Oxford	N812PDL	Southern Vectis	N950NAP	Stagecoach South	NUW671Y	Stagecoach South
N614XJM	First Beeline	N812XJH	Reading Buses	N951NAP	Stagecoach South	NUW672Y	Stagecoach South
N615DWY	First Citybus	N813PDL	Southern Vectis	N952NAP	Stagecoach South	NWT639P	Charlton Services
N615FJO	City Line, Oxford	N813XJH	Reading Buses	N953NAP	Stagecoach South	OAP16W	Home James
N615XJM	First Beeline	N814PDL	Southern Vectis	N954NAP	Stagecoach South	OBN502R	Carterton
N616FJO	City Line, Oxford	N815PDL	Southern Vectis	N955NAP	Stagecoach South	ODL438M	Gange's Coaches
N616XJM	First Beeline	N855DKU	Luckett	N956DWJ	Hellyers	ODL678	Seaview Services
N617FJO	City Line, Oxford	N901ABL	Fleet Coaches	N956NAP	Stagecoach South	OGL849	Cheney Coaches
N617XJM	First Beeline	N901PFC	Stagecoach Oxford	N957NAP	Stagecoach South	OHV688Y	Stagecoach South
N618FJO	City Line, Oxford	N902ABL	Fleet Coaches	N958NAP	Stagecoach South	OHV697Y	Stagecoach South
N618XJM	First Beeline	N902PFC	Stagecoach Oxford	N959NAP	Stagecoach South	OHV711Y	City Line, Oxford
N619FJO	City Line, Oxford	N903ABL	Fleet Coaches	N960NAP	Stagecoach South	OHV724Y	Stagecoach South
N619XJM	First Beeline	N903PFC	Stagecoach Oxford	N961NAP	Stagecoach South	OHV731Y	Stagecoach South
N61KBW	Stagecoach Oxford	N905NAP	Stagecoach South	N962NAP	Stagecoach South	OHV743Y	Stagecoach South
N620FJO	City Line, Oxford	N906NAP	Stagecoach South	N963NAP	Stagecoach South	OHV744Y	Stagecoach South
N620XJM	First Beeline	N907NAP	Stagecoach South	N964NAP	Stagecoach South	OHV759Y	Stagecoach South
N621FJO	City Line, Oxford	N908DWJ	Buddens	N965NAP	Stagecoach South	OHV761Y	Stagecoach South
N621XJM	First Beeline	N908NAP	Stagecoach South	N966NAP	Stagecoach South	OHV769Y	Stagecoach South
N622FJO	City Line, Oxford	N909DWJ	Buddens	N967NAP	Stagecoach South	OHV784Y	Stagecoach South
N622XJM	First Beeline	N909NAP	Stagecoach South	N968NAP	Stagecoach South	OIW5198	Oakley Coaches
N623FJO	City Line, Oxford	N910DWJ	Buddens	N969NAP	Stagecoach South	OIW5798	Solent Holidays
N623XJM	First Beeline	N910NAP	Stagecoach South	N970NAP	Stagecoach South	OJD401R	Worth's
N624ATF	Reading Buses	N911DWJ	Buddens	N971NAP	Stagecoach South	OJD877R	Frimley
N624FJO	City Line, Oxford	N911NAP	Stagecoach South	N972NAP	Stagecoach South	OJI3907	Charlton Services
N624XJM	First Beeline	N912DWJ	Buddens	N973NAP	Stagecoach South	OJO835M	Chiltern Queens

Registration	Operator
OKE141P	Priory of Gosport
OPE613W	Oakley Coaches
OSF939M	Tappins
OSK774	Buddens
OUF262W	Stagecoach South
OUF863W	Stagecoach South
OXI9100	Charlton Services
P7WMS	Worth's
P11BSL	Bennetts Silverline
P12BSL	Bennetts Silverline
P13BSL	Bennetts Silverline
P18CCL	Courtney
P31KWA	Hellyers
P36KWA	Burghfield Mini
P37KWA	Burghfield Mini
P76MOR	Easson's
P77EAS	Easson's
P77ECL	Easson's
P81VDL	Wight Bus
P82VDL	Wight Bus
P83VDL	Wight Bus
P97GHE	IoW Tours
P102GHE	Hellyers
P120GHE	Luckett
P122GHE	Buddens
P124GHE	Buddens
P124RWR	Marchwood
P124TDL	Wight Bus
P125GHE	Buddens
P125RWR	Marchwood
P125TDL	Wight Bus
P126GHE	Buddens
P126RWR	Marchwood
P130GHE	Luckett
P137TDL	Wight Bus
P138TDL	Wight Bus
P139TDL	Wight Bus
P140GHE	Luckett
P140TDL	Wight Bus
P141TDL	Wight Bus
P142TDL	Wight Bus
P159FJO	Grayline
P167ANR	Horseman
P168ANR	Horseman
P190PBP	Marchwood
P191PBP	Marchwood
P193KJM	Buddens
P194KJM	Buddens
P224PTP	Brijan Tours
P231TDL	Wight Bus
P237NLW	First Beeline
P238NLW	First Beeline
P239NLW	First Beeline
P242KJM	Buddens
P244VDL	Southern Vectis
P245VDL	Southern Vectis
P246VDL	Southern Vectis
P247VDL	Southern Vectis
P250AUT	Amport & District
P260WPN	Stagecoach South
P261WPN	Stagecoach South
P262WPN	Stagecoach South
P263WPN	Stagecoach South
P264VPN	Stagecoach South
P265VPN	Stagecoach South
P266VPN	Stagecoach South
P267VPN	Stagecoach South
P268VPN	Stagecoach South
P269VPN	Stagecoach South
P276VPN	Stagecoach South
P277VPN	Stagecoach South
P278VPN	Stagecoach South
P279VPN	Stagecoach South
P281VPN	Stagecoach South
P282VPN	Stagecoach South
P283VPN	Stagecoach South
P284VPN	Stagecoach South
P285VPN	Stagecoach South
P286LOW	Jacobs
P286VPN	Stagecoach South
P287VPN	Stagecoach South
P288VPN	Stagecoach South
P289VPN	Stagecoach South
P290VPN	Stagecoach South
P291KPX	First Citybus
P291LOW	Jacobs
P292KPX	First Citybus
P293KPX	First Citybus
P294KPX	First Citybus
P295KPX	First Citybus
P296KPX	First Citybus
P321JND	Stagecoach Oxford
P322JND	Stagecoach Oxford
P323JND	Stagecoach Oxford
P324JND	Stagecoach Oxford
P325JND	Stagecoach Oxford
P326JND	Stagecoach Oxford
P327JND	Stagecoach Oxford
P328JND	Stagecoach Oxford
P330JND	Stagecoach Oxford
P331JND	Stagecoach Oxford
P332JND	Stagecoach Oxford
P334JND	Stagecoach Oxford
P336CDF	Horseman
P382ARY	Jacobs
P385ARY	Home James
P404KOW	First Citybus
P405KOW	First Citybus
P406KOW	First Citybus
P407KOW	First Citybus
P407MLA	First Beeline
P414HRB	Tappins
P415HRB	Tappins
P483GTF	Luckett
P492LLU	Horseman
P493LLU	Horseman
P494LLU	Horseman
P525YJO	City Line, Oxford
P526YJO	City Line, Oxford
P527YJO	City Line, Oxford
P616LTP	County Travel
P625PGP	Stagecoach Oxford
P626PGP	Stagecoach Oxford
P627CGM	First Beeline
P627PGP	Stagecoach Oxford
P628CGM	First Beeline
P628PGP	Stagecoach Oxford
P629CGM	First Beeline
P629FFC	City Line, Oxford
P629PGP	Stagecoach Oxford
P630CGM	First Beeline
P630PGP	Stagecoach Oxford
P631CGM	First Beeline
P631FFC	City Line, Oxford
P632CGM	First Beeline
P632FFC	City Line, Oxford
P633FFC	City Line, Oxford
P634FFC	City Line, Oxford
P635FFC	City Line, Oxford
P636FFC	City Line, Oxford
P637FFC	City Line, Oxford
P638FFC	City Line, Oxford
P639FFC	City Line, Oxford
P640FFC	City Line, Oxford
P641FFC	City Line, Oxford
P642FFC	City Line, Oxford
P643FFC	City Line, Oxford
P668GJB	Luckett
P677CUD	Pearces
P677NOJ	Stagecoach Oxford
P722KCR	First Provincial
P723KCR	First Provincial
P724KCR	First Provincial
P725KCR	First Provincial
P726KCR	First Provincial
P727KCR	First Provincial
P728KCR	First Provincial
P729KCR	First Provincial
P774BJF	McLeans
P775BJF	McLeans
P776BJF	McLeans
P778BJF	McLeans
P781BJF	Hellyers
P866ADO	Brijan Tours
P881MTR	Luckett
P901EGM	Reading Buses
P902EGM	Reading Buses
P903EGM	Reading Buses
P904EGM	Reading Buses
P905EGM	Reading Buses
P906EGM	Reading Buses
P907EGM	Reading Buses
P908EGM	Reading Buses
P909EGM	Reading Buses
P910EGM	Reading Buses
P911GJM	Reading Buses
P912GJM	Reading Buses
P913GJM	Reading Buses
P914GJM	Reading Buses
P915GJM	Reading Buses
P921SJH	Reading Buses
P922SJH	Reading Buses
P923SJH	Reading Buses
P924SJH	Reading Buses
P933KYC	Priory of Gosport
P953DNR	Hellyers
P977HWF	Buddens
P988HWF	Buddens
P989HWF	Buddens
P991RNW	Cheney Coaches
P992RNW	Cheney Coaches
PAZ3270	Jacobs
PBP224S	First Citybus
PBP225S	First Citybus
PBP228S	First Citybus
PBP229S	First Citybus
PBP230S	First Citybus
PBP231S	First Citybus
PCD73R	Stagecoach South
PCD79R	Stagecoach South
PCD80R	Stagecoach South
PCG920M	First Provincial
PCR305M	Newnham Coaches
PDL230	Seaview Services
PDL298	Seaview Services
PDN873	Cheney Coaches
PEX620W	Stagecoach South
PEX621W	Stagecoach South
PFN873	Stagecoach South
PIL2249	John Pike
PIW5455	Bennetts Silverline
PJH582X	Chiltern Queens
PJI6394	Princess Summerbee
PJJ344S	Stagecoach South
PJT262R	County Travel
PJT271R	County Travel
PMT199X	Stagecoach South
PPJ65W	Chiltern Queens
PRE36W	Frimley
PSU951	Priory of Gosport
PTR238S	First Provincial
PVS828	Reading Mainine
PVV316	Heyfordian
PWL999W	City Line, Oxford
R1OXF	City Line, Oxford
R2HLC	Luckett
R2OXF	City Line, Oxford
R3OXF	City Line, Oxford
R4HLC	Luckett
R4OXF	City Line, Oxford
R5BSL	Bennetts Silverline
R5HLC	Luckett
R5OXF	City Line, Oxford
R6HLC	Luckett
R6OXF	City Line, Oxford
R7OXF	City Line, Oxford
R8OXF	City Line, Oxford
R8WMS	Worth's
R9BJT	Brijan Tours
R9OXF	City Line, Oxford
R10HLC	Luckett
R10OXF	City Line, Oxford
R11OXF	City Line, Oxford
R12OXF	City Line, Oxford
R46FFC	City Line, Oxford
R63GNW	Marchwood
R63UFC	Stagecoach Oxford
R64GNW	Marchwood
R64UFC	Stagecoach Oxford
R65GNW	Marchwood
R65UFC	Stagecoach Oxford
R111TAY	Travel Taylor
R146COR	Hellyers
R163GNW	County Travel
R164GNW	County Travel
R176TKU	Burghfield Mini
R180BDT	Altonian
R192LBC	McLeans
R193LBC	McLeans
R204STF	Horseman
R204WYD	Priory of Gosport
R219AOR	Home James
R291HCD	Stagecoach South
R292HCD	Stagecoach South
R293HCD	Stagecoach South
R294HCD	Stagecoach South
R295HCD	Stagecoach South
R296HCD	Stagecoach South
R297HCD	Stagecoach South
R298HCD	Stagecoach South
R299HCD	Stagecoach South
R301BDL	Wight Bus
R301HCD	Stagecoach South
R302BDL	Wight Bus
R303BDL	Wight Bus
R304BDL	Wight Bus
R329VJO	Pearces
R401FFC	City Line, Oxford
R402FFC	City Line, Oxford

Reg	Operator	Reg	Operator	Reg	Operator	Reg	Operator
R403FFC	City Line, Oxford	R621YCR	First Provincial	R796WOY	Horseman	RHT503S	First Provincial
R404FFC	City Line, Oxford	R622YCR	First Provincial	R797WOY	Horseman	RHT504S	First Provincial
R405FFC	City Line, Oxford	R623YCR	First Provincial	R801YUD	Stagecoach Oxford	RIA1445	Solent Holidays
R407FFC	City Line, Oxford	R627SJM	Reading Buses	R802YUD	Stagecoach Oxford	RIB4313	Altonian
R408FFC	City Line, Oxford	R628SJM	Reading Buses	R803YUD	Stagecoach Oxford	RIB5124	Cheney Coaches
R408WPX	First Citybus	R629SJM	Reading Buses	R804YUD	Stagecoach Oxford	RIB6581	Angela
R409FFC	City Line, Oxford	R633VLX	First Beeline	R805YUD	Stagecoach Oxford	RIB6582	Angela
R409WPX	First Citybus	R634VLX	First Beeline	R807YUD	Stagecoach Oxford	RIW8799	Solent Holidays
R410FFC	City Line, Oxford	R636VLX	First Beeline	R808YUD	Stagecoach Oxford	RJI1647	Priory of Gosport
R410WPX	First Citybus	R636VYB	Priory of Gosport	R809YUD	Stagecoach Oxford	RJI6612	Carterton
R411WPX	First Citybus	R637VLX	First Beeline	R810YUD	Stagecoach Oxford	RJI6617	Altonian
R412WPX	First Citybus	R638VLX	First Beeline	R811YUD	Stagecoach Oxford	RJI8610	Priory of Gosport
R413WPX	First Citybus	R639VLX	First Beeline	R812HCD	Stagecoach South	RJI8726	Priory of Gosport
R414WPX	First Citybus	R640VLX	First Beeline	R812YUD	Stagecoach Oxford	RJI8919	Travel Taylor
R414XFC	Stagecoach Oxford	R641VLX	First Beeline	R813HCD	Stagecoach South	RJI8920	Travel Taylor
R415WPX	First Citybus	R642TLM	First Beeline	R813YUD	Stagecoach Oxford	RJI8921	Travel Taylor
R415XFC	Stagecoach Oxford	R643TLM	First Beeline	R814HCD	Stagecoach South	RJI8922	Travel Taylor
R416WPX	First Citybus	R644TLM	First Beeline	R814YUD	Stagecoach Oxford	RJI8923	Travel Taylor
R416XFC	Stagecoach Oxford	R645TLM	First Beeline	R815HCD	Stagecoach South	RJT146R	Stagecoach South
R417WPX	First Citybus	R646HCD	Stagecoach South	R815YUD	Stagecoach Oxford	RJT147R	First Provincial
R417XFC	Stagecoach Oxford	R646TLM	First Beeline	R816HCD	Stagecoach South	RJT148R	First Provincial
R418WPX	First Citybus	R647HCD	Stagecoach South	R816YUD	Stagecoach Oxford	RLW778R	White Bus
R418XFC	Stagecoach Oxford	R647TLM	First Beeline	R817HCD	Stagecoach South	RMO71Y	Reading Buses
R419WPX	First Citybus	R648HCD	Stagecoach South	R817YUD	Stagecoach Oxford	RMO72Y	Reading Buses
R419XFC	Stagecoach Oxford	R648TLM	First Beeline	R818HCD	Stagecoach South	RMO73Y	Reading Buses
R420WPX	First Citybus	R649HCD	Stagecoach South	R818YUD	Stagecoach Oxford	RMO74Y	Reading Buses
R420XFC	Stagecoach Oxford	R649TLM	First Beeline	R819HCD	Stagecoach South	RMO75Y	Reading Buses
R421WPX	First Citybus	R650TLM	First Beeline	R819YUD	Stagecoach Oxford	RMO76Y	Reading Buses
R421XFC	Stagecoach Oxford	H651TLM	First Beeline	R820HCD	Stagecoach South	RMO77Y	Reading Buses
R422WPX	First Citybus	R652TLM	First Beeline	R821HCD	Stagecoach South	RMO78Y	Reading Buses
R422XFC	Stagecoach Oxford	R653HCD	Stagecoach South	R821YUD	Stagecoach Oxford	RMO79Y	Reading Buses
R423WPX	First Citybus	R653TLM	First Beeline	R822HCD	Stagecoach South	RUF37R	First Provincial
R423XFC	Stagecoach Oxford	R654HCD	Stagecoach South	R822YUD	Stagecoach Oxford	RUF970M	Stagecoach South
R424WPX	First Citybus	R674HCD	Stagecoach South	R823HCD	Stagecoach South	S6WMS	Worth's
R424XFC	Stagecoach Oxford	R675HCD	Stagecoach South	R823YUD	Stagecoach Oxford	S371DFC	Stagecoach Oxford
R425WPX	First Citybus	R676HCD	Stagecoach South	R824HCD	Stagecoach South	S372DFC	Stagecoach Oxford
R425XFC	Stagecoach Oxford	R677HCD	Stagecoach South	R824YUD	Stagecoach Oxford	S373DFC	Stagecoach Oxford
R426WPX	First Citybus	R678HCD	Stagecoach South	R825YUD	Stagecoach Oxford	S374DFC	Stagecoach Oxford
R426XFC	Stagecoach Oxford	R679HCD	Stagecoach South	R826YUD	Stagecoach Oxford	S375DFC	Stagecoach Oxford
R427WPX	First Citybus	R680HCD	Stagecoach South	R827YUD	Stagecoach Oxford	S376DFC	Stagecoach Oxford
R466GUA	Reading Buses	R701DNJ	Stagecoach South	R828YUD	Stagecoach Oxford	S377DFC	Stagecoach Oxford
R524EUD	Grayline	R702DNJ	Stagecoach South	R829YUD	Stagecoach Oxford	S377SET	Hellyers
R551UOT	Marchwood	R703DNJ	Stagecoach South	R835VLX	First Beeline	S378DFC	Stagecoach Oxford
R552UOT	Marchwood	R704DNJ	Stagecoach South	R867SDT	Hellyers	S379DFC	Stagecoach Oxford
R553UOT	Marchwood	R705DNJ	Stagecoach South	R868SDT	Hellyers	S380DFC	Stagecoach Oxford
R554UOT	Marchwood	R706DNJ	Stagecoach South	R902GGO	Pearces	S381DFC	Stagecoach Oxford
R556UOT	Marchwood	R706YUD	Stagecoach Oxford	R904XFC	Stagecoach Oxford	S382DFC	Stagecoach Oxford
R557UOT	Marchwood	R707DNJ	Stagecoach South	R905XFC	Stagecoach Oxford	S383DFC	Stagecoach Oxford
R558UOT	Marchwood	R708DNJ	Stagecoach South	R906XFC	Stagecoach Oxford	S431SLF	Horseman
R559UOT	Marchwood	R709DNJ	Stagecoach South	R907XFC	Stagecoach Oxford	S432SLF	Horseman
R560UOT	Marchwood	R710DNJ	Stagecoach South	R908XFC	Stagecoach Oxford	S433SLF	Horseman
R561UOT	Marchwood	R710NMO	Burghfield Mini	R909XFC	Stagecoach Oxford	S434SLF	Horseman
R562UOT	Marchwood	R711DNJ	Stagecoach South	R910XFC	Stagecoach Oxford	S435SLF	Horseman
R563UOT	Marchwood	R711NMO	Burghfield Mini	R911XFC	Stagecoach Oxford	S913CFC	Stagecoach Oxford
R564UOT	Marchwood	R720YUD	Stagecoach Oxford	R912XFC	Stagecoach Oxford	S914CFC	Stagecoach Oxford
R565UOT	Marchwood	R737XRV	Solent Blueline	R916SJM	Reading Buses	S915CFC	Stagecoach Oxford
R608YCR	First Provincial	R738XRV	Solent Blueline	R917SJH	Reading Buses	S916CFC	Stagecoach Oxford
R609YCR	First Provincial	R739XRV	Solent Blueline	R918SJH	Reading Buses	S917CFC	Stagecoach Oxford
R610YCR	First Provincial	R741XRV	Solent Blueline	R919SJH	Reading Buses	S918CFC	Stagecoach Oxford
R611YCR	First Provincial	R752GDL	Southern Vectis	R920SJH	Reading Buses	S919CFC	Stagecoach Oxford
R612YCR	First Provincial	R753GDL	Southern Vectis	RDL686X	Southern Vectis	S920CFC	Stagecoach Oxford
R613YCR	First Provincial	R754GDL	Southern Vectis	RDL687X	Southern Vectis	S921CFC	Stagecoach Oxford
R614YCR	First Provincial	R755GDL	Southern Vectis	RDL688X	Southern Vectis	S922CFC	Stagecoach Oxford
R615YCR	First Provincial	R756GDL	Southern Vectis	RDL689X	Southern Vectis	S923CFC	Stagecoach Oxford
R616YCR	First Provincial	R757GDL	Southern Vectis	RDL690X	Southern Vectis	S924CFC	Stagecoach Oxford
R617YCR	First Provincial	R791WOY	Horseman	RDL691X	Southern Vectis	S925CFC	Stagecoach Oxford
R618YCR	First Provincial	R792WOY	Horseman	RFC10T	Chiltern Queens	S926CFC	Stagecoach Oxford
R619YCR	First Provincial	R793WOY	Horseman	RFC12T	Chiltern Queens	S927CFC	Stagecoach Oxford
R620YCR	First Provincial	R794WOY	Horseman	RFC443W	Cheney Coaches	S928CFC	Stagecoach Oxford
R621VNN	Grayline	R795WOY	Horseman	RFM894M	Newnham Coaches	S929CFC	Stagecoach Oxford

Duple-bodied Dennis Javelin G283BEL from the Hellyers fleet is seen on an excursion passing through london's Parliament Square. The vehicle index shows four vehicles from this index sequence are used by operators featured in the book. As with other parts of the country, the reduced number of 'H'-reg PCVs is notable. *Colin Lloyd*

Reg	Operator	Reg	Operator	Reg	Operator	Reg	Operator
S930CFC	Stagecoach Oxford	SJI8118	Buddens	TAZ5002	Cheney Coaches	TJI8784	Southern Vectis
S931CFC	Stagecoach Oxford	SJI8120	Buddens	TDL563K	Southern Vectis	TJI8788	Travel Taylor
S932CFC	Stagecoach Oxford	SJI8122	Buddens	TDL564K	Traditional	TOK65	Easson's
S933CFC	Stagecoach Oxford	SJI8123	Buddens	TDL856	Seaview Services	TPX41T	First Provincial
S934CFC	Stagecoach Oxford	SJI8124	Buddens	TEL490R	Stagecoach South	TRN160V	Solent Blueline
S935CFC	Stagecoach Oxford	SJI8125	Buddens	TIB4901	Angela	TRN161V	Solent Blueline
S936CFC	Stagecoach Oxford	SJI8127	Buddens	TIB8562	Princess Summerbee	TRN162V	Solent Blueline
S937CFC	Stagecoach Oxford	SJI8128	Buddens	TJI4820	First Beeline	TRN163V	Solent Blueline
S938CFC	Stagecoach Oxford	SJI8129	Buddens	TJI4822	First Beeline	TRN164V	Solent Blueline
S939CFC	Stagecoach Oxford	SJI8131	Luckett	TJI4823	First Beeline	TRN165V	Solent Blueline
S940CFC	Stagecoach Oxford	SJI8132	Luckett	TJI4826	First Beeline	TSU648	Luckett
S941CFC	Stagecoach Oxford	SKG406Y	Worth's	TJI4828	First Beeline	TSV804	Chiltern Queens
SAZ4959	Princess Summerbee	SKL680X	Stagecoach South	TJI4829	First Beeline	TVH135X	Horseman
SBK740S	First Provincial	SKL681X	Stagecoach South	TJI4830	First Beeline	TXI8764	Courtney
SBL70Y	Reading Buses	SKL682X	Stagecoach South	TJI4831	First Beeline	UCT838	Jacobs
SBZ1621	Brijan Tours	SKL683X	Stagecoach South	TJI4832	First Beeline	UCW162X	Island Coach
SDL638J	Southern Vectis	SKL685X	Stagecoach South	TJI4833	First Beeline	UDZ7334	County Travel
SDL638J	Westbrook	SMY621X	Priory of Gosport	TJI4834	First Beeline	UF4813	Stagecoach South
SFJ101R	First Provincial	SNK255N	White Bus	TJI4835	First Beeline	UFG48S	Stagecoach South
SIB3054	Bennetts Silverline	SNS827W	First Provincial	TJI4836	First Beeline	UFX505S	Southern Vectis
SIB3272	Marchwood	SPR39R	First Provincial	TJI4838	First Beeline	UFX506S	Southern Vectis
SIB3273	Marchwood	SPR40R	First Provincial	TJI4926	Hellyers	UFX630X	Marchwood
SIB8243	Stagecoach South	SPR41R	First Provincial	TJI4927	Hellyers	UFX847S	First Provincial
SIB8342	Courtney	SPV860	Grayline	TJI4929	Hellyers	UFX848S	First Provincial
SIW1934	Solent Holidays	ST158W	First Provincial	TJI6278	Charlton Services	UFX856S	Traditional
SJI1960	Bennetts Silverline	STL725J	White Bus	TJI6301	Bennetts Silverline	UFX858S	Westbrook
SJI2764	Cheney Coaches	SVK627G	Stagecoach Oxford	TJI6302	Bennetts Silverline	UJI1759	City Line, Oxford
SJI4428	Heyfordian	SVL171W	Travel Taylor	TJI6303	Heyfordian	UJI1760	City Line, Oxford
SJI4431	Home James	SWX534W	First Provincial	TJI6304	Heyfordian	UJI1761	City Line, Oxford
SJI5861	Heyfordian	SYC852	Stagecoach South	TJI6305	Heyfordian	UJI1762	City Line, Oxford
SJI7473	Burghfield Mini	TAZ4988	Cheney Coaches	TJI6307	Bennetts Silverline	UJI1763	City Line, Oxford
SJI8099	Travel Taylor	TAZ4990	Cheney Coaches	TJI6308	Bennetts Silverline	UJI2184	Burghfield Mini
SJI8115	Buddens	TAZ4999	Cheney Coaches	TJI7513	Hellyers	UJI2436	Charlton Services
SJI8116	Buddens	TAZ5001	Cheney Coaches	TJI7520	Southern Vectis	UJI6316	Burghfield Mini

Reg	Operator	Reg	Operator	Reg	Operator	Reg	Operator
UJI6317	Burghfield Mini	VPF742	Cheney Coaches	WWL208X	City Line, Oxford	YCD74T	Stagecoach South
UPO232T	First Citybus	VPP958S	Charlton Services	WWL209X	City Line, Oxford	YCD76T	Stagecoach South
UPO233T	First Citybus	VSF438	Heyfordian	WWL210X	City Line, Oxford	YCD77T	Stagecoach South
UPO234T	First Citybus	VTK254	Jacobs	WWL211X	City Line, Oxford	YCD82T	Stagecoach South
UPO235T	First Citybus	VTW600	Angela	WWL212X	City Line, Oxford	YDL671T	Newnham Coaches
UPO236T	First Citybus	VUD33X	City Line, Oxford	WWM930W	Charlton Services	YDL672T	Brijan Tours
UPO237T	First Citybus	VWL766V	Tourex	WXI6274	Charlton Services	YDL674T	Newnham Coaches
UPO238T	First Citybus	WAS766V	First Provincial	WXI6291	Seaview Services	YDL675T	Brijan Tours
UPO239T	First Citybus	WBW736X	Bennetts Silverline	WYJ169S	Stagecoach South	YDL676T	Solent Blueline
UPO240T	First Citybus	WCA941W	Cheney Coaches	WYJ857	Reading Mainine	YFC18V	Chiltern Queens
UPO241T	First Citybus	WCA942W	Cheney Coaches	XCT550	Heyfordian	YFS306W	First Provincial
UPO242T	First Citybus	WCR474	Coliseum	XDL696	Seaview Services	YHR702	Jacobs
UPO243T	First Citybus	WCR833	Coliseum	XIA586	Stagecoach South	YIB9072	Altonian
UPO244T	First Citybus	WDL142	Southern Vectis	XIA857	Stagecoach South	YIB9073	Altonian
UPO245T	First Citybus	WDL692Y	Southern Vectis	XJJ650V	Stagecoach South	YIB9078	Altonian
UPO246T	First Citybus	WDL693Y	Southern Vectis	XJJ651V	Stagecoach South	YIB9079	Altonian
UPO443T	First Provincial	WDL694Y	Solent Blueline	XJJ652V	Stagecoach South	YJB68T	Reading Buses
UPO444T	First Provincial	WDL695Y	Southern Vectis	XJJ653V	Stagecoach South	YJB69T	Reading Buses
URH13R	Cheney Coaches	WDL696Y	Southern Vectis	XJJ654V	Stagecoach South	YJN166	Tourex
URT682	Cheney Coaches	WDL748	Southern Vectis	XJJ655V	Stagecoach South	YLC896S	Fleet Coaches
UTO836S	First Provincial	WFM823L	Frimley	XJJ657V	Stagecoach South	YLJ332	Stagecoach South
UVX2S	First Provincial	WFX257S	First Provincial	XJJ658V	Stagecoach South	YNN33Y	Island Coach
UVY412	Brijan Tours	WIB3420	Brijan Tours	XJJ659V	Stagecoach South	YPB834T	Grayline
UWV621S	Stagecoach South	WJI1727	Angela	XJJ660V	Stagecoach South	YPJ501Y	John Pike
UWV623S	Stagecoach South	WJM829T	Stagecoach South	XJJ661V	Stagecoach South	YRN816V	Stagecoach South
UWY66X	First Provincial	WJM832T	Stagecoach South	XJJ662V	Stagecoach South	YRN821V	Stagecoach South
VBW581	Chiltern Queens	WLO471	Altonian	XJJ663V	Stagecoach South	YRV247V	First Citybus
VCL461	First Provincial	WLT316	Reading Mainine	XJJ664V	Stagecoach South	YRV248V	First Citybus
VDL613S	Traditional	WLT577	Reading Mainine	XJJ665V	Stagecoach South	YRV249V	First Citybus
VER262L	Tourex	WLT621	Reading Mainine	XJJ667V	Stagecoach South	YRV250V	First Citybus
VFB617T	County Travel	WLT790	Reading Mainine	XJJ668V	Stagecoach South	YRV251V	First Citybus
VFJ687	Coliseum	WLT848	Reading Mainine	XJJ669V	Stagecoach South	YRV252V	First Citybus
VFX980S	First Provincial	WLT879	Reading Mainine	XJJ670V	Stagecoach South	YRV253V	First Citybus
VFX984S	Stagecoach South	WLT937	Reading Mainine	XKR469	Mervyn's Coaches	YRV254V	First Citybus
VGJ317R	Charlton Services	WLT938	Reading Mainine	XKV488S	Worth's	YRV255V	First Citybus
VIJ68	Easson's	WLT993	Reading Mainine	XSK144	Worth's	YRV256V	First Citybus
VJO201X	City Line, Oxford	WNR63	Easson's	XSL220A	Reading Mainine	YRV257V	First Citybus
VJO202X	City Line, Oxford	WRD162T	Reading Buses	XVS319	Reading Mainine	YRV258V	First Citybus
VJO203X	City Line, Oxford	WSV489	Fleet Coaches	XVS830	Reading Mainine	YRV259V	First Citybus
VJO204X	City Line, Oxford	WTS102A	Reading Mainine	XVS839	Reading Mainine	YRV260V	First Citybus
VJO205X	City Line, Oxford	WTS186A	Reading Mainine	XYJ440	Reading Mainine	YRV261V	First Citybus
VJO206X	City Line, Oxford	WUD815T	Chiltern Queens	XYK976	Stagecoach South	YRX481	Travel Taylor
VLT44	Reading Mainine	WVS423	Reading Mainine	YAY537	Heyfordian	YSU975	Cheney Coaches
VOI890	Coliseum	WVT618	Stagecoach South	YBK132	Wight Bus	YTS973A	Reading Mainine
VPF285S	Travel Taylor	WWL207X	City Line, Oxford	YCD73T	Stagecoach South	YUE338	Tappins
						YXI2841	Island Coach

Home James operates a Dennis Dominator on School services, his only double-deck bus. Like most Dominators, East Lancashire bodywork is fitted as, at that time, both companies were connected with the same holding company. As we go to press the sale of Dennis to Volvo/Henly or Alexander's parent, Mayflower, is predicted.
Robert Edworthy